Paths to the American Past

Paths to
the American Past

J. R. POLE

New York   Oxford
OXFORD UNIVERSITY PRESS
1979

Copyright © 1979 by Oxford University Press, Inc.

Library of Congress Cataloging in Publication Data
Pole, Jack Richon.
Paths to the American past.
Includes index.
1. United States—Historiography—Addresses, essays, lectures.
2. United States—Politics and government
—Revolution, 1775–1783—Addresses, essays, lectures.
3. United States—Race relations—Addresses, essays, lectures.
I. Title.
E175.1.P64   973'.07'2   79-830   ISBN 0-19-502579-2

Printed in the United States of America

For
Rogers Albritton

Acknowledgment

I would like to express my appreciation to the Woodrow Wilson International Center for Scholars for the Guest Scholarship which provided me with the facilities in which this volume was completed.

Contents

Section Three

selves for the stories that maintain their own society's culture
—that supply its understanding of itself. Written history—a comparatively recent but immensely important addition to humanity's
means of understanding itself—greatly increases the information
available and the possible subtleties of analysis; but written history, while it increases our range and perhaps our dependence,
does not, I think, by virtue of the writing alone, introduce any
fundamentally new principle. In other words I do not think that
the practice of history needs to be defended against the charge that
non-literary societies have been able to manage themselves completely without the support of history; this would be an error into
which such societies have not fallen.

Yet 'a concept of history' is itself an expression which obviously
permits those who explore its recesses to indulge themselves in
widely varying and extremely contrasting ideas of the content and
meaning of the past. The differences reflect, and in turn maintain,
fundamentally differing social, intellectual, and political purposes, a
state of affairs which seems likely to continue as long as people
have differing opinions and temperaments. Some of the essays collected in this book were written to advance the interests of what I
regard as legitimate historical method, and legitimate historical
engagement, against certain forms of intellectually dangerous
trivialization, often undertaken by skeptical pragmatists and hard-
nosed demystifiers, or by historians deeply attached to conclusions
to which more critical—indeed more skeptical!—methods of
analysis would not lead. The arguments involved are sufficiently
complex and difficult to have engaged the attention of philosophers
as well as historians at least—to date the problem from modern
times, since F. H. Bradley's *Presuppositions of Critical History*,
published in 1874. The arguments would certainly be interesting
enough to engage critical attention even if they could be detached
from their social and political consequences. It is often said that
even the survival or destruction of historical records is subject to
chance, but it would be an error to let this obvious truth deflect
our attention from the historically more important reflection that

the records that survive are themselves the direct *consequences* of past social and political decisions: Domesday Book, Westminster Abbey, the Debates held in Philadelphia in 1787, newspaper advertisements for runaway slaves, to offer examples. They present the present mind with a choice that is vast and variable but never merely random. We bring to the past our interests, tastes, and preferences—sometimes our passions. We bring our own autobiographies, sometimes subtly recasting the past to advance or protect some cherished or threatened aspect of our own identity. No historian can confine himself to writing history, as it were, 'as he finds it,' because what he finds will depend so largely on what he looks for. Rather too often perhaps the historian finds history as he is already determined to write it. This has generally been the case when historians have embarked on some historical enterprise in order to establish a thesis already firmly set in their minds, or to supply perpetual warmth to a glowing emotion.

When I began to open the books of American history as an undergraduate shortly after the Second World War, the subject was in a conceptually more primitive state than it is now. Although many American historians were steeped in learning and were no doubt aware of the significance in history of the unstated alternative, these were not the features that attracted readers or commanded the dominant interests of the profession of American history itself. American history was an epic, a panorama, a concatenation of heroics; or it was a series of clashes between mighty opposites, in which the reader was usually left quite clear as to whose side he was supposed to be on. Or again it was presented in sweeping, single-minded interpretations, among which the grip of the frontier was only beginning to be unfastened. The concept of Freedom glowed brightly in American skies, its light rekindled by recent victories. The word 'Freedom' actually appeared in the titles of an extraordinary number of books on American history. But the concept was rarely subjected to any analysis. There was either more freedom (the Revolution, Jefferson, Jackson, Emancipation) or less (the British Empire, the Constitution in some views,

Hamilton, the Bank, the Confederacy) but justice and therefore happiness always consisted in more. The skeptical student could begin quite early in life to wonder how a country that began its career in freedom could go on indefinitely getting freer and freer, and how it would all end.

I was fortunate in coming on the scene as many of these things were beginning to change. One can see easily enough how the postwar generation of American historians was influenced by its own times and by the urgent pressures of contemporary social needs: Oscar and Mary Handlin's and Louis Hartz's analyses of the role of government in early American states; Arthur Schlesinger, Jr.'s protective history of the New Deal; Kenneth Stampp's attack on the Phillips tradition of paternalistic slavery; Hofstadter's critique of the Populists and of anti-intellectualism—and previously his *American Political Tradition;* Vann Woodward's profound rethinkings of the South's complex burdens; David Potter's absorption in the qualities and sources of national character—all these interests could be explained with some degree of reference to the social and economic biographies of the writers and their times. But one can also see a critical sophistication that would never be content merely with a new set of two-dimensional views to take the places of the old ones.

This emerging critical subtlety was in itself an intellectual phenomenon of the highest value and interest; but it can best be understood as a product of the economic and psychological impact of the Great Depression, the New Deal, and the Second World War. Nearly every historian of the United States whom one met in those days—and particularly those whose works were coming to influence their generation—was a New Dealer. There existed nothing like the spectrum of political opinions that one regularly encountered among members of the same profession in Europe. The Depression and the New Deal were essentially internal events, each producing forms of division and recrimination. As an influence on American social and historical thought, the War differed from both of them, because it struck Americans as an essentially external event, and after the bitter divisions of recent years, it produced an extraordinary degree of national unity—a unity that persuaded many former Marxist or left-wing critics to perceive in American society greater virtues than they had given it credit for. The 'consensus' school could not have emerged to achieve any significant influence had it not been for the sense of justified ideological nationhood of the war years. That civilization, in the Western sense of the word—and the West did not then include Germany—had powerful enemies, was a truth which did not need further demonstration. But for committed New Dealers under the rising onslaught of McCarthyism from within and the Cold War without, the survival of free institutions left a position charged with painful complexities. The New Deal was beginning to acquire the ambiguous and not previously expected credit inherent in its conservatism: it had saved American political society but it had hardly transformed it. The achievements of Roosevelt's presidency needed defence against a fierce and embittered attack; yet it was equally clear that much remained to be done. American liberalism could hardly repose on the laurels of the Wagner Act, the TVA, and Social Security followed by the Fair Deal. These seem to me to have been among the forces, felt or sensed, that impelled the interests and commitments of that powerful generation—among whom I have mentioned only a handful of familiar names.

Within a few years, though I think for reasons that were more internal to the interests of the historical profession, significant changes also began to take place in the study of colonial America, beginning simply with a revival of professional interest. The late J. H. Easterby, Archivist of South Carolina, remarked to me when I visited the archives in 1953 that younger men were too impatient to occupy themselves with local studies. 'They want a wider field,' he observed; but, he implied, it was only through a sound grasp of local conditions that any sound general view could be built up. I took note of this remark, which accorded with a view I was already forming. General interpretations must henceforth be built on the firm foundations of research in the archives of the states, and where necessary of the counties and the towns.

A similar thought had occurred to Robert E. Brown, who was then engaged in research towards his influential books on democracy in early Massachusetts and (with his wife, B. Katherine Brown) on Virginia. At one level their interpretation was certainly an application of the 'consensus' view of American history to both colonial and revolutionary America. Since I felt that their conception of the social structures and political directions of eighteenth-century American society was badly astray (for the reasons, see 'Historians and the Problem of Early American Democracy' below), I should say here that they did valuable service to the raising of professional standards of research by insisting on the fundamental importance of local records. Very little of that type of research was being done at the time, and the historians who objected to the Browns' conclusions at least had to follow them into the archives.

This, then, was a promising atmosphere in which to begin a professional career, however little prospect of employment there might have seemed to be for a trained Americanist in the history departments of British universities. After leaving Oxford, I was fortunate in getting the Procter Visiting Fellowship at Princeton, where I was given the opportunity of remaining to complete a Ph.D. and of beginning my career as a university teacher. Back at home, however, after those four years, it was clear that something was missing. British interest was beginning to stir, the British Association for American Studies was formed, and we found that there were perhaps slightly more of us than each individually had been inclined to imagine. But American history still formed very little part of the normal conception of a history syllabus. British historians in general, if they thought about America at all, seemed to suppose that it had been carrying on quite separately, far from the mainstream of historical development. This sense of distance, moreover, reflected a quite unmistakable cultural preference. Intellectual circles in Britain were unwilling to take America seriously; they were affected by a strain of popular anti-Americanism which took its roots in the mutual strains and contrasting costs of the War and its aftermath, but was reanimated by the feverish rage of McCarthyism. It was at least comforting to settle back from all this and reflect, as so many Europeans did, that America, for all its wealth and power, was pathetically 'immature.' It is easy to forget how widely that word was used of the United States by British intellectuals. Unfortunately, there was some truth in this notion. McCarthyism was not a phenomenon which can be dismissed as a mere aberration. In foreign affairs, American opinion was overwhelmingly committed to what the late Sir Denis Brogan called 'The Myth of American Omnipotence.' But I am not sure that this reflected the thrust of the current British tone of criticism, which sprang, I suspect, from a need to assuage our own somewhat nettled sense of national status.

This complacent notion that American history belonged to a separate compartment, which could be safely ignored by those who preferred to study real history, was defective in at least two respects. In the first place it missed the point that there might be something inherently interesting and instructive—to the extent that the same might be said of Tudor England or any other phase of historical experience—in a mass civilization whose record brought together such ingredients as the most rapid economic development of the industrial era, the earliest and most widespread modern democracy, and the world's greatest mixture of peoples under a single political roof. And all this under a remarkably stable federal form of republican government. The second point was that it would really have been very odd if all this had been going on without affecting the Old World. The truth, of course, was that ever since the sixteenth century Europe and America had been locked into a growing complex of economic, demographic, and political systems, from which none of them could ever escape. (And so was Africa, although white racial attitudes made this side of the truth more difficult to acknowledge.)

British historians with primarily American interests therefore had mission work to do, and some of them felt, with some reason, that their principal task was to interpret America to British audiences. But in the long run a new academic subject can gain respect among its older neighbours in only one way, and that is the way of research and the advancement of knowledge. Research, however, was slow to develop. After a promising doctoral thesis or a good start, people became easily stalled, or sidetracked into operations which yielded quicker or more conspicuous rewards. There were practical difficulties about travel, of course, but more fundamentally I think there were difficulties about what questions to ask. The solid and permanent advance of the subject would always depend on those who were prepared to forgo other excitements to the extent of spending their best efforts reading the published and archival records of American history, and it was this kind of work that began in due course to make its impact on the interpretation of critical issues. I continue to regard W. R. Brock's *An American Crisis: Congress and Reconstruction* (1963) as a pathbreaking example of this new work. Books which any student of American history would be required to read in order to get an adequate grasp of the literature of the subject—always excepting, of course, the phenomenon of Sir Denis Brogan, whose *American Political System* was published in 1933—appeared from British hands only in the 1960s, which was long after the establishment of the first British chair, and even then they did not come thick and fast. It remains true that some of the most scholarly British contributions have appeared in the form of articles, which may continue to be the medium of those who find difficulties in arranging prolonged research in the United States.

The research problems that now attract graduate students sometimes seem more demanding than those that occupy the incumbents of the secure ground of established positions. As an intellectual development this offers a reassuring prospect for the future, provided always that the interest is maintained, which has not always been the case in the past. In British universities the general state of American studies, and in particular of American history, is incomparably better than it was thirty, or twenty, years ago; but I doubt whether it is much advanced on what it was ten years ago. It is a basic mistake for the British or Continental historian to limit himself to the view that his problem is to find questions that can be asked and answered within the limitations of a base in Europe; the critical problem will always be to ask difficult and important questions, and then to find ways of answering them.

When I began to attend history courses in America I was faintly disturbed by what seemed to me to be a note of apology for history, a disquiet about their own standing which led professors to explain to classes that we study history 'to understand the present.' We shall never learn anything worth knowing from the study of history unless we begin by trying to understand the past, a fascinating and by no means easy exercise of imaginative intelligence. The historian's point of departure must necessarily be present, but his task calls for an unusual power of abstracting himself from the present. This is not to say that historical writing is a mere exercise in abstraction. There can be no doubt that the writing of history has consequences, and that the historian is responsible for the contribution he makes to the structure and movement of ideas on which his generation's intellectual synthesis rests. Or, if there is no such agreed synthesis, historians contribute their theories of society and change to the struggles to influence the minds of their generation.

The question of consequentiality acquired new and dramatic implications during the years of student unrest, and more so in the United States than in Britain. The cant expression on which most of the argument turned was 'relevance,' but as far as I could ever make out, the word 'relevance,' when it had any meaning, was interchangeable with 'interesting,' if the interest was coloured by significance or importance. The gravest intellectual error into which so many young men and women fell, as did some older ones who had failed to learn by teaching, was that of confusing *relevance* with *recency.* In this connection it is worth recalling the course of preparation undertaken by Thomas Hobbes when as a young man he was appointed tutor to the Earl of Devonshire's son. His pupil was expected to enter public life according to his rank; it was therefore important to educate him in the ways of men, and Hobbes prepared himself for his duties by translating Thucydides' *History of the Peloponnesian Wars,* on the judgement that Thucydides had made the most profound contribution to the understanding of human behaviour in times when choices, freely made after elaborate debate, led to events that destroyed the civilization in which free choice was possible. So far as I can judge the matter, Hobbes's view would still be correct now. In the best sense of the word, Thucydides' *History* remains the most 'relevant' work of history ever written.

To say this is not to detract from some of the forms of consciousness-raising aspects of historical writing that have become popular. Where a group, clearly identified within a nation, has been the victim of a severe cultural deprivation of group consciousness, that deprivation is likely to be reflected in its members' view of their social position, their personal possibilities, and their self-respect. An attempt at compensation seems a reasonable remedy, and such compensation may take the form of the stabilizing influence of long historical perspectives. The word 'roots,' often used in this connection, is a metaphor, which it is just as well to remember; each individual grows separately, and often at great psychological distance from his forebears. But individuals also grow up in social, familial, economic, and educational environments, and self-respect and self-confidence are difficult to acquire when the environment itself is starved of them.

But the aim of restoring these attributes, especially by the creation of a specific historical legend, is best considered a transitional aim. The class under consideration, whether it be the English working class, the Croats in Yugoslavia, the Negroes in America, the female sex nearly everywhere, is integral to the wider society. And it is particularly to the point that except where minority territorial bases exist, the specified class and the wider society can never be separated from each other because they are in truth part of each other. In any of these cases, the specified class has its own inner life, its private rules and codes, ambitions, and achievements, which are worthy of attention for their own sake, as examples of human vitality, inventiveness, endurance, and culture. But they are also worthy of attention because, once their contribution is understood, the larger social and economic arrangements to which they belong can no longer be understood without them.

No experienced historian is likely to find these reflections particularly subtle, but students enter into the study of history before they are experienced. It is precisely in the confusion of 'relevance' with mere recency, or even topicality, and precisely in the demand that historical studies should be directed in some mysterious way to obtaining concrete results, that these dimensions are missed. American students are still in particular need to liberate themselves from the false and shallow notion that the only history from which they can learn anything of value is the history that dates back no farther than their parents' lifetimes.

American civilization is itself a highly complex fusion of transatlantic influences and domestic circumstances. One of the most valuable things that has been happening in fairly recent years has been the growing consciousness of a genuine transatlantic historical culture. Colonial American historians no longer ignore what used to be called the 'English background' to American history, and my impression is that the best American historians of the period are often better and more comprehensive scholars of the totality of Anglo-American history than their British contemporaries who specialize in British history. American history has been growing rapidly less parochial as Americans have joined the international community—a process that has followed the abandonment of American diplomatic and political isolation in a manner that suggests the possibility of some psychological connection (however furtively recognized).

The best work being done in the United States thus looks much farther back into the past than used to be the case with the more popular writers of history. One result of this has been a subtle reversal of the oldest and in some ways the most confident theme in the older American historical tradition. I mean the theme that American historical development has been the direct result of *willed* progress. We see clearly enough now that the founders of New England were intent on *restoring* lost or enfeebled traditions in church and village; nothing would have shocked them more than the assertion that they were engaged in a great departure from the ways and morals of their ancestors. The idea of Progress would literally have made no sense to them.

This increase in historically minded, unsentimental realism about the past, this willingness to recognize the profound differences in motives and morals that divide us from forebears who lie only three or four lifetimes away from us, is an advance whose benefits are being increasingly handed on to new generations of students. But it is a difficult message to grasp. To some it must appear pessimistic, or even slightly treacherous. To such naïve skeptics the past has no answer; after all, we may listen to it, but as I began by observing, it is not listening to us.

We can listen to it, however, with new sophistication because we possess new methods of analysis. The first school of 'New Historians' in the United States, who flourished for some quarter-century after the appearance of James Harvey Robinson's book on the theme in 1912, loudly proclaimed the importance of the social sciences, but they achieved little or no intellectual advance either because they were too preoccupied with publicizing and repeating their original assertions to address themselves to the problems of learning and applying these methods, or because, like Charles Beard, they moved in other directions. But much more recently we have witnessed the rapid development of methods and even styles of thought derived from disciplines as diverse as anthropology and statistics. In the hands of historians these methods are capable of being more than techniques, for they suggest the possibility of new questions.

History for all these reasons seems to me to be in an intellectually prosperous condition. It has much to teach the society which it serves, and it is better equipped to do so than ever before. Is modern society ready to listen? That is a question whose significance ranges far beyond the enrollments in university history courses—the point which causes the most direct concern to university teachers of the subject. There is an obvious, if superficial, difference between the interests of the university student working with course assignments and examinations in view, and those of the wider public, but the first should merge into the second. When the student becomes a member of that wider public there is no good reason why he should renounce the benefits of his university education. As the work of historians continues and extends, so should the interest of former students and present readers. To inform the intelligent public of the content of the past itself is an ambition worthy of the historian's engagement, and in this too there is mission work to be done.

The Woodrow Wilson   J. R. P.
International Center for Scholars
Washington, D.C.
12 November 1978

Section One

1

Representation and Authority in Virginia
from the Revolution to Reform
(1958)

One of the most distinctive features of the American Revolution in Virginia was the skill with which it was led. The quality and the underlying unity of this leadership not only helped to make Virginia the first province to declare for independence, but exerted a formative influence on the character of the new state government. It is true that certain ardent separationists feared that there would be altercation before independence was adopted, but in the event no resistance materialized; and it is true again that the movements for ecclesiastical and land reform, undertaken by Thomas Jefferson at the earliest opportunity in the history of the new state, met with varying degrees of opposition, some of it weak, some severe. But the more significant fact is that Jefferson's proposals for broadening the distribution of political power by extending the suffrage and reforming the basis of representation in the assembly met with complete defeat. The traditional leadership of Virginia, despite serious internal divisions over specific issues of policy and personality, despite, indeed, the varieties of interest within its own membership, never allowed the Revolution to get out of hand.

It would be easy, however, to exaggerate the element of paradox in this situation; to say, in effect, that the Revolution in Virginia produced a social upheaval without giving rise to any political consequences of the same order. The old system, which stood so firm against the shocks of revolution, drew its strength from the fact that, although it was far from being fully representative of the people in the modern sense, it was in a high measure representative of the prevailing social order. To call it a system of government by the consent of the governed would be a trifle romantic. That familiar phrase implies the existence of some explicit compact among the people. Certainly the freeholders, who participated freely and frequently in elections, were, in a sense, affirming their consent to the system when they did so. But socially and economically below the independent station of the freeholders there were many Virginians who had no vote in elections for the Assembly and who, nevertheless, do not seem to have felt themselves violated or aggrieved by the political system. 'Consent' implies a more positive attitude of acceptance than this. It would be more accurate to call it government with the acquiescence—or without the manifest dissent—of the governed.

At the time of the Revolution, the elections of the province were still governed by the election law of 1736.[1] Under this law, the vote for elections to the House of Burgesses was open to all freeholders owning either twenty-five acres of land with a plantation and a house on it, or one hundred acres with no settlement, and also to freeholders in the towns. The preamble referred to the need to check the practice of making fraudulent conveyances for the purpose of multiplying the number of voters at election times only, and it was to this end that the law contained the rather vague qualification that the property must be in the possession of the

1. William Waller Hening (ed.), *The Statutes at Large; Being a Collection of all the Laws of Virginia* [1619–1792] (13 vols., Richmond, 1809–23), IV, pp. 475–78; IX, p. 115.

freeholder 'for a term of years.' It was under this law also that Virginia offered the remarkable fractional vote to joint tenants, who, if they could agree, might unite to cast one single vote if their freehold was big enough to satisfy the qualification.[2] A significant innovation was made with regard to residence. Earlier laws had required that the voter be a resident of the county in which he voted;[3] but this restriction was now dropped, with the effect that larger landowners, whose holdings satisfied the minimum requirements in more than one county, could vote in each of them. Those who had acquired their land by other means than those of inheritance and marriage were required to have enjoyed one year's possession before they were allowed to vote.

Before 1736 both religious and racial intolerance had made their appearance, religious intolerance first. In 1699 the class of persons known as recusants convict were barred both from voting and from office.[4] Recusants were simply those who failed to attend their parish church, and so, in the strictest sense, the term might have been held to include nonconformists as well as Roman Catholics; but this double sense was rare, and by the Virginia legislators was almost certainly not intended.[5] The constitution of 1776 offered no explicit relief to the Catholics,[6] and as late as 1784 Madison expressed uncertainty about their rights;[7] the religious disability was dropped in 1785.[8] Indians, mulattoes, and Negroes had been excluded from the polls in 1723.[9]

2. A. E. McKinley believed this feature to have been unique. *The Suffrage Franchise in the Thirteen American Colonies* (Philadelphia, 1903), p. 40.
3. October 5, 1705, Hening, *Statutes*, III, p. 238.
4. *Ibid.*, pp. 172–75.
5. The word 'recusant' was not used to describe dissenters when they were made the subject of repressive legislation in England under Charles II. Sir Charles Grant Robertson, *Select Statutes, Cases and Documents* (London, 1947), pp. 32–53, 67–74.
6. McKinley states that the exclusion of Catholics 'was continued until the Revolution.' *Suffrage Franchise*, p. 35.
7. James Madison, *Writings*, ed. by Gaillard Hunt (9 vols., New York, 1910), II, 54n.
8. Hening, *Statutes*, XII, p. 120.
9. *Ibid.*, IV, pp. 133–34; J. A. C. Chandler, *History of Suffrage in Virginia* (Baltimore, 1901), p. 12.

The comparatively small number of townsmen enjoyed a more generous franchise than those of the country, despite the fact that prevailing political ideas attributed a superior virtue to country life. Under the charters of Williamsburg and Norfolk, a freehold bearing a house 'in tenantable repair' and of the modest dimension of twelve feet square, as required by law, would qualify the owner to vote; and it would do so whether held in single or in joint tenancy, joint tenants being entitled to a single vote between them. Even a nonfreeholder of twelve months' residence could vote if he possessed a 'visible estate' worth fifty pounds in current money. Moreover, persons who had been apprenticed for five years to a trade within the city, and had got a certificate to that effect from the court of hustings, could vote if they were inhabitants and housekeepers in the city. Indentured servants were excluded.[10]

But although the law of 1736 remained until the Revolution as the definitive election statute of the province, it by no means continued to represent the will of the House of Burgesses, in view of which fact its influence over the electoral process should be regarded with skepticism. In 1762 the burgesses decided that the General Assembly should have the same fixed term of office as the British Parliament, and accordingly they passed a law limiting the life of assemblies to seven years and ordering that a new assembly was to meet not more than three years after the dissolution of the old one.[11] The action of a colonial legislature in attempting to regulate the duration and frequency of its own meetings was an encroachment on the royal prerogative—a fact of which the members of the Virginia Committee of Correspondence showed some appreciation when, in writing to their agent in London, they protested the Assembly's innocence of any such intention.[12] Governor Francis Fauquier shared the opinions of the burgesses, but

10. May 1742, Hening, *Statutes*, V, p. 206.
11. November 1762, *ibid.*, VII, pp. 517–30.
12. *Virginia Magazine of History and Biography* (Richmond, 1893–   ), XI (1903–04), 133–35. (Hereafter *VMHB*.)

thought it his duty to draw the attention of the Board of Trade to the possibility of an infringement of the prerogative, a point, however, of which their lordships had no need to be reminded.[13]

This statute also embodied an attempt to alter the suffrage qualifications. It contained a new provision, by which the area of freehold land, without house or plantation, to be held in order to qualify the owner for the vote for burgess, was reduced from one hundred to fifty acres. The act contained no indication of the motive for the change. The Committee of Correspondence seems to have regarded the point as secondary to the main consideration of legislative terms, and commended it to the agent without elaboration: 'The Reasons for the Several other amendments will readily occur to you by comparing this Act with those that are repealed by it.'[14] The committee wrote later to the agent hoping that even if the act were disallowed, the burgesses might have leave to re-enact such parts as were not disapproved of, but it gave no further details.[15] The measure was duly condemned by Sir Matthew Lamb, counsel to the Board of Trade, as an infringement of the prerogative;[16] the Board, noting that the measure contained a suspending clause, agreed to await further argument from the agent,[17] but its journal records no further discussion of this act, which accordingly failed of the royal assent.

No objection was raised in Britain to the extension of the suffrage as proposed in this act. Indeed, a letter from Robert Carter, who attended a meeting of the Virginia Assembly's Committee of Correspondence at which its London agent's letters on the subject were read, not only makes it clear that the infringement of the prerogative was the ground of rejection, but strongly implies (although this portion is somewhat mutilated) that the section on the

13. Francis Fauquier to Board of Trade, March 20, 1763: Colonial Office (hereafter CO5), *vol.* 1330, pp. 395–97 (Public Record Office, London).
14. *VMHB*, XI, 133–35.
15. *Ibid.*, XII (1904–05), 5.
16. CO5, 1330/403–5.
17. *Journal of the Commissioners of Trade and Plantations, 1759–1763* (London, 1935), 365, 369. (Hereafter *JCTP*.)

qualifications of voters if passed again would meet with approval.[18]

Most of the provisions of the rejected law of 1762 were in fact repeated in a new act of the session of 1769, actually passed in June 1770.[19] The same amendment to the suffrage qualifications was proposed, and the period of previous tenure was reduced from one year to six months, but although no objection was raised on points of substance, the act failed to be approved.[20]

Although the preambles to these acts contained no effort to explain the motives for their intended reform of the suffrage, it is not difficult to see why they would have been generally popular, and why, therefore, the reasons for them would 'readily occur' to the colonial agent by comparison with former acts. One effect of the reduction, from one hundred to fifty acres, of the unoccupied land required for the vote for the lower house would have been an increase in the voting power of the larger landowner, who could already take advantage of the absence of a residence requirement;[21] but another and no less significant effect would have been an in-

18. Robert Carter to Landon Carter, January 21, 1764, in Landon Carter Papers (University of Virginia Library). McKinley gives a detailed account of the act of 1762 but omits to mention that it failed of royal assent. *Suffrage Franchise*, pp. 40–42.

19. Hening, *Statutes*, VIII, pp. 305–7.

20. *JCTP*, 1768–75 and 1776–83 (London, 1937 and 1938), *passim*. Under this act, as under the inoperative measure of 1762, certain placemen were made ineligible to sit in the House of Burgesses. These acts, of 1762 and 1770, were the first to place sheriffs and under-sheriffs in this category with the inspectors of tobacco, first excluded in 1742. It was expressly provided as early as 1742 that persons so excluded might not sit as members of the House of Burgesses until two years after ceasing to hold office (Hening, *Statutes*, V, p. 206). It seems rather troublesome of the Board of Trade to have queried the new act on the ground that, although it could see the reason for the exclusion of the placemen, it could not understand the extra two years' exclusion after ceasing to hold office. No other objection was offered. An adequate and indeed an interesting explanation was received from Dunmore in October 1773. Board of Trade to Dunmore, March 11, 1773, CO5, 1369/323–25; Dunmore to Board of Trade, July 9, 1773, CO5, 1372/252–53. In the MS. copy of the letter, in this latter volume, the act of 1770 is incorrectly dated 1772.

21. This was considered by Sydnor to be the probable motive for the measure. Charles S. Sydnor, *Gentlemen Freeholders* (Chapel Hill, 1952), p. 164.

crease of voters among the pioneer and poorer farmers, especially
in the Western country, where it might be expected to take some
time to bring the first twenty-five acres under cultivation. The
former effect would undoubtedly have been palatable to some—
not all—large landowners, but the latter effect would of course
render the back country more attractive to settlers, an object in itself to be desired by those speculative landed interests ambitiously
engaged in the promotion of Western values. Indeed, the rivalry
between these interests called forth an anonymous charge, in July
1770, that the governor and council had made immoderate grants
of land west of the Alleghenies; to which William Nelson, who as
president of the council was senior official in the interim between
governorships, replied that the grants, which had been made before 1763, were made to 'men of consequence who were most
likely to be able to procure settlers.' [22] At this phase of settlement,
therefore, the interests of the many Tidewater planters who were
engaged in land speculation were at one with those of the settlers,
who would desire active political powers. This common interest
was not long to survive the Revolution. The price of the land mentioned by Nelson was only three pounds (Virginia) for a hundred
acres. Another advantage of this reform for the larger landowners
was that it would enable them more easily to enfranchise their sons
by conveying land to them.

The under-representation of the back country was already a
well-recognized problem, but it was not of Virginia's making. It
was forced on the province by the royal policy of disallowing laws,
passed by the General Assembly, seeking to establish new counties
with representation in the House of Burgesses. This grievance was
charged against George III by Jefferson in the Declaration of Independence. The reasonableness of the demand was acknowledged
by Lord Dunmore, who as governor was sharply criticized by the
Board of Trade for putting his signature to such a provincial law. In
self-defence he replied that, although he would not have given his

22. Nelson to Board of Trade, October 18, 1770, CO5, 1372/125–37.

assent if he had considered the full force of his instructions, he was induced to do so by 'the necessity of the thing.' The back counties were vast and were rapidly filling up by settlement and by natural increase; there was much turbulent and refractory behaviour; he thought these steps the only method of establishing order and regularity there.[23] But in due course the men who controlled the legislature of Virginia from their fastnesses in the Tidewater and Piedmont regions were to become the true heirs and successors to the royal government in their determination to deny an equality of representation to the back country.

Electoral contests under the pre-Revolutionary system were, on occasion, energetically conducted and carefully planned. Despite the statutory limitations, colonial elections in Virginia could arouse widespread participation; and it was long ago pointed out that a higher percentage of the population sometimes went to the polls even than in Massachusetts, where the franchise was notoriously liberal.[24] The reluctance often expressed by established gentlemen to take part in promoting their own election was overcome at an early stage by George Washington, who lost his reticence after it had cost him his first political campaign.[25] Such contests reflected the rival ambitions, and the rivalry for social standing, of different members of the gentry; claims of ability most effectively to represent local interests were naturally involved in these rivalries. But seldom if ever is there recorded evidence of dissatisfaction with the system itself. It seems to have been commonly accepted that the gentry exercised their traditional leadership by a right as natural as that by which the freeholders participated in elections. Not, however, that the burgesses always stood

23. Board of Trade to Dunmore, March 2, 1773, CO5, 1336/469–73; Dunmore to Board of Trade, May 25, 1773, CO5, 1372/241–43.
24. J. Franklin Jameson, 'Did the Fathers Vote?' in *New England Magazine* (Boston, 1884–1917), IX (January 1890), 6n., and 'Virginia Voting in the Colonial Period,' in *Nation* (New York, 1865–   ), LVI (April 27, 1893), 309–10.
25. Douglas S. Freeman, *George Washington* (6 vols., New York, 1948–54), II, p. 147.

very high above their electors. Richard Henry Lee heard from a correspondent in 1758 that he knew no better way to support the independence of the legislature and guard the liberty of the subject than by now and then shifting the representatives of the people, 'especially those who have neither natural nor acquired parts to recommend them: for this reason we have sent two new Burgesses from King William.'[26] But the central control of political affairs was not subject to such chancy arrangements. Of more than a hundred members who regularly attended the House of Burgesses before the Revolution, only about twenty took any leading part, and these were of well-established families; three families, indeed, the Robinsons, the Randolphs, and the Lees, provided most of the leaders.[27] The burgesses in general accepted among themselves the conventions of a hierarchy no less effective than that to which they in turn owed their own membership in the lower house.

In the progress of the revolutionary crisis, in Virginia as in other provinces, the General Assembly lost its grip (in Virginia its last meeting was from March to May 1776), and all effective authority was seized by the revolutionary provincial conventions. The first of these conventions met in August 1774, after county elections probably called by members of the late House of Burgesses, and in general it was the former members of that house who became delegates to the convention. Elections to this and the succeeding conventions were governed by the same rules as those for the legislature, and the delegates were usually men of long legislative experience.[28]

These elections, held in April 1776, of delegates to the convention that was duly to declare Virginian independence, were the

26. Alexander White to Richard Henry Lee, 1758, in Lee Papers (University of Virginia Library).
27. Robert LeRoy Hilldrup, 'The Virginia Convention of 1776' (Ph.D. thesis, University of Virginia, 1935).
28. Charles R. Lingley, *The Transition in Virginia from Colony to Commonwealth* (New York, 1910), pp. 72–82.

scene of great excitement. If indeed one were to look for evidences of something like a revolt against the traditional leadership in politics, this episode provides more fertile ground than any in the recent colonial past. Many well-known public men either lost their seats or experienced the humiliation of winning narrowly after a determined contest.[29] George Mason, himself soon to be one of the architects of the new state constitution, was nearly deprived of the privilege of representing his county. Robert Wormeley Carter complained that he and Colonel Thomas Lee 'after near 7 years faithful services were shamefully turned out. Surprising that Colo. Lee who was judged by Convention a proper Person to go to Congress should be rejected by Richmond County as not fit for Convention.'[30]

The reports give no indication that the rival candidates stood for opposed policies. The strenuousness of these elections, however, is not hard to explain; for it was already understood that the new convention would make the choice of independence—that issue was no longer at stake—and would have power to instruct the delegates to the Continental Congress accordingly; after which it would proceed to make a new constitution for the state. Ambitious men must have been eager to be members of so powerful a body.

The work of the convention, when it turned to the construction of a new form of government, was at all events far from revolutionary. The new constitution announced that the suffrage was to remain 'as at present' for both houses of the legislature.[31] Senators and members of the lower house, now to be called the House of Delegates, were to be freeholders and residents respectively of

29. Robert Brent to R. H. Lee, April 28, 1776, in Lee Papers (University of Virginia Library).

30. Robert Wormeley Carter diary (Archives of Colonial Williamsburg). The most probable explanation of the contest for Colonel Thomas Lee's seat, here referred to, is that the freeholders felt that a man already away in the Continental Congress could not properly represent his constituents in the provincial convention. The same problem affected Colonel Braxton in King William County. William Aylett to R. H. Lee, April 20, 1776, in Lee Papers, where Aylett notices the similarity between the two cases.

31. Hening, *Statutes,* IX, p. 115.

their counties and districts, 'qualified according to law.'[32] The law, when it spoke on the subject, merely said that all who were qualified to vote might serve as delegates or senators[33]—a liberality that contrasted sharply with the system adopted in Massachusetts, where the suffrage was almost unrestricted but the legislature was guarded by property qualifications.[34] It does not follow that Virginian society was more fluid than that of Massachusetts; rather the reverse. The political leadership of Virginia felt too strong to need the safeguard of special property qualifications for membership of the legislature; and it was quite right. Not for over thirty years was its control subjected to any dangerous political challenge.

From 1776 to 1850, a longer period than in any other state, both suffrage and representation were governed by this first independent constitution. The general principle was laid down by George Mason in a famous clause of the Declaration of Rights: 'That elections of members to serve as Representatives of the people in Assembly, ought to be free; and that all men, having sufficient evidence of permanent common interest with, and attachment to the community, have the right of suffrage.'[35]

It was generally agreed in 1776 that this 'permanent common interest and attachment' was best assured by the freehold ownership of land. The most advanced views in the convention were those of Jefferson, who wanted to extend the suffrage to freeholders owning a quarter of an acre in a town, or twenty-five acres in the country, and who would have granted fifty acres to all those of full age who did not already possess so much.[36] Jefferson was also in favour of what was then the comparatively novel idea of apportioning the representatives of the people on a basis of population. He did not actually advocate abandoning the counties, but of giving each county one representative for every four hundred qualified elec-

32. *Ibid.*, p. 114.
33. *Ibid.*, XII, pp. 121–22.
34. Francis N. Thorpe, *Federal and State Constitutions, Colonial Charters, and Other Organic Laws* (7 vols., Washington, D.C., 1909), III, p. 1895.
35. *Ibid.*, VII, pp. 3812–19.
36. Dumas Malone, *Jefferson the Virginian* (Boston, 1948), p. 238.

tors.[37] If Jefferson's views had been adopted, the constitution of Virginia might have had a very different future, for it was the basis of apportionment, not the suffrage, that was the central issue of the protest that led to the convention of 1829. The proposal offered by Mason in the committee on the constitution is interesting because it presumably embodies his own interpretation of the concept of 'interest and attachment.' He would have given the suffrage to all men aged twenty-four with an estate of inheritance of land worth £1000; to all such having leases in which there was an unexpired term of seven years, and to every father of a household with three children.[38] The last provision reminds one of the importance of the family in the social life of Virginia.[39] Mason differed from Jefferson over the basis of representation. Mason contended, successfully, for a fixed ratio of two members from each county, regardless of the differences in population.[40] Jefferson had had the opportunity of observing the justice of the case for proportional representation in Albemarle, a large Piedmont county capable of supporting a large population; but Mason lived in Fairfax, bordering the Potomac River, where there seemed (at that time) little prospect of expansion.

For the purpose of representation in the Senate, which was intended to be a much smaller body than the House, the counties were grouped into twenty-four districts and each district elected one senator. The district lines did not cut across county lines, and the polling and all electoral arrangements continued within the counties, so that a district made up of three counties would have three independent elections, one in each county, to make its choice.

37. Julian P. Boyd and others (eds.), *The Papers of Thomas Jefferson* (13 vols. to date, Princeton, 1950–   ), I, pp. 341, 348, 358–59; Paul L. Ford (ed.), *The Writings of Thomas Jefferson* (10 vols., New York, 1892–99), II, p. 14.
38. Boyd, *Papers of Jefferson*, I, pp. 366–69. There is an interesting discussion of Mason's proposals here.
39. Cf. Sydnor, *Gentlemen Freeholders*, p. 37.
40. Lingley, *Transition in Virginia*, pp. 171–72.

There may have been a few supporters in the committee on the constitution of Jefferson's suffrage proposals; there were certainly severe differences of opinion about the Declaration of Rights.[41] But there was no popular movement to support him. Jefferson at this phase and on this issue was in the strange position of being an advocate without clients.

The reform of the suffrage planned in the disallowed acts of 1762 and 1770–that is, the reduction from one hundred to fifty acres of the area of unimproved land required to qualify a voter—can hardly have seemed a matter of urgency to the legislators. It was eventually passed, in a comprehensive election law, in 1785.[42] The religious disability against Catholics was then dropped. The suffrage was expressly restricted to white males, however. An attempt was made to introduce compulsory voting, and anyone failing to vote was made liable to a fine amounting to one quarter of his annual tax; but it is doubtful whether this was ever enforced. No registration machinery was established, and it was left to a candidate or his agent to challenge a voter of doubtful qualification; a voter refusing to give his oath in answer to such a challenge was to have his name entered in a separate book, but must be permitted to vote if his claim was sustained after scrutiny.

The towns received separate attention. In Williamsburg and Norfolk, the vote was now conferred on owners of freehold houses—'housekeepers'—of six months' residence and fifty pounds' visible estate. Freeholders in these cities enjoyed the exceptional privilege of voting in both town and county polls in the same election, an advantage they did not lose until 1831, although by a statute of 1787[43] it was withheld from all towns to be incorporated in the future. In other cities incorporated by the Assembly, a man would become a qualified voter by virtue of having possessed a freehold lot for six months. But if the lot was held by descent,

41. Thomas Ludwell Lee to R. H. Lee, June 1, 1776, in Lee Papers (University of Virginia Library).
42. Hening, *Statutes*, XII, pp. 120–29.
43. *Ibid.*, pp. 642–43.

devise, or marriage, the six months would be waived; unearned property had not lost its magic.

The laws governing municipal elections were various; but only in Norfolk and Williamsburg did municipal electors have the right to vote by the same token in general elections. Indeed the Richmond charter was so restrictive on this head that it had to be amended, as late as 1852, to give the municipal vote to townsmen already enfranchised for state elections by the new state constitution.

The election statute of 1785, moreover, exhausted the interest of the legislature in the possibilities of reform without doing anything to remedy the already apparent defects in the apportionment of representatives. The amendments were not adventurous; they remained consistent with the interests of a powerful leadership which, despite sharp internal divisions, despite the accession of new forces, had made use of the opportunities of the Revolution to adjust the social economy of Virginia to its own demands far more decidedly than it had found it necessary to adjust itself to the threatening emergence of a changed social order. The new social order was held at bay for more than a generation.

The property qualification for freeholders was low; but freeholders alone could vote, nor do they seem to have shown any inclination to share their powers. The failure of the legislatures of the Revolutionary era to break with the freehold basis is matched by another failure—that of the unenfranchised class to make any effective protest. The issue was not agitated as it was in other states. [44] Yet it has recently been found that in the 1780s no fewer than half, perhaps as many as three-quarters, of the adult white

---

44. Property qualifications were opposed in several Massachusetts towns. Massachusetts Department of Archives, vols. 276 and 277. They were at issue in New York before independence. Carl L. Becker, *The History of Political Parties in the Province of New York* (Madison, 1909). In New Jersey the freehold tenure qualification was discarded in the Revolutionary constitution after a specific attack on it in the press and by petition. J. R. Pole, 'Suffrage Reform and the American Revolution in New Jersey,' in *Proceedings of the New Jersey Historical Society* (Newark, 1845–   ), LXXIV (July 1956), 184–87.

males were landless,[45] and all who were landless were of course voteless. The political weight of these people was evidently feeble; they may even have been, in this period, comparatively indifferent to all such questions. But it is not surprising that they should have also been low in military enthusiasm. They may well have suspected, without the help of the 'designing dangerous characters' discerned by one of R. H. Lee's correspondents, that the Revolutionary war was 'a war produced by the wantonness of the Gentleman, and that the poor are very little if any interested.'[46]

The leadership of the Revolution in Virginia remained throughout peculiarly the concern and responsibility of the prevailing leadership of society. The point could not well be more strikingly impressed than by catching the assumptions behind the remarks of another of R. H. Lee's correspondents of the same summer, Mann Page, who wrote: 'The spark of Liberty is not yet extinct among our People, & if properly faned [sic] by the Gentn. of Influence will, I make no doubt, burst out again into a Flame.'[47] Page was afraid that the defeat of Jefferson in the House election for speaker, and the success of Colonel Benjamin Harrison, whom he described as an 'aristocratical Gentleman,' might have a disturbing popular effect. He wanted Lee to explain 'to our Republican Friends' that it had been due to the presence of a majority of members from the lower counties upon the James and York rivers. The incident could be explained, enthusiasm rekindled, but only through proper exertions by 'the Gentn. of Influence.'

These gentlemen maintained their position by the ownership of vast estates, by controlling every aspect of local government (except the churches after disestablishment), the judiciary, and the central political machinery of the Commonwealth. Great landed

45. Jackson Turner Main, 'The Distribution of Property in Post-Revolutionary Virginia,' in *Mississippi Valley Historical Review* (Cedar Rapids, 1914–   ), XLI (September 1954), 241.

46. John Augustine Washington to R. H. Lee, June 20, 1778, in Lee Papers (University of Virginia Library).

47. Mann Page to R. H. Lee, May 15, 1778, *ibid*.

property naturally induced such power in an agrarian community. This authority, both among those who gave the law and those who obeyed, was largely a matter of unchallenged social habit, and it was maintained through an extensive network of family connections. The system was not centralized; there was no one instrument of control; there was no unified controlling group. But all the important political and social functions within the state were dominated by men of similar interests and disposition, and in any one county the responsibilities of leadership would in all probability be shared among themselves by the same group of men. The prevailing system of political representation served this social order. Claims of a right to representation by all who paid taxes made little impression in Virginia in the Revolutionary era. The main source of organized discontent was among the religious sects, whose wishes prevailed in what has been called 'The Jefferson Revolution.'[48] The voteless section of the population acquiesced in what must be called a hitherto unrecognized American variation of government by virtual representation.

Such a description would hardly have been welcomed, still less offered as a defence of contemporary institutions, by the generation which took part in the Revolution. Yet in 1812, before those institutions had been modified, before the state constitution had been amended—but after the changing distribution of social forces had begun to arouse pronounced discontent—Benjamin Watkins Leigh, who was making his mark as the new generation's leading exponent of political conservatism, quietly but unmistakably affirmed this very principle when expounding the right of the state legislature to instruct its representatives in the United States Senate. Writing with special reference to the American situation, where the senator or representative was obliged to be an inhabitant of the state in which he was chosen, Leigh subtly advanced the doctrine of virtual representation under cover of the familiar

48. By David J. Mays in his great work of historical biography, *Edmund Pendleton, 1721–1803* (2 vols., Cambridge, Mass., 1952).

principle of government by consent: 'It is a maxim of all governments founded on contract, that no man can be bound by laws to which he has not given his assent, either directly; or mediately by his representative, or virtually thro' representatives chosen by his fellow citizens, among whom he dwells; having the same local and general interests with himself.'[49] It was, perhaps, a little like introducing one's mistress as a member of one's wife's family, but it was shrewdly done, and the statement was there for all who would read to the end of what began as a very ordinary sentence.

The requirement, noted earlier by Leigh, that in America the representative must be an inhabitant of his constituency, was oddly enough of comparatively recent vintage in Virginia itself. Before the Revolution it was common for members of the lower house to represent counties in which they held enough land to qualify as voters but did not reside; the requirement of residence was introduced by the constitution of 1776, but the earlier practice did not immediately come to an end.[50] It is not certain that residence would have been required of candidates for Congress under the Federal Constitution but for the anxiety of Patrick Henry to keep Madison from representing the state. Henry had enough power in the legislature to secure the passage of a law requiring a representative to have resided in the constituency for the twelve months previous to the election, and then went on to affix Orange County, in which Madison lived, to a constituency composed largely of counties where Madison, or his cause, was thought to be unpopular.[51] The stratagem failed; but the residence principle was soon sanctified by custom.

No student of Virginia is likely to make the mistake of regarding

49. Benjamin Watkins Leigh, *Substitute, Proposed by Mr Leigh, of Dinwiddie, to the Preamble and Resolutions, on the subject of the right of the State Legislatures, to instruct their Senators in the Congress of the U.S.* (n.p., n.d. [1812]), pamphlet in the Library of Congress.
50. Sydnor, *Gentlemen Freeholders*, pp. 70–71, 164.
51. Edward Carrington to James Madison, November 9, 15, 1788; Madison to Jefferson, December 8, 1788; Burgess Ball to Madison, December 8, 1788, in James Madison Papers, vol. 10 (Manuscripts Division, Library of Congress).

the process of elections to the General Assembly as the one key to
the government. The county courts, with their power to fill their
own vacancies, and their extensive authority over local affairs, bore
much more closely on the everyday lives of the people than did
the distant Assembly, and were a veritable—if on the whole a
tolerable—oligarchy.[52] But all the responsibilities of government
that reposed in the Assembly were exercised by men who owed
their authority to the process of Assembly elections. To this process the election laws provide the basic guide. The laws, however,
form a kind of text, upon which a valuable and illuminating commentary is found in the records of disputed elections, for the intentions of the legislature were interpreted in a startling variety of
practices. Petitions complaining of electoral irregularities came up
regularly at the beginning of legislative sessions. In 1804 the
House of Delegates accepted a set of rules for the adjudication of
such cases.[53] These rules placed the burden of proof, in cases of
alleged illegal voting, on the plaintiff, who must show the land
book or provide other proof to disqualify the voter. They laid down
that the voter would be duly qualified if he had held his land for
six months on the day of the election; and that the citizen was entitled—as he had always been since 1736–to vote in any county in
which he owned the required freehold, though he might be a
nonresident of the county.

The commonest grievance was that unqualified persons had
voted. In May 1799 the candidates who had been declared elected
in West Liberty, Ohio County, were unseated after a lengthy hearing in which it was shown that nonfreeholders, nonresidents, and
aliens had voted.[54] In 1800 two remonstrants from Wood County
were seated when they claimed that they had originally been returned, but that after a counterclaim by the other side, the sheriff
had given the certificate to their opponents. Twenty-five names

52. Mays, *Edmund Pendleton*, in general, and especially vol. I, ch. iv.
53. *Journal of the House of Delegates*, 1804, p. 46. (Hereafter *JHD*.)
54. Ohio County petition, May 1, 1799 (Virginia State Library [hereafter VSL]);
    JHD, 1799–1800, pp. 86–88.

were listed in this case as 'Bad voters' because they had no free-hold.[55] A voter in Monroe County in 1804 was held to have been ineligible to vote because, although he had lived on and improved a lot of one hundred acres given him by his father eight or ten years before, the transaction was unrecorded.[56] These investigations, which, as in other states in this period, were conducted by a special committee of the House, went painstakingly into the details of titles from documents and local knowledge. A candidate who gained his election through fraud might reasonably expect to be challenged, and in something like one-third of the cases the plaintiff was upheld and awarded the seat; but how many may have been restrained from fraud by the prospect of investigation, we do not know.[57]

The very frequency of these abuses indicates that an appreciable section of the white male population was in fact disfranchised. Complaints of illegal voting by unqualified persons were extremely rare, by contrast, in Massachusetts, where nevertheless a very high percentage of the adult male population frequently went to the polls. But the disfranchised in Virginia, whose numbers and whose feelings are difficult to judge in the Revolutionary era and its aftermath, become more distinguishable in the presidency of Jefferson and particularly of Madison. The change was not only in numbers but in character. Years before the revisionist constitutional convention was held in 1829, it was clear that the old, unreformed system of representation was working a grievous injustice upon a widespread and capably led minority who were no longer content to be subordinate to a government in which they had no voice.

55. Wood County petition, 1800 (VSL); *JHD*, 1800, pp. 16–17.
56. Monroe County, petition of John Woodward, 1804 (VSL).
57. The scale of illegal practices was certainly generous. In Giles County in 1824, 114 votes were challenged in all. The game of challenge and counter-challenge multiplied the labours of the special committee. In Bedford County in 1828, the remonstrant objected to 195 votes, to which his rival retorted with objections to 127. In addition to a large number of minors and nonfreeholders, it was alleged that votes had been recorded in the names of thirty-four persons who did not exist.

The popular protest, however, was preceded by the more intellectual strictures of Jefferson and Madison, both of whom advocated constitutional reform in the 1780s. Jefferson's criticisms are well known from the *Notes on Virginia*. Comparing the militia and the tax-gatherers' rolls with those of the freeholders entitled to vote, he actually found that the majority of men in the state, who paid and fought for its support, were unrepresented in the legislature.[58] Jefferson also attacked the unequal apportionment of representation, showing that nineteen thousand men, living below the fall line, controlled half the Senate and were only four members short of a majority in the House of Delegates, giving the law to upwards of thirty thousand living in other sections. Jefferson, however, was not exempt from special pleading; in at least one Piedmont county, Powhatan, every man had as much influence as four in the Tidewater county of Fairfax.[59] There was substantial truth in his argument, however, and more truth as time went on. But it was a long time before the movement gathered weight. A demand for a constitutional convention from Frederick county in 1796 pointed out that the government deprived the people of representation in proportion to their numbers, and objected to the mode of electing senators.[60] About two hundred signatures were attached to the petition of the freeholders and others of Patrick county in 1806.[61] They confined their protest to the suffrage arrangements. The fullest statement of this period came from Pittsylvania, whose 'sundry Citizens, Inhabitants of the County'—not freeholders, be it noted—advanced a forceful, if repetitive, argument. Other states had profited by experience, and

> . . . it is a Matter of Surprise, that, Virginia, who stood foremost in the late Revolution, both in the Declaration of her Rights and Independence, who, we trust has kept face with the Knowledge of those Rights with other parts of America, should so long have acquiesced under the Imperfections of

58. Ford, *Writings of Jefferson*, III, pp. 222–23.
59. Hilldrup, 'The Virginia Convention of 1776,' 138–39.
60. Frederick County, petition no. 3576 A, November 18, 1796 (VSL).
61. Patrick County, petition no. 5033, December 12, 1806 (VSL).

her first Essay on the Subject.—We are well aware that it is
the Interest of part of the Community to oppose any Reform;—and have expressed fears lest a Government should be
obtained equal to the present—in plain terms they are afraid
to trust the People—This has been and ever will be the Language of Aristocracy;—the object of which is—to degrade the
Mass of the People and sacrifice *Public Rights* to private *Interest*. . . .[62]

The demand for suffrage extension was grounded in the rights of
those who paid taxes and were called on to fight for their country.
The petition also demanded that the sheriffs and other county
officers be made subject to popular suffrage, and that militia
officers up to the rank of captain be elected by their companies.

The demand for suffrage reform became insistent as a result of
the War of 1812. By 1815 the practice had been developed of
printing a form of petition declaring that, in a recent militia call-
out, only a certain fraction of the total muster consisted of men entitled to vote in Assembly elections. A blank space was left for the
actual figure in each case. In a Shenandoah muster of 1,000, only
300 men claimed to be voters; not more than one third could vote
out of 800 in Rockingham; only 200 out of 1,200 could vote in that
of Loudoun;[63] and so on. But despite the force of these demands,
it was the system of apportionment of representatives that was in
far greater peril than the suffrage restrictions. Not only did the petitions on that score also pour into the legislature on printed forms,
but the protest had more political power behind it. The unofficial
convention held at Staunton in 1816 adopted resolutions putting a
strong case for revision, and these resolutions were themselves
printed, as petitions, for distribution among the counties, from
which they reappeared before the legislature.[64]

The demand for reform of the basis of representation was a char-

62. Pittsylvania County, petition of December 24, 1807 (VSL).
63. Shenandoah County petition, 1816; Rockingham County petition, 1816; Lou-
    doun County, petition no. 6563, 1815 (VSL). The Loudoun County petition,
    however, is handwritten.
64. Hardy County, petition no. A 8306, 1816, and others (VSL): J. A. C. Chandler,
    History of Representation in Virginia (Baltimore, 1896), p. 24.

acteristic product of regional development; it proceeded from a populace rapidly changing in both geographical distribution and social character. The recently settled people of the West were gaining in wealth. In the convention of 1829 it was pointed out that slavery was already moving into the Valley and even beyond.[65] Moreover, as slavery spread in the interior beyond the Tidewater, it came to be adopted by a larger number of farmers working average-sized farms, while at the same time the general prosperity of the Tidewater declined.[66] The demand for reform in Virginia was in one way analogous to the contemporary movement for parliamentary reform in Great Britain, where the rise of new centers of population had rendered the old distribution of seats wholly anachronistic. It was natural that in the Valley and across the Alleghenies, the new men of local substance should want a redistribution of members that would give them weight in the Assembly proportionate to their numbers. But the demand for suffrage extension was not regionally confined. In the old Tidewater the poorer classes were increasing in numbers and diminishing in wealth as slavery moved westward; in the Piedmont, the Valley, and the West, and in the growing city populations of Richmond, Norfolk, Alexandria, Williamsburg, and Petersburg, a large, increasing, and resentful aggregation of nonfreeholders demanded the right to vote. From about 1810 the two strands joined to make a formidable, at times indeed a threatening, volume of protest. But they were not made of the same stuff; and the movement for reapportionment included elements that were actually afraid of and hostile to the extension of the suffrage.

The antagonism between the two elements appeared sharply in the debates of the Staunton convention of 1816. Archibald Stuart of Augusta County, a member of the Virginia ratifying convention of 1788 and a judge, presidential elector, and influential state politician who had been associated with the Richmond *Enquirer*, gave in a letter to William Wirt a most revealing account of the division:

---

65. *Proceedings & Debates of the Virginia Convention of 1829–1830* (Richmond 1830), 423–24. (Hereafter *Convention, 1829–1830*.)

66. Main, 'The Distribution of Property in Post-Revolutionary Virginia,' 253–56.

Johnson [Chapman Johnson of Augusta] used his whole efforts
in recommending a Convention whose powers should be limited to equalize the representation—he was powerfully aided
by Tucker—their efforts were herculean but the question was
lost by a considerable Majority—The public feeling on this
subject has become too strong to be resisted, the people appear determined that the minority in the state shall not continue to hold the reins of government. . . .

My wish is that the senatorial districts should be perfectly
equalized, let the counties remain as they are & have no Convention—I think this may be done constitutionally, but the
objection to this is not only on constitutional grounds but
because the representation in the house of delegates would be
too large as well as unequal depend upon it something must
be done—if the people cannot be satisfied with reform in the
Senate the next stand must be made for a Convention with
limited powers—if we lose this I fear the right of suffrage will
be extented [*sic*] this would be to sow the seeds of destruction
in our country, I view this subject with Horror—if we look
forward but a few years we must see that for one land holder
there will be many who have none, the rights then of those
who own the country will be invaded by those who have no
part of it & it will become in the progress to [of?] that state of
things an objection to a candidate to be either a Man of Talents or property, The darkness and confusion which would
ensue would even reach the counsels of the U States

Experience has taught us how even free holders who are in
a state of dependence may be influenced to commit foolish
acts what then might be expected if the idle and vicious &
worthless are to have an agency in carrying on our government?[67]

It is not without interest that Stuart had been a presidential elector
for both Jefferson and Madison and a public supporter of Jefferson's administration.[68]

An attempt to fob off the discontent of the West was indeed

67. Archibald Stuart to William Wirt, August 25, 1816 (photostat in William and
Mary College Library); printed in *William and Mary College Quarterly* (Williamsburg, 1892–   ), 2d Ser., VI (1926), 340–42.
68. Hugh Blair Grigsby, *The History of the Virginia Federal Convention of 1788* (2
vols., Richmond, 1891), II, pp. 9–16.

made when the legislature, in 1817, passed a limited reapportionment in the Senate. The West received nine senators instead of its
previous four; but Eastern representation in the Senate also went
up from thirteen to fifteen.[69] The pressure for reform was not
relaxed for long. A new Staunton convention, held in July 1825,
demanded apportionment of the General Assembly based on the
free white population, a reduction of the total numbers of the
House of Delegates, and an extension of the right of suffrage.[70]
Bills for a constitutional convention were defeated in 1826 and
1827, but the reformers did not cease their efforts, and at length a
referendum, late in 1827, gave a majority of more than five thousand in favour of a convention.[71] The truly striking thing about
these long-drawn-out preliminaries is the parliamentary adroitness
and the fervent obstinacy with which the inevitable convention
was delayed by the conservatives.

Of these conservatives the acknowledged leader in the convention was Benjamin Watkins Leigh, who represented Chesterfield
County, in which he had been born.[72] Leigh was later a member
of the United States Senate. He was a landowner, but was also a
professional lawyer. This was, of course, by no means an uncom-
mon combination, but Leigh's case is nevertheless representative
of a change that was coming into the character of the Virginia leadership in this generation. Leigh lived most of his life in the county
of his birth; he spoke and fought in the political affairs of Virginia
as one who was deeply attached to the land and who looked with
dismay on the drift of a restless young population seeking its own
advancement in the West and disloyal, as he seemed to feel, to its
ancestry and origins. Yet throughout his lifetime more and more
men of the traditional planting families were coming to support
themselves by entering the professions, especially the law. The

69. Chandler, *Representation*, p. 26.
70. *Ibid.*, p. 27.
71. *Ibid.*, p. 30.
72. But had not always resided. In 1812 he was 'of Dinwiddie.' See Leigh, *Substi-
    tute*.

depleted and encumbered lands of the older settlements could no longer support an independent aristocracy; though great landed property continued to be the major single determinant of power, it now faced previously unknown competition, both from the wider distribution of land within the state and from the professional alternatives that, having been adopted to eke out the enfeebled resources of the land itself, could soon offer their own means of accumulating wealth and exerting political influence. Some of the most powerful men in early nineteenth-century Virginia politics were closely associated with the Richmond *Enquirer*. Land must make terms not only with the law but with the press.

The opposition of the landed powers of the Tidewater to a constitutional reform that would either reapportion the representation or extend the suffrage in effect began after the passage of the election law of 1785. In 1784 a legislative committee, reporting on a petition for reform, recommended further measures; but no action followed.[73] The efforts of later petitioners met with uniform failure. Though the extension of the suffrage in 1785 may still have been held to be consistent with the interests of the ruling planters, it was clearly the last measure to be regarded in that light. Against the challenge that arose about 1810 they fought desperately to keep the majority in the legislature, which was their only guarantee of power over the political economy, and not least over the taxation policy, of the state. Their policy represented a profound change in the attitude of Eastern leadership to Western development since the days when the provincial Assembly had sought to extend both representation and the suffrage franchise to the pioneer farmers.

The calling of the convention in 1829 was preceded by a long legislative struggle over the representation upon which that body should itself be based. Both sides well knew that the constitution was not much in danger of reform by an assembly that closely resembled the unreformed legislature. Equality would not spring

73. Augusta County, petition no. A 2083, May 25, 1784 (VSL).

from inequality. The basis at last agreed upon was not fully satisfactory to the reformers; but the conservatives had reason to feel
that in submitting to compromise they had lost their cause beyond
recovery.

It has often been remarked that the convention of 1829–1830
represented a very great assembly of talents, wisdom, and experience. Its proceedings also gave occasion for a mercifully unusual
demonstration of sustained oratorical energy. When it was all over,
the agreements reached represented, not a set of acknowledged
principles, but a common degree of exhaustion. There was little to
be added to the argument on either side by, or indeed long before,
that time.

For the reformers, one of the best statements to reach the convention was made in a petition from the nonfreeholders of the city
of Richmond,[74] presented (without comment) by Chief Justice
John Marshall. The petitioners claimed to be 'a very large part,
probably a majority, of the male citizens of mature age.' The burden of their plea was that the nonfreeholders were responsible,
self-respecting citizens, fully equal to the freeholders in their civic
capacities, but unable to call themselves free while they were denied any right to participate in the government. Attachment to
property, often a sordid sentiment, was not to be confused with
patriotism. If the landless citizens were ignominiously driven from
the polls in times of peace, they had at least been generally summoned, in time of war, to the battlefield. The generality of mankind desired to become property owners; there was no danger that
they might attack the rights of property. The petitioners ridiculed
the idea that moral and intellectual endowments could be ascribed
to a landed possession; and many cultivators were not proprietors.
The horror often expressed by conservatives that large manufactures would develop, bringing into existence a large, dependent
proletariat who, if enfranchised, would merely vote at their mas-

74. *Convention, 1829–1830*, 25–31.

ters'[75] bidding, was answered with the assertion that such establishments must for a long time remain at the mercy of those
who affected to dread them. For how many centuries must disfranchised citizens be deprived of their rights because a remote posterity might abuse them? The petitioners agreed that suffrage was a
social right, but denied that the existing social limitations were
proper. It was said to be expedient to exclude nonfreeholders; but
expedient to whom? Society was not composed only of the holders
of certain portions of land. The convention did not consist of the
representatives of the people but was the organ of a privileged
order. The many later reformist speeches did little more than
amplify this forceful opening plea.

The labourer in the West shared the grievances of the Richmond
petitioners and probably had worse to endure in the service of a
Commonwealth that refused to recognize him as a politically responsible person. Philip Doddridge, the uncouth but able de-
fender of the rights of the unprivileged,[76] said that the poor man in
the West often had to walk fifteen miles with his spade and ax to
do his required labor on the roads; in many places ten or twenty
days' work was required from journeymen who had not yet enough
stock to commence for themselves.[77] One of the most persuasive
and tactically soundest of the reformist arguments was that society,

75. The same fear was expressed when the Massachusetts constitution was under
debate in 1830–21. *Journal of the Debates of the Convention To Revise the
Constitution of Massachusetts, 1820–1821* (Boston, 1853), 250–52.

76. 'Dodridge is an old disepated dog of whom you have often heard me speak. He
was once dead and his wife brought him back to life by pouring brandy into his
throat. He is from Brook County, a little narrow neck of land in the extreme
north western part of Va running up into Pennsylvania. He has none of the
bland and polished manner belonging to the South. He is a low thick broad
shoulder'd uncouth looking man having an uncommonly large head & face with
cheaks overloaded with flesh. . . . He speaks in the broad Scotch-Irish dialect
although he is an excellent scholar & a man of extensive and profound research.' He was gifted with an excellent memory and powers of argument. John
Campbell to James Campbell, February 1, 1829, in David Campbell Papers
(Duke University Library); reproduced by permission of the library.

77. *Convention, 1829–1830*, 425.

far from being endangered or undermined, would really be strengthened if its base were made broader. Chapman Johnson, in one of the cleverest and one of the most unpleasant speeches of the convention, expressed his conservative instincts when he recommended 'a prudent limitation of the right of suffrage.' Johnson in 1816 had fought against suffrage reform; and he continued for some years to be associated with Leigh in defending the *status quo*. But by now he had changed sides, slightly. He admitted that he spoke as one with a foot in both camps, and said that he wanted the qualification fixed so low that the industrious of all classes, professions, and callings could acquire it in a few years of persevering labour; but he would still have preferred real to personal property if that were possible. Johnson's speech, which lasted two full days and occupies thirty-seven pages of fine print, began with a note of brutal, if refreshing, realism:

> We are engaged, Mr Chairman, in a contest for power—disguise it as you will—call it a discussion of the rights of man, natural or social—call it an enquiry into political expediency—imagine yourself, if you please, presiding over a school of philosophers, discoursing on the doctrines of political law, for the instruction of mankind, and the improvement of all human institutions—bring the question to the test of principle, or of practical utility—still, Sir, all our metaphysical reasoning and our practical rules, all our scholastic learning and political wisdom, are but the arms employed in a contest, which involves the great and agitating question, whether the sceptre shall pass away from Judah, or a lawgiver from between her feet.[78]

Johnson, anticipating the rise of towns in the Tidewater, suggested limiting their representation in advance to a prescribed number; proposing thus to establish for future urban populations the injustice he was attacking. As to the others who would still be denied the franchise, he thought that slaves, children, daughters, and wives would not resent their exclusion, and neither would widows, because they had learned, in heaven's best school, the

78. *Ibid.*, 257.

vanity of human power and the necessity of seeking happiness in devotion. In expressing these meretricious sentiments, as in rejecting the claims of both aliens and free colored—he remarked that there was no apprehension of them—Jonnson was in no danger of being answered. Who else, he asked, was excluded? Individuals of all classes who were still laying the foundations of their property; the sons of freeholders who had not yet come into their estates and had not earned one of their own. The imprudent and unfortunate had no right, in his opinion, to complain of exclusion from public affairs if they could not manage their own[79]—as though the management of public affairs might not have borne some responsibility for their plight.

Johnson was still in essential agreement with Leigh that political society ought to include the main body of property owners, but Leigh insisted that their loyalty to the state should be firmly grounded in the freehold ownership of land. All agreed to exclude free Negroes, aliens, and women—although Philip P. Barbour observed from history that it was nonsense to suppose women politically incapable.[80] Beyond this, Johnson showed that in Virginia there survived the idea that membership of society was to be earned through the acquisition of property by hard work. A man not born to privilege could prove himself economically capable and make himself independent, thereby earning his place in political society. There were indeed, and there have always been, occasions to which this brand of conservative economic egalitarianism aptly applied; but its exponents too often used it only as a sentimental substitute for what was more fundamentally needed—a rigorous examination of the social conditions which governed the chances of self-advancement and made opportunity the handmaiden of privilege.

The convention accepted without amendment the Declaration of Rights of 1776.[81] This was a favourite document with the reformers,

79. *Ibid.*, 284.
80. *Ibid.*, 92.
81. *Ibid.*, 32, 44.

who promptly asserted that all that was now required was that it be sincerely fulfilled for the first time.[82] To this optimistic argument the conservatives had no great difficulty in replying that the Declaration of Rights was adopted by the very men who had been content to continue the colonial suffrage laws; they, apparently, had considered that those laws satisfied the provisions as to 'permanent common interest and attachment.' The reformist reply to this was one familiar among pleas for the revision of the early state constitutions: the instrument of 1776 was a temporary measure, adopted in the heat of revolution, when harmony was essential but experience limited and conditions for debate unfavorable.[83] This argument was unfortunately reversible: the same was presumably true of the Declaration of Rights.[84] And both sides, equally, of course, could claim that the convention had adopted the Declaration in the spirit in which it had been intended by the Fathers. The reformist case was historically thin. Experience of self-government, though restricted by certain British limitations, was deep-rooted in 1776; the truth, as has been seen, was that there was no popular demand for a more democratic system at that period. The reformists also insisted that the right of suffrage was a natural and underived right, while the conservatives asserted that it was merely conventional and social. Lucas P. Thompson of Amherst sensibly remarked that he did not care whether a right was natural or social provided that it was valuable; he somewhat strengthened the reformists' theoretical position by asserting, first, that suffrage

---

82. *Ibid.*, 58, 84, 85, 413.

83. *Ibid.*, 79, 109–10, 413.

84. Mason himself, it is amusing to note, had a decidedly poor opinion of the circumstances in which the constitution was framed, but not for the reasons later advanced by the reformers: 'The Committee appointed to prepare a plan is, according to custom, overcharged with useless Members—you know our Convention—I need only say that it is not mended by the late Elections—We shall, in all probability, have a thousand ridiculous and impracticable proposals, and of course a plan form'd of hetrogeneous [*sic*], jarring and unintelligible ingredients.' But he went on to say that this could be prevented if men of ability, integrity, and patriotism undertook the business. George Mason to R. H. Lee, May 18, 1776, in Lee Family Papers, vol. 4 (Virginia Historical Society).

was the inherent right by which people agreed to make society—it underlay all other rights—but then by adding: 'Natural rights may be transplanted into the civil, political or social state and yet they are still natural rights.' But would this mean votes for women, minors, paupers, slaves? His answer again was practical: test no rule by extreme cases.[85] The reformists were on strong ground tactically when they pleaded that a great many of those who were at present disfranchised did in fact have a stake in society and shared the interest in and attachment to Virginia of which the freeholders claimed a monopoly. Thus a resolution offered by Alexander Campbell of Brook County declared simply that 'all free white males of twenty-three years of age, born within the Commonwealth and resident therein, have sufficient evidence of permanent common interest with, and attachment to, the community, to have the right of suffrage.'[86]

The conservatives insisted that different people bring different possessions into the social compact; some their persons only, others their persons and their property. The property owners deserve a larger share of responsibility just as they require a higher degree of protection. But this view was fully, if briefly, answered by a delegate who pointed out that each brings his *all*.[87] Madison remarked: 'It would be happy if a state of society could be found or framed, in which an equal voice in making the laws might be allowed to every individual bound to obey them. But this is a theory, which like most theories, confessedly requires limitations and modifications.'[88]

This was perhaps the simplest statement of the interest of society as a whole in its own government. Drawing upon thought that had not changed for forty years,[89] Madison went on to distinguish persons and property as the two great interests on which govern-

85. *Convention, 1829–1830*, 410–14.

86. *Ibid.*, 43.

87. *Ibid.*, 95, 106.

88. Madison, *Writings*, IX, p. 359.

89. Cf. *ibid.*, V, p. 287 (1788).

ment was to act, whose respective rights it was to protect. He saw that these rights could not well be separated: 'The personal right to acquire property, which is a natural right, gives to property, when acquired, a right to protection, which is a social right.' He was still occupied with protecting minority rights from the abuse of majority power, but now the minority consisted of Virginia slaveowners, in whose form of property the majority had no interest. He advocated the adoption by Virginia, for purposes of representation, of the federal ratio, by which representatives were apportioned, not on the basis of free population, but on free population together with three-fifths of the slaves.[90]

The belief that property and persons were distinct types of interest was, indeed, at the core of the conservative argument. The argument had a respectable history. It was an assumption of the political thought of the early republic; Jefferson, in his *Notes on Virginia*, treated as acceptable the arrangement by which the two houses of other state governments were intended to represent these separate interests, and even criticized the Virginia Senate for being 'too homogeneous with the house of delegates.'[91] But early in the proceedings of the convention Samuel Taylor, from Leigh's own county of Chesterfield, argued that a representative derives his position only from his constituents, who are men: property could not vote, nor delegate power—'and yet we are told that it is to have a representative.'[92] But the conservatives were not disposed to re-examine the doctrine.

One speaker complicated the position by denying that slavery was the only form of property concerned, and asserted that nineteen-twentieths of the visible taxable property of the state was held by freeholders.[93] The representatives of the larger slaveowning interests repeatedly made it clear that their greatest fear was of a hostile policy of exorbitant taxation, exercised by an assembly

90. *Ibid.*, IX, pp. 360–63.
91. Ford, *Writings of Jefferson*, III, p. 223.
92. *Convention, 1829–1830*, 51.
93. *Ibid.*, 400.

dominated by Western representatives. Their own ascendancy, they argued, had always borne mildly upon the weaker and more exposed members of the Commonwealth, but it was all too clear that they did not trust the raw, undisciplined Western farmers to exercise such restraint. Yet the conservative flank was turned by the practical argument that slave property was already moving into the West; it had reached the Valley and was pressing beyond. The Tidewater and Piedmont need not fear the intentions of the Valley or even the trans-Allegheny region, which would soon share its interest in slavery.[94] These remarks were based on very careful comparisons of the census statistics; but they did not impress Watkins Leigh, who made a long, able, and at times moving defence of an order that he felt to be doomed. His argument constantly assumed that the superiority of the Eastern landed proprietors was a benevolent superiority, that they were entitled to hold power because their relation with the smaller farmers was protective, not competitive. In defending the existing system of representation he was defending an entire social order, the leading members of which were the rightful and proper spokesmen for the whole community. But that social order had already changed so much since the making of the state constitution that threats of a secession on the part of what was indeed later to become West Virginia were already forming an undertone of the debate.

If such a secession had occurred in 1830, the great slaveowners for whom Leigh spoke would probably have found it easier to maintain their power over the remainder of the state; the West might indeed have lost more weight in the councils of the Union through separation from the great state of Virginia than it would have gained from having two senators of its own. But it is far from clear that such a separation would have been the disaster, for either side, that in prospect it seemed. The Western members were evidently less deeply attached to the state than their rivals, and for them the problem of separation was perhaps as much practical as

94. *Ibid.*, 280–81.

sentimental. But the earnestness of the planters' desire to keep the
state intact, though it sprang in large part from a strong sense of
personal and family commitment to Virginia history, must also
have been a manifestation of pride. A smaller Virginia, from which
a large section had voluntarily withdrawn, would in every sense
have been a lesser Virginia. The planters would have suffered an
unmistakable loss of authority.

With such a secession the East would assuredly have been
threatened in earnest if it had been prepared to make no concessions. The struggle over apportionment in large measure repeated
an earlier legislative struggle over the basis to be used in the elections for the convention itself. There were two basic plans. That of
the reformists was for the 'white basis,' under which representatives would have been distributed according to the entire white
population. The other was for some agreed compromise between
population and wealth, though the details fluctuated with the debate. It was called a 'mixed basis.' But in the end the convention
abandoned any attempt to find or preserve an underlying principle
of adjustment, and simply allotted a certain number of seats in
each house to each section, giving the East a majority of twenty-
seven on the joint ballot.[95] The only way in which the convention
could agree as to future adjustments was to give the General Assembly the authority to make reapportionments after the 1840
census and every ten years thereafter. The suffrage was extended
to leaseholders and to householders who paid taxes, but was subjected to a list of reservations so tortuous and confused as to baffle
successive attempts at elucidation.[96]

The convention fulfilled the fears of the conservatives by opening the floodgates of democracy; but the flood refused to flow. Instead it trickled. In the referendum, in 1827, on whether to hold a
convention, 28 per cent of the adult white males of the state took
part, in all 38,533.[97] Philip Doddridge said in debate that the total

95. Thorpe, *Federal and State Constitutions*, VII, pp. 3821–23.
96. *Ibid.*; Chandler, *Suffrage*, pp. 37–42.
97. See table appended.

number entitled to vote was 44,320, and that only one-seventh of
the qualified voters had failed to turn out, which was not far wrong
as a round figure. His own proposals, incidentally, would grant the
vote to another 30,236.[98] The new constitution was ratified in an
election attended by 29 per cent of the adult white males. Yet only
31 per cent appear to have voted in the re-election of Jackson in
1832. No constitutional amendment was passed between 1830 and
1840; but in the presidential election of the latter year there occurred an astonishing leap of nearly 20 per cent, giving a measure
of participation that was barely surpassed until after the further
constitutional amendment of 1850. It would seem, then, that the
pressure for suffrage extension before 1829 came from a comparatively small section of the disfranchised class, albeit a highly conscious and politically active section, but that it was the achievement of this minority that made way for the numbers who voted in
the election of 1840. But if suffrage extension had not been linked
with the discontent of the West about representation in the General Assembly, there is no knowing how long the nonfreeholders
might have had to wait for the vote.

The unsatisfactory nature of the compromise of 1830 made further agitation inevitable. It was like a peace treaty which immediately creates an irredentist problem threatening future war. But
the Eastern political leaders now began to reverse the position
taken by their predecessors. They saw the force of the demand for
white manhood suffrage, and accepted it as tolerable to their interests provided that the basis of apportionment could remain undisturbed.[99] The chances of suffrage reform were strengthened by the
growth of a strong Whig minority in the East, which, lacking political control, thought it might be able to exploit a larger electorate.[100]

The constitution at length drawn up by the new convention of
1850 was fully the most democratic instrument yet known to the

98. *Convention, 1829–1830,* 423–24.

99. Chandler, *Suffrage,* p. 45.

100. Charles A. Ambler, *Sectionalism in Virginia* (Chicago, 1910), p. 259.

state. It at last becomes possible to recognize the ingredients of modern democracy. The suffrage was opened to all adult white males except paupers; judges and county officials, as well as the governor, were to be elected by the people.[101] The ancient system of county government seemed to have been breached at last. A new distribution of seats, which the East had failed to resist, gave the West for the first time a majority in the House, the East, however, keeping its majority in the Senate. Provision was made for a reapportionment in 1865, by which date, however, Virginia was a different state. The new suffrage basis was used for purposes of ratification; but the vote in percentage was actually lower than in any of the previous three presidential elections.[102] After 1850 the percentage of voters steadily increased, reaching 70 in the presidential election of 1860.

Great property and family connections had certainly not ceased to count in the Virginia of the middle-nineteenth century; but the part they played had changed since the Revolution. Their position was, perhaps, less easily taken for granted, and their support had to be mobilized in different, and less dignified ways. It was, moreover, a leadership whose structure had changed, and which combined in itself a greater variety of interests.[103] But the system of representation then, as in the earlier era, did much more than af-

101. Thorpe, *Federal and State Constitutions*, VII, pp. 3836–37.

102. Chandler, *Suffrage*, p. 53, says that the new constitution extended the suffrage over 60 per cent, and argues that the 110,000 voters in the election for governor in 1851 represented 13 per cent of the people, as against only 8 or 10 per cent in former years. The presidential polls noted in the table appended below, however, actually show a higher level of participation in several earlier years. The general significance of these proportions is not affected by the fact that Chandler's figures are percentage of the whole population while mine are of adult white males. Incidentally, the *Journals of the Senate and House of Delegates*, 1852, p. 204, show the total poll to have been 124,571. (Information kindly supplied by the Virginia State Library.)

103. A valuable contribution has been made by Anthony F. Upton, 'The Road to Power in Early Nineteenth Century Virginia,' in *VMHB*, LXII (July 1954), 359–80.

ford the voters the opportunity to express their preferences in elections: it continued, in its altered form, to represent, and therefore, if sympathetically observed, in some measure to explain, the social order. Within that order the leadership, though forced to share its powers, had succeeded in maintaining unmistakable lines of continuous descent from its predecessors. Familiar family names appeared again and again. The operation of this leadership and, equally interesting, its processes of recruitment are in their way no less remarkable and not less worthy of examination than is the achievement of suffrage extension and the redistribution of representatives in Virginia after it had lost the touch of the eighteenth century.

Statistical Note

In the following table, the population figures have been taken from the federal census. The estimates for years between census years have been obtained by subtracting the earlier from the later figure, dividing by ten, and adding one-tenth for each successive year. To find the number of free adult white males and of total free adult males (including free coloured), I have adopted a similar principle. For example, where the census breaks the returns at sixteen and twenty-six, the total number in that age group has been divided by ten, and half the remainder (that is, the total over twenty-one) has then been added to the rest of the total over twenty-six. (I should like to express my thanks to Mr. N. H. Carrier, Reader in Demography in the London School of Economics, for his care and patience in going over my statistical problems. I am confident as a result of his help that my methods are not liable to yield more than minor errors, such as will not affect the general significance of the inferences for the purpose of this study. At the same time, Mr. Carrier is in no way responsible for any errors that may have survived in my own mathematics or for the conclusions I have drawn from these calculations.)

Year	Free Adult White Males	Total Free Adult Males	Election	Votes	% White Males	% All
1800	104,837	109,868	P	27,177	25	24
1804	108,345	114,420	P	12,843	11	11
1808	111,853	118,972	P	19,914	17	16
1812	115,999	123,471	P	20,803	18	17
1816	120,787	127,919	P	6,956†	6	5
1820	125,575	132,366	P	4,321†	3	3
1824	132,931	140,734	P	15,335*	12	11
1827	138,448	147,010	Conv. ref.	38,533	28	26
1828	140,287	149,102	P	38,719	28	26
1829	142,126	151,194	ratif.	41,618	29	28
1832	146,768	156,264	P	45,325**	31	29
1836	152,376	162,228	P	53,629	35	33
1840	157,984	168,192	P	86,394	55	51
1844	174,913	185,546	P	95,539	55	51
1848	191,837	202,902	P	92,004	48	45
1850	200,299	211,580	ratif.	86,811	43	41
1851	203,990	215,319	G	124,571	61	58
1852	207,677	219,055	P	132,604	64	61
1855	218,738	230,263	G	156,629	72	68
1856	222,425	233,999	P	150,233	68	64
1859	233,486	245,207	G	148,656	64	61
1860	237,176	248,944	P	166,891	70	67

† A few counties may have been missed in these returns.
* No return for Grayson County.
** No returns for Giles, Hardy, Prince Edward, and Floyd counties.

The voting figures are derived from three sources: before 1824, Archives of the Virginia State Library (I am indebted to Mr. William J. Van Schreeven for the help of his department in putting these figures together); 1824–32, Edward Stanwood, *History of the Presidency* (2 vols., Boston, 1916); 1836–60, W. Dean Burnham, *Presidential Ballots, 1836–1892* (Baltimore, 1955).

2

The Emergence of the Majority Principle in the American Revolution
(1966)

Recent judgments of the Supreme Court of the United States, coming nearly 200 years after the American Revolution, have declared as a constitutional doctrine that the majority principle must be regarded as fundamental to republican government.[1]

The majority whose rights have thus been confirmed by the Supreme Court is clearly understood to be a purely numerical majority—a majority of persons in each constituency under a system in which the constituencies are all made up of equal numbers. On this basis, each representative in the legislature is held to represent a majority of his constituents, so that when a division takes place in the chamber, the majority of members will represent a majority of the electorate outside.

The main importance of this view both in history and in consti-

1. The leading case is *Baker v. Carr*, No. 6, October term, 1961.

This essay was first published in *Études sur l'histoire des Assemblées d'États*, Travaux et Recherches de la Faculté de Droit et des Sciences Economiques (Paris, 1966). The essay as originally published drew on material from my *Political Representation in England and the Origins of the American Republic* (New York: St. Martin's Press; London: Macmillan & Co., 1966).

tutional law lies in its necessary effect of displacing the claims of any other kind of majority. A majority of corporations, of unequal size but held to be equal to each other in their corporate capacity; a majority of 'interests,' economic or religious; or a majority of persons where each vote is compounded of property in addition to the person who owns it—all of these have historically contributed to the theory and practice of different forms and degrees of representative government.

The opinion of the Supreme Court—like so many other judgments affecting American constitutional law—requires a reconsideration of the formative period between 1774, when the Continental Congress began to meet in Philadelphia, and 1787, when the Constitution was drawn up in the same hall. The issues which were to enter into subsequent American history are to be sought among the internal struggles for the representation of different domestic interests, not in the American struggle with Britain or in the older story of the conflicts between the estates of the realm and the Crown.

Representation in the American colonies was never based on any single, uniform principle. In Massachusetts, the constituencies of the legislature, or General Court, were the corporate towns of which the province was made up. These towns, which were unequal to each other in population and wealth, were held to be equal within very narrow limits for purposes of representation. Each town was entitled to send one member to the General Court, with the exception of Boston, which was allowed four.

At times when the apportionment of representatives was being considered it seemed to be generally agreed that a correct representation would take account of both property and persons. The weight of property was to be assessed in accordance with taxation. This attitude was in no way confined to Massachusetts. In 1752 Philadelphia petitioned the Assembly of Pennsylvania for the right to increase its membership on the ground of its tax payments; and all Pennsylvania counties asking for increased representation mentioned their tax payments in support of their claims. In Massachusetts, Essex County also based a demand for a greater share of representatives on a statement of its proportion of the tax burden of the province.[2]

American colonial institutions were not based on any assumption that political society was composed of autonomous individuals. An element of such political individualism was indeed present, partly because the suffrage was generally extensive, partly because the elector stood rather closer, socially and in fact numerically, to his representative, than could usually be the case in England. This element gained decisive strength during the period of the Revolution. By the time the Philadelphia Convention of 1787 had completed its labours, political individualism had emerged as the major principle among the interests competing for recognition. The character of this transformation can be followed most clearly in Massachusetts, where the responsibilities of electoral legislation and finally of constitution making produced, between the years 1775 and 1780, a distinct transition from a representative system based on corporations to one which, still using the corporate structure, used numbers of population to determine representation in the Assembly.

The leadership in Massachusetts politics had long lain with the eastern seaboard towns, dominated by Boston. These towns, for example, almost invariably gave the Assembly its speaker.[3] But the leadership was exercised at the cost of considerable suspicion and hostility among the towns of the interior, and as the imperial crisis deepened, the domination of the seaboard depended to a large extent on the primacy of the question of relations with Britain over domestic issues. Even while western towns protested their determination to defend their liberties against Britain, they remained acutely suspicious of the intentions of the dominant group in the Assembly.

2. *Pennsylvania Archives,* 8th series, IV, 3486; VI, 5419–20; VIII, 6779–80; *Acts & Resolves of Massachusetts,* 1775–1776, ch. 6, pp. 432–33.
3. *Journals of the House of Representatives.* The election of the Speaker is recorded at the beginning of each session.

Representation in the Assembly was not the only issue. Much feeling was aroused by the distribution of patronage. But representation was the basic problem; and the Assembly juggled furiously with it in the crucial year before Independence was declared. The subject was regulated twice, in divergent senses, by acts of August 1775 and May 1776.[4]

Unfortunately the military emergency reduced the output of newspapers and there is little information to be had about these measures from other sources.

The first Act, that of August 1775, was intended to correct the injustice that had developed gradually as a result of the eighteenth-century practice of incorporating new towns without granting them the right of representation. This was the Massachusetts equivalent to the deliberate under-representation of the newer settlements as practised by the older counties in Pennsylvania; it was less effective, because Boston itself was restricted to four members by the Massachusetts charter of 1691—but the intention should not be mistaken. The new Act granted the right of sending one representative to every town or district of thirty or more qualified voters—which meant approximately 150 inhabitants. Towns of 120 voters were to send two; Boston alone was entitled to four. Every district which had been invested with the rights and privileges of a town was declared to be a town for the purpose of representation; but only towns and recognized 'districts' could be represented, so that unincorporated plantations and settlements still lacked this privilege.

This step restored the basic position of 1691. The result was a great increase in the number of representatives from the towns of the interior. The obvious inference is that the measure was intended to rally support throughout the province—to give the townspeople a sense of attachment to their Assembly. If it achieved that, however, it also succeeded in producing great consternation on the seaboard.

4. *Acts and Resolves of Massachusetts*, V, 1st session, ch. 3, pp. 419–20; ch. 26, pp. 502–3.

The rejoinder came from Essex County, where a convention, held in April 1776, presented the legislature with a memorial holding out the new basis of representation as a major grievance.[5] The memorialists declared that they would be satisfied with 'equality of representation, whether it has respect to numbers, or property, or both.' It was argued that a single town in Essex paid more taxes than thirty other towns and districts; though under the new distribution, a majority of the General Court could be obtained from towns which did not pay one-fourth of the total taxes. Essex paid one-sixth of the taxes but sent only one-tenth of the representatives.[6]

Property, or numbers, or both. The claim deserves attention. It was the first public challenge to the venerable tradition of town representation. The basic interest at stake, as the tax statement makes clear, was the great concentration of mercantile and city property on the seaboard; and this wealth was allied to the higher concentration of population. Thus a numerical scale could be introduced to undermine the principle of corporate representation. And, after all, was not the connection between taxation and representation the crux of the American case against Britain? To the memorialists of Essex, the principle seemed very clear cut; a plain matter of equality.

The tactical problem was how to get the basis of representation changed by an Assembly elected under the very Act that was to be attacked. The accomplishment of this delicate task showed much understanding of the management of representative bodies. The memorial appeared at the end of the session. It is clear from subsequent criticisms that the majority of members from the interior towns had already gone home when, in response to the petition, a new bill for reapportionment was introduced; the measure was propelled through its three readings in a single day.[7]

The preamble of this new Act stated that representation in the

5. *Acts and Resolves*, V, pp. 542–43.
6. *Acts and Resolves*, VI, pp. 432–33.
7. *House Journal*, session 1775–76, 235 and 242.

colony was 'not as equal as it ought to be,' and the reform was drastic. Each town of 220 freeholders was thenceforth to be entitled to no fewer than three representatives while each additional hundred freeholders gave one additional member. Moreover the measure was to come into force at once, in time for the oncoming elections.

This last provision aroused as much protest as the substance of the Act. In the short interval before the election, the law was not properly circulated; one writer alleged that there were towns within twenty miles of the Court that had never heard of it—while others scorned to act on it, holding the measure to be illegal.[8] A county convention held a year later in Worcester declared that the Act, passed 'in a very thin house, at the close of the Session, when members in general were returned home, expecting no further business of importance would be attended to, and even after writs were issued for a new choice,' was contrary to the general sentiments of the people; and ended by recommending the towns to instruct their representatives to vote for repeal.[9] Two towns later used the unsatisfactory basis introduced by this Act as a reason for holding the General Court unqualified to draw up a new constitution for the State.[10]

However, the composition of the new House, in consequence of the new basis, was highly satisfactory to the defenders of property. The number of members at the session of May 1776 rose from 201 to 266, the increase from the seaboard being enough to account for the whole of the difference.[11] The representation of Boston immediately went up from the traditional four to twelve.[12]

One effect of this Act was to produce a House of unwieldy size.

8. *Massachusetts Spy*, January 16, 1777.

9. *Massachusetts Spy*, April 24, 1777.

10. Returns of towns ot Ashby and Topsfield; Massachusetts Department of Archives, vol. 156, folios 183, 184.

11. Harry A. Cushing, *The Transition in Massachusetts from Province to Commonwealth* (New York, 1896), p. 203, n. 2.

12. Alden Bradford, *History of Massachusetts from 1775 to 1789* (Boston, 1825), p. 107.

A Boston member gave it as his opinion that the object was to produce a period of confusion after which the leading men of property would be left in charge.[13] The principal long-term result was to give the advantage in the making of policies to the commercial interests of the eastern section.

The General Court failed to satisfy the towns with a new draft constitution drawn up in 1777, and it was not until late in 1779 that a new convention, based on universal adult male suffrage, met to form a State constitution. The Constitution was adopted on ratification by the towns in 1780. By that time, the numerical principles of representation had gone far to undermine the older concept of corporate units. Towns were still to be represented: but on the basis of their populations.

The issue was not determined by size of population alone. There were no political demonstrations based on the rights of the majority. The determining factor was that the men of property who habitually exercised authority in the Assembly were allied by their interests with that of the numerical majority. The old corporation system was outflanked by this crucial combination of the interests of numbers and property. The fact was that much the greatest concentration of numbers occurred in the seaport cities where the great shipping and commercial interests were also centred. Effective political power was controlled by these interests. This combination of forces is the key to the advance of the principle of the numerical majority.

The Constitution of 1780 still recognized the need for an institutional safeguard for property. The Senate established by that Constitution was based on districts—actually the existing counties—and in each district, representation was based, not on numbers, but on taxes paid into the State treasury. The numerical basis of town representation in the House was thus made safe when the protection of property was confided to the Senate on a county basis. The numerical principle had not been established as the

13. Benjamin Kent to Samuel Adams, May 24, 1776; Samuel Adams papers, New York Public Library.

exclusive principle of representation in Massachusetts; but it had emerged as the dominant force—and subsequent political history would continue to confirm that domination.

Turning to the very different field of the organisation of the continental government, the same essential combination can be found at work.

At the Continental Congress, which began to meet at Philadelphia in September, 1774, each of the thirteen provinces was represented separately by its own delegation, appointed by a congress held in the province. Each province therefore amounted to a constituency, giving a Congress of thirteen very unequal units, each casting a single vote.

The delegates at Philadelphia accepted the prevailing view that weight of property was always a factor of major importance in determining the political power to be exercised by any particular 'interest.' It proved to be the case that the large states held the essential combination: weight of property together with greatest numbers. It was these elements, moreover, which put forward the strongest arguments for basing the representation of the entire country on the numerical principle.

The problem of representation presented itself on the first day of the first meeting in 1774. Was each delegation to vote as a unit? Or should each province be apportioned a number of votes in accordance with its wealth and population—its 'weight' or 'importance'? The argument was settled, not on principles, but on the practical consideration that the material for a differentiated system was simply not available. But in order to avoid prejudicing future discussion the Congress recorded this difficulty, stating that the decision to give each colony one vote was taken because it was unable at the moment to 'procure proper materials for ascertaining the importance of each colony.'[14]

When the debate was resumed, in 1776, the committee of the Congress which had been delegated to draw up Articles of Confed-

14. L. H. Butterfield, ed., *Diary and Autobiography of John Adams* (Cambridge, Mass., 1961), II, 123–24. *Journals of the Continental Congress*, I, 25.

eration reported its opinion that financial requisitions should be drawn on the states in proportion to the numbers of their inhabitants (except Indians); that a census should be taken every three years; but that 'In determining questions each colony shall have one vote.'[15]

The view that the assessments of the states for requisitions to the Congress should be based on population was supported by the feeling that, on the whole, under the conditions prevailing in America, population was a fairly reliable guide to property. But it was not reliable enough to satisfy the delegates. The Articles of Confederation settled instead on the rule that each state was to be assessed according to the value of its land.[16] The practice of limiting each state to one vote was maintained on the insistence of the smaller states, who were in the position of being able to exercise a kind of veto. The Articles incorporated the principle of state sovereignty, which necessarily meant state equality in the Congress.

This principle, for a variety of reasons, proved unworkable. A strong nationalist group of men whose experience had taught them to look on American government on a continental scale determined on a revision of the frame of government. In this movement the principal theoretical mind and the most effective parliamentarian were combined in the person of James Madison of Virginia, who has been called 'The Father of the Constitution.'

Shortly before the opening of the Convention at Philadelphia in 1787 he put his views to his colleague, Governor Edmund Randolph of Virginia. After noting the need to reform the system of representation and the danger of a splitting up of the states, he went on:

> I hold it a fundamental point that an individual independence of the States is utterly irreconcileable to the idea of an aggregate sovereignty. I think at the same time that a consoli-

15. *Journals of the Continental Congress*, VI, 1098, 1101. The references to the debates are from pp. 1098–1105.
16. This rule, however, was never effectively operated: E. James Ferguson, *The Power of the Purse* (Chapel Hill, 1961), p. 209.

> dation of the States into one simple republic is not less unattainable than it would be inexpedient. [This view he was to modify after three weeks of struggle in the forthcoming Convention.] Let it be tried then whether any middle ground can be taken which will at once support a due supremacy of the national authority, and leave in force the local authorities so far as they can be subordinately useful.
>
> The first step to be taken, is I think a change in the principle of representation.

Here Madison went on to argue in some detail for a system under which individuals, throughout the nation, would be represented on a numerical basis in a single, national legislature, whose composition would not be affected by state boundaries.

> The change in the principle of representation [he concluded] will be relished by a majority of the States, and those too of the most influence. The Northern States will be reconciled to it by the *actual* superiority of their populousness: the Southern by their *expected* superiority in this point. This principle established, the repugnance of the large states to part with power will in great degree subside, and the small states must ultimately yield to the predominant will. . . .[17]

Madison, before the Convention assembled, had thought his way through the major problems that were to confront it.

A new form of government was offered by the delegation from Virginia to the Constitutional Convention. This draft became known as the Virginia Plan. In presenting this Plan the Virginian delegation assumed that, in accordance with the conventional view, the main objects requiring representation were the separate interests of *persons* and *property.* This well established doctrine of American whiggery embodied a pale reflection of the British distinction between Lords and Commons, and issued forth in the two houses of legislature, between which the Senate would represent the interests of property, the House of Representatives those of persons.

17. Madison to Randolph, April 8, 1787; Madison Papers, Library of Congress.

This Plan assumed that the whole of the national legislature would be put on a national basis—and therefore on a numerical basis. The nationalists, most of whom actually represented large states, had no fear of constituting the new Congress from numerical majorities on a popular basis. But when the small states, which feared for their independent existence, challenged this scheme and insisted on a compromise resulting in the specific, institutional representation of the states, then the Senate lost its original character as the house of property.

The great compromise adopted the principle of proportional representation in the House of Representatives. The electoral districts, equal in population, were to be drawn up by the state governments within the several states.

It was more on grounds of expediency than of democratic doctrine that this flat numerical ratio found favour with the Convention. The difficulties and disputes that would arise during the investigation and adjustment of apportionment on any mixed basis of numbers and wealth added to uncertainty as to whether any significant political value would be maintained, swung most of the delegates to the numerical side. In practice, the method adopted was bound to strengthen the interest of 'persons' and weaken that of 'property.' For property had lost almost its last institutional safeguard in the electoral system. Not quite its last, however: slave property was specially protected by the Federal ratio, which enumerated three-fifths of the slaves as persons for computation of representatives. Nevertheless the voters who were to be consulted under the Federal Constitution were to be consulted as persons, not as the owners of specified amounts of property. Their state governments might and usually did impose property qualifications, but these were not the result of anything in the Federal Constitution. Once the Federal government was in operation, its electoral system gave a possibly unintentional but nevertheless an unmistakable impetus to the idea of political democracy.

After settling the dispute between large and small states, and the question of representation in Congress, the Convention nearly foundered on the problem of how to constitute the executive. And the question of the presidency was closely connected in principle with that of representation in Congress: the Nationalists, who had been ardent for proportional representation in both houses, were also strongest for popular election of the executive.[18]

The Virginia Plan had envisaged an executive elected by the lower house of the legislature. But the objection to this proposal was that it would make the executive unduly dependent on the legislature, offending the doctrine of the separation of powers. The problem became extremely difficult. The Nationalists tended to favour a general election by the people at large; but this was firmly opposed by the defenders of the interests of small states and of local self-government, who argued that the people scattered over the country could not possibly know the characters of the candidates in states remote from their own, and that the elections would fall into the hands of small groups of intriguers. Eventually, at a very late stage, the Convention agreed to establish the College of Electors. Voters in presidential elections would not vote directly for presidential candidates; instead they would simply elect members of the electoral colleges in the several states; and these colleges, meeting separately, would proceed to give their own ballots for the president and vice-president, the winners being the candidates gaining the most electoral votes all over the country.

The system reflected a certain distrust of direct popular action. But the constitution of the electoral colleges in fact reflected the trend towards giving power to electoral majorities among the people. Each state was to be entitled to as many members in its own electoral college as it had members of the House of Representatives and senators; so that voting strength in the full College of Electors would turn on population. Each state was free to decide how to elect its own electoral college—some did it by legislative appointment, others by popular election. It later became the custom for the winning side in each state to take *all* the electoral votes

18. Farrand, *Records of the Constitutional Convention* (New Haven, 1937), I, pp. 36, 193; II, pp. 55–56, 111.

in that state; so that a narrow popular majority would result in a unanimous slate of voters in the state electoral college. The system therefore produced, in presidential elections, some marked distortions of the majority principle.

The Nationalists—or National Whigs, as they might better be called—showed no fear or hesitation about the wholesomeness of the popular will. They had undertaken to model a government based on the consent of the governed. Though such consent had long stood, in some form, as an English constitutional principle, it was a distinctive American contribution to insist that consent could no longer rest on legal fiction. American whiggery required more explicit procedure for the implementation of consent.

In the search for a procedure of consent, those who wanted special safeguards for property did not persist in the demand for the representation of property by itself but rather tried to find some way of mixing property with persons. It was this sort of mixture that gave to a state, or district, what was called 'weight' or 'importance.' And a decisive step had been measured in the forming of democratic institutions when it was decided that this great element of political authority was adequately determined by proportional representation—in short, by the majority.

In Massachusetts, the majority principle had made its decisive advance through the conjunction of the interests of mercantile wealth and the city populations of the seaboard. Something very similar happened in Maryland, under the dominating influence of Baltimore, and in New York. It was not population that carried the day, but population allied to the leading interests of the most politically influential form of property.

On the continental scene the operative principle, though not identical, was similar in character. The National Whigs, for a variety of reasons, saw the United States as a nation. The allegiance of every citizen, then, had to be drawn towards the national authority, and that authority had to draw its strength from the people of the Union, not from a congregation of unequal units exercising equal powers. The interests that brought the Convention into being were diverse, sometimes inharmonious; but the most powerful of those making for a stronger and more national form of government were in general (though not without exceptions) connected either with the larger states, or with the business interests more intimately allied to the leadership in those states than in their own.

The majority principle thus emerged as the one which would give a proper representation to 'weight' in the Union, as it had done in the states where, sooner or later, it was to gain a leading place in each constitution. But in spite of this victory, the principle of majority rule emerged from the Philadelphia Convention with an ambiguous authority in American government.

The truth was that a residual element of interest representation was frozen into the American Constitution. The form it took was that of the direct representation of the states on an equal basis in the Senate. As new interests, embodied in the great geo-economic sections of the growing Union, took shape during the next half-century, they took shelter beneath the interest principle in the Constitution. But even this procedure was made possible because, within the states themselves, the trend was towards more and more popular elections: wider suffrage (already extensive at the Revolution); wider eligibility to political office; numerical apportionment of legislative seats.

Thus, although the corporate or interest principle remained embedded in the Constitution, the course of American history gradually made it more anachronistic.

3

Slavery and Revolution:
The Conscience of the Rich
(1978)

> The late resolution of the Quakers in Pennsylvania to set at
> liberty all their negro slaves may satisfy us that their number
> cannot be very great. Had they made any considerable part of
> their property, such a resolution could never have been
> agreed to.
>
> ADAM SMITH, The Wealth of Nations,
book three, chapter two.

Adam Smith's ironical comment appears at first sight to be a reflection on the power of property. But it is set unostentatiously in a
paragraph which begins by saying that the pride of man makes him
love to domineer, and concludes that the sugar and tobacco
planters can afford the costs of slave labour because their profits
are so high—not that their profits are high because slave labour is

This essay is a revised version of a review article on two important but widely differing books: *The Problem of Slavery in the Age of Revolution 1770–1823*, by David
Brion Davis (Ithaca: N.Y., Cornell University Press, 1975); and *American Slavery,
American Freedom: The Ordeal of Colonial Virginia*, by Edmund S. Morgan (New
York: W. W. Norton, 1975). The attempt to combine them was an intellectual experiment which in slightly different circumstances would not have occurred to me,
and which I risked only after much deliberation. I would not now wish to stand by
all of my earlier comments on Professor Morgan's book, and this revision has been
influenced by a correspondence between us. The main burden does seem to me to
survive, but I would like to express my appreciation of the generous spirit in which
he replied to my argument.

The review originally appeared in *The Historical Journal*, vol. 20, no. 2 (1977).

superior. Men will not voluntarily get rid of large numbers of slaves when those numbers are the visible sign of the power of domination; but they may do so—Quakers no more nor less than others—when the smallness of numbers makes little difference.

The author of *The Wealth of Nations* understood far better than many economists, social scientists, and historians who have succeeded him that the concept of self-interest is complex and that, though property must always be a large element, it is not the only point from which self-interest can be defined. It was to appear later, very gradually, that when the self-interest of slave-owners ceased to be connected to the dominant interests of society, there existed for the first time the possibility of a flanking movement which could isolate slavery, exposing it to attacks which it could not survive.

Considered from Professor David Brion Davis's deep perspectives, the problem of slavery was a special case of the conscience of the rich. It began as the problem of how slavery was justified, and turned into the problem of how it came to be an abomination, no longer to be tolerated by civilized morality. The solution that began to emerge in the first of his two magnificent works[1] centred eventually on the emergence of the doctrine of benevolence—which is to be found, incidentally, in Pope's *Essay on Man* as well as in Shaftesbury and Hutcheson. Benevolence was based on the belief that people naturally preferred freedom. The burden of justification therefore fell on those who would enslave their fellow men. After the decline of all forms of slavery in the West, it posed a special problem because of its massive revival in the New World. Arguments for involuntary service as a form of social control, to be found in certain seventeenth-century political thinkers including Pufendorf, and surviving even into the thought of Francis Hutcheson, really did not apply to the conditions of labour exploitation in the Americas. The whole of the argument for New World slavery was brutally materialistic. Wherever slaves were

1. David Brion Davis, *The Problem of Slavery in Western Culture* (Ithaca, N.Y., 1966).

held on a large scale, the institution created a society which would have the greatest difficulty in absorbing the consequences of emancipation—making voluntary emancipation extremely improbable, as Adam Smith perceived. In the New World, moreover, this problem was greatly exacerbated by the fact that long before the end of the eighteenth century the very definition of slavery was bound up with race.

Professor Davis's aim in this second volume is to trace the impact of the revolutions of the Western world on both the concept and the practical vitality of slavery. He tells us, however, that he does not aim to explain the exact processes but rather the enveloping circumstances that weakened slavery's defences against its enemies. The political responses to slavery followed similar patterns in the different institutions of Great Britain, France, and the United States; the crucial difference followed from the opportunities available to the slave-holding classes and from their influence over constitutional structures; this is the basic reason why Britain and France, unlike the United States, found it possible to abolish slavery in their empires without civil convulsion at home. This elaborate framework enables Professor Davis to follow in detail the changing attitudes of upper-class or educated people to the use and discipline of labour, which he suggests as a legitimating condition for the rise of the anti-slavery movement. One inevitable consequence of these patterns is the structural complexity of the book, which continues the story of the general weakening of the defences of slavery in America during the Revolution, explains the consequences of the French revolution in both the French and British empires, and traces the mounting strength and gradual triumph of the abolition movement in Britain. A sort of coda is provided by a study of the Somerset case and its successors—a passage that might have been placed earlier in the text to assist the reader in following the decline of slavery's standing in English law.

Mansfield's celebrated judgement in *Somerset*[2] has often been

2. *Somerset* has generally been held to have been the test case for the doctrine that slavery could not exist on English soil. The case arose in 1769 after the slave

the subject of romantic treatment; but (unlike Camden!) he was not a romantic man, and no recent scholarly opinion seems to have held that his decision abolished slavery even in England. Mansfield wished to avoid rendering £700,000 worth of slave property held in Britain insecure, he recognized that British courts upheld contracts for slave property in the colonies and at sea, and he might have added that British colonies, which were forbidden to make laws repugnant to the laws of England, had protected slavery in laws which the Privy Council had never disallowed. Moreover, Mansfield had before him the joint opinion of the law officers Sir Philip Yorke (Lord Hardwicke) and Charles Talbot in 1729 in which they declared that a slave brought into England remained a slave—a view thought necessary to maintain Britain's good faith with its slave-holding colonies. This opinion was intended to modify that of Lord Chief Justice Holt, who held in *Smith v. Gould* (1706) that the fact of being a Negro could not establish slavery since English law knew of no difference between Negroes and other men; in the later view, it was not the fact of being black but the condition of being slave that the law must consider.

Yet Mansfield did not follow these precedents. When every allowance has been made for the inescapable conclusion that he held his opinion down to the narrowest grounds compatible with the facts on the record, from which he hoped it would not escape into

James Somerset had escaped from his master, Charles Stuart, a Virginian who had brought him to London. When Stuart's agents found Somerset they seized him and placed him in irons on board a vessel bound for Jamaica, where Stuart intended to sell him. Before the ship sailed, anti-slavery people in London heard of the incident and obtained a writ of *habeas corpus* from Lord Mansfield, Chief Justice of the King's Bench. Mansfield himself would have preferred an out-of-court settlement avoiding any pronouncement of general principles, but this proved impossible, partly because Granville Sharp, who was active for Somerset behind the scenes, dissuaded him from accepting manumission as part of a compromise. Eventually, in 1772, Mansfield gave his judgement, which concluded with the celebrated statement that the case could not be allowed by the laws of England. He did not, however, specifically declare that *slavery* in all circumstances could not be allowed. Modern scholarship recognizes that Mansfield's reasoning in *Somerset* was too narrow to serve as a precedent for full-scale emancipation in Great Britain.

the political atmosphere, the judgement was undoubtedly a triumph for anti-slavery. For the historian there appear to be two questions: What considerations influenced Mansfield's decision? And what did his decision determine?

They may be taken in order. Professor Davis, whose researches amount to the most thorough *investigation* yet made into the reports, arguments, and general debate on the case, argues that a hundred years of political ideology lay behind Mansfield's conclusion that an act representing total domination by one man over another's person was intolerable under English law. This should help, incidentally, to explain why Mansfield went out of his way to remark that positive law could be preserved in immemorial usage: the point being that *no* such usage could be found to protect slavery anywhere in English law. 'Personal dominion was the point at issue in Somerset,' says Professor Davis (p. 480), and Mansfield's phrase, 'so high an act of dominion' (which echoes Somerset's counsel) refers, not to slavery in general, but to Charles Stuart's action in seizing Somerset's body and putting him in irons on board a vessel with the intention of transferring him as a slave to Jamaica.

That was not all, however. According to Howell,[3] Mansfield concluded with the words: 'Whatever inconveniences therefore, may follow from the decision, I cannot say this case is allowed or approved by the law of England; and therefore the black must be discharged.' If—as Professor Davis implies—the law permitted Stuart to hold Somerset as a slave but not to transport him abroad, or if, following a suggestion in the third edition of Blackstone's *Commentaries*,[4] the master had a right to the service though not to the person, it seems that one result might have been to release Somerset from the confinement imposed by Stuart but not actually set him at liberty. Why, for example, should Stuart (who was leav-

3. T. B. Howell, *State Trials* (London, 1814), p. 82.
4. Blackstone warned Granville Sharp not to rely on the more outright version in the first edition, which declared that English law freed a slave who set foot in England. Davis, *Age of Revolution*, p. 485.

ing the country) not have sold him in England? The possibility
might have followed from Mansfield's use of the word 'discharged,'
which need not have meant more than that the black was to be
taken out of confinement. He did not explicitly say that the black
was to be given his liberty. Professor Davis does not consider this
question, to which no answer seems yet to have appeared either
on the face of the record or in subsequent scholarship. But the abolitionists knew that for all Mansfield's caution they had won a
famous victory, and proceeded to attribute to the Lord Chief Justice those famous but highly uncharacteristic words about the pure
air of England that were actually spoken by Serjeant-at-law William Davy. Professor Davis next goes to the Scottish case of *Knight
v. Wedderburn* (1778) in which Mansfield's implied doctrine becomes the law of liberty in Britain; but he further shows that as
late as 1827 Lord Stowell, sitting in the Court of Admiralty, found
it necessary to correct misinterpretations of the Somerset precedent, and confirmed the slave status of Grace Jones, who had been
brought to England but returned later to Antigua.[5]

The anti-slavery movement could not feed on tendencies. As
Professor Roger Anstey has observed, 'An intellectual climate fa-
vourable to abolition, though important, was in no way sufficient to
secure it.'[6] Much of the growing power and relentless determina-

5. I am grateful to Dr. David Yale for a letter on the interpretation of Somerset and
related cases. It is clear that even in the light of Somerset, residence in England
did not make a slave free if that slave left British shores without compulsion; and
yet a master, though entitled by law to the slave's service, could not compel the
person. The contradiction (it seems to me) was inherent in the condition, and no
logical resolution was possible. Lord Stowell avowed himself an abolitionist;
another anti-slavery judge, Joseph Story of the United States Supreme Court,
regretfully accepted his opinion as binding precedent for American law.
   I would like also to record my sense of indebtedness to the late Jacob Viner of
Princeton University, who in the course of long conversation in 1957 pointed out
to me that James Somerset was the only slave freed by Lord Mansfield's famous
decision and that both slavery and slave sales continued in Britain.
6. Roger Anstey, *The Atlantic Slave Trade and British Abolition, 1760-1810* (London, 1975), pp. 406-7. In his analysis of the tactics by which Grenville and the
abolitionists urged the importance of cutting off the slave trade to captured
foreign islands as a precaution against enhancing their value against their possi-

tion of the abolition movement was owed to what might be called the Quaker International. The sense of urgency which impelled these men and the Clapham sect who overlapped with them had perforce to make its accommodations with political realities and to accept the necessity of gradualism. It must be said here that Professor Davis's method does not supply an explanation of how the abolition of the slave trade was actually achieved in Britain, and it has been left to Professor Anstey to clinch the connection between idealism and politics; the full implications of Davis's work become clearer in the light of Anstey's, and students will be well advised to keep them side by side.

Professor Davis is at his most concrete when he demonstrates that when in 1794 the French National Convention finally decreed universal emancipation they were moved not by the ideals of Brissot or the now enfeebled *amis des noirs* but by the consideration that only Toussaint's black army could save the island from British invasion. On the whole, however, he is more interested in the complex task of re-creating a changing intellectual climate in which anti-slavery takes its place among a variety of trends in the relationship of people to work, time, and property. The development of a wage-based economy itself helped to establish the preference for freedom. Under advanced industrialism this very freedom was to become 'wage slavery'; but Professor Davis takes note of the need to avoid 'the simplistic impression that "industrialists" promoted abolitionist doctrine as a means of distracting attention from their own forms of exploitation' (p. 455). But he has already said quite baldly that 'The anti-slavery movement, like Smith's political economy, reflected the needs and values of the emerging capitalist order.' And after some qualification he adds that the abolitionists 'succeeded in making a sincere humanitarianism an integral part of

ble return at the end of the war, Anstey observes in a brilliant aside, which has some bearing on Davis's thesis, that the situation is 'perhaps harder to discern because one is so conditioned to expect interest to masquerade as altruism that one may dismiss altruism when concealed beneath the cloak of interest.' *Ibid.*, pp. 407–8.

class ideology, and thus of British culture' (p. 350). One can agree that 'Because the slave system appeared to be dominated by an un-mitigated drive for wealth, it could symbolize all the forces that threatened to unravel the fabric of traditional deference, patronage and hereditary status' (pp. 453–54). But why does he say only that it 'could' have symbolized these forces? The question is whether it *did*, and if so what part that symbolism actually played in shaping the fears and motives of abolitionists. This choice of a non-commit-tal word is significant of a certain inconclusive suggestiveness which Professor Davis sometimes strikes while seeming to say more. He sees the record of English capitalism as making English-men particularly sensitive to the dangers of such disintegration; but after all, West Indian slavery was a long way from England, and in any case English society had absorbed its consequences for over a century. Slavery itself was not likely to be a greater force for disintegration merely because of the rise of industry. Professor Davis adds a comment on the probability that 'anti-slavery experi-ence ultimately taught many Englishmen to recognize forms of sys-tematic oppression that were closer to home' (p. 455). He affirms—though it looks a little like an admission—that 'the rise of anti-slavery represented a major advance in the moral consciousness of mankind.' Yet almost irresistibly he slides towards some of the simplifications against which he has warned himself, and concludes with ambivalent firmness that 'although the abolitionist movement helped to clear an ideological path for British industrialists, it also bred a new sensitivity to social oppression' (p. 467).

These remarks are connected to the argument that the early forms of the new industrialism, notably in the rules enforced by Josiah Wedgwood, tended to substitute a contractual and individ-ual set of relationships for the old, organic, and customary ones. Now every one of these observations may be true. They help us to see much more clearly the extraordinary complexity of the social and intellectual circumstances in which the anti-slavery movement arose; and they probably mean that anti-slavery was likely to con-verge with a new industrial consciousness, linking the rights of property with the discipline of labour and requiring a much tighter form of human control. St. Monday was on its way out. But it does not follow that anti-slavery was promoted, even unconsciously, to advance the interests of that order, to furnish it with a clear conscience or to mediate its emergence in British law and culture. I cannot help feeling that when Professor Davis remarks that 'Anti-slavery was a transitional social movement that served to mediate values and to prepare the way for the largely unforeseen things to come' (p. 361), he betrays a sense of the vulnerability of his own argument. The anti-slavery movement cannot conceivably have been motivated by a desire to prepare the way for things it could not foresee; and the facts that its leaders tended to be gentry or professional persons who knew and spoke the same language as the country's rulers and argued their case in terms of values held in common rather than attacking the social order, do not establish a connection between the motives of anti-slavery and the interests of industrial capitalism. This issue brings out a conflict of views between Davis and Anstey in which Anstey's method of sticking close to political history should not escape notice. His analysis of the parliamentary votes on abolition and other issues in 1791 and 1796 discloses 'not a trace' in abolitionist ranks 'of parliamentary support representing the rising forces in the economy.'[7]

The topography that Professor Davis re-creates should not be taken for a map. He suggests immanent possibilities where he may lead readers to think he has established firm lines of communication. In his view the freedom to which British abolitionists were attached was a disciplined, work-conscious, utilitarian freedom. With this argument, which he develops with great subtlety and a wealth of evidence, including Bentham's vision of the industrial panopticon, one can surely agree; the error would be to accept the implication that the connection is required to *explain* the rise of the anti-slavery movement—that in effect the one could not have happened without the other. The immorality of slavery as it

7. Anstey, *Atlantic Slave Trade*, p. 285.

seems to emerge from this picture was not domination but merely waste: an inefficient use of labour. But Sharpe, Stephen and Clarkson, Wilberforce and Thornton, did not take their moral bearings from Josiah Wedgwood—and neither did the Quakers of Pennsylvania or of the London Meeting for Sufferings; and it stretches the economic imagination of the Saints to suggest that their changing perception of the labour potential of the poor in the British Isles inspired the condemnation of slavery in the Caribbean. Such a criticism would have been vulnerable to the alternative view that slavery needed not to be abolished but to be improved. Professor Davis has foreseen and even warned his readers against these objections, only, I think, to involve himself in arguments that could be taken in either direction. Bentham's panopticon, for example, might have been admired as the perfect moden for *more efficient* slavery.

Great Britain's experience differed in two important respects from America's. Britain did not depend on a domestically based slave economy, and did not share in the revolutions of the era. The American War of Independence may have had some of the secondary but it had none of the primary effects of a revolution. In America, on the other hand, public commitment to liberty and equality of rights forced the new republicans to attend to the problem of slavery in their midst, but—as Duncan MacLeod has shown—this also had the effect of defining the limits of human rights. Professor Davis holds, with Dr. MacLeod, that the problem had a firmly racial connotation at the time of the Revolution, and that the Revolution was therefore bound to define not only the expectation of eventual emancipation but the geographical limits within which it could hope to work. Though Professor Davis disclaims any intention to criticize the views of Winthrop Jordan [8] and William Freehling, [9] his argument that Jefferson and the other

8. Winthrop D. Jordan, *White Over Black: American Attitudes toward the Negro, 1550–1812* (Chapel Hill, 1968).
9. William Freehling, 'The Founding Fathers and Slavery,' *American Historical Review*, LXXVII (February 1972).

Southern founders were basically controlled by the economic needs and psychological ties of the planter class, and that their anti-slavery gradualism gradually became mere impotence, is at the very least distinct from theirs; and for all the respect we may have for the subtle agonies of the Jeffersonian conscience, Professor Davis makes a case from which it is difficult to dissent.

Jefferson, Hamilton, and Jay, as he points out, all deplored slavery, all of them were aware of the obstacles to emancipation, and none was free of racial prejudice. Hamilton and Jay gave their support to anti-slavery causes; Jefferson hardly lifted a finger. The fundamental difference lay not in their psychologies but in their situations. It is important, however, to link this argument with another finding that comes out elsewhere in Professor Davis's work: that of the extreme gradualism which dominated the Northern branches of the American anti-slavery movement. An immense optimism about America's capacity to solve the problems that had troubled so much of human history tended to diminish the urgency of slavery. When one has compared the satisfied gradualism of Noah Webster of Massachusetts, who regarded slavery as an abomination to be wiped out in the course of the next two centuries, with the painful helplessness of Jefferson and his Virginian contemporaries, one has gained a perspective from which the Virginian position, though far from admirable, becomes a little less merely self-serving. Professor Davis, who quotes Webster, is too absorbed in his critique of Jefferson to pause over the light this passage casts on Jeffersonian gradualism, and absorbs this transition into a concept which he entitles 'The Perishability of Revolutionary Time.' The concept of 'revolutionary time' deserves more attention; for some branches of historical study it may have profound importance.

One of the most illuminating contributions of these monumental books has been the analysis of the new philosophy of benevolence and its role in altering the moral climate of human obligations. This, as we saw in the first volume, has as much as anything to do with the otherwise inexplicable rise of the anti-slavery movement in the mid-eighteenth century, when no economic indications had seriously begun to question its utility. It may be suggested that in concentrating on business and labour Professor Davis gives rather less than its due to the moral momentum built up by that movement. But the American Revolution accelerated that momentum and raises the question as to why 'benevolence'—if we are to attribute force to ideas—failed to curb slavery in the South. The basic answer is of course economic: Southern leadership could no longer contemplate the future without either slave labour or some near equivalent, while the racial factor confirmed the system. In a very sensitive analysis, Professor Davis shows how in the light of white beliefs—and needs to believe—in racial superiority, benevolence became a philosophy of trusteeship; a view that slid easily into the paternalism to which Eugene Genovese has recently given a new explanatory depth for a later generation of slaveholders.

The concept of benevolence, however, plays a diminished part in Davis's revolutionary era. He is aware of a need to link his earlier emphasis on benevolence with the emerging ethics of capitalism and utilitarianism, and he remarks of British anti-slavery that it 'helped to ensure stability while accommodating society to political and economic change; it merged Utilitarianism with an ethic of benevolence, reinforcing faith that a progressive policy of laissez faire would reveal men's natural identity of interests' (p. 384). Satisfaction with the functional efficiency of this formation should not have impeded its author from reminding his readers that British opponents of slavery did not *know* they were doing all this and did not embark on their passionate crusade against evil for these chilly and abstract reasons. Yet beyond this there remains a certain discrepancy when we turn back to the explanatory force which Davis attaches to the idea of benevolence in his first volume, and compare its effects with those of the colder ethics of utility which in his second volume seem to carry the dynamic charge which really gets things done. It may well be that if the convictions which sustained the writing of *The Problem of Slavery in Western Culture* had been maintained, we should have seen a much stronger interpretation of the operation of benevolence as a political force; and if the new emphasis on labour time and economic utilities is correct, we may well be tempted to ask how mere benevolence could have achieved such decisive changes of preliminary attitude *before* the age became revolutionary.

Professor Davis's argument overlaps with Professor Morgan's, and although the essence of the first begins where the latter leaves off, Davis links them to reinforce his own. Professor Morgan's theme has developed through two phases, each resulting in a paradox. It is Phase One to which Professor Davis refers, and in this, published in 1972,[10] Professor Morgan concluded that by virtue of her peculiar dependence on slavery, Virginia had in effect bought her liberty at the price of black slavery. To this Davis attaches a corollary, valuable for Virginia, dubious for Britain: 'the Virginians could defend man's inalienable rights because Negro slavery had precluded the need to discipline a white proletariat; Englishmen could later condemn the principle of slavery, as a demonstration of their own liberality, because they were beginning to find new uses for the idle poor, who . . . could be molded into a compliant working class.' Justice is not done to the abolitionists by suggesting that they were demonstrating their own liberality, nor does this sort of argument explain why some people became abolitionists while others did not; and it may be significant that Professor Davis would not be likely to transfer it to William Lloyd Garrison, the sisters Grimké, Theodore Parker, or Theodore Weld.

He is on much safer ground in accepting Morgan's Paradox Phase One, which had some of the force of a truism. In the mid-nineteenth century George Fitzhugh placed the argument that high civilizations had always been raised on forced or exploited labour at the centre of his sociological defence of Southern slavery. The real importance of Professor Morgan's book is his second paradox, that Virginians bought not only their political independence

10. Edmund S. Morgan, 'Slavery and Freedom: The American Paradox,' *Journal of American History*, LIX (June 1972).

but their libertarian ideology with Negro slavery. This he regards as a tragic conclusion to a process that had little if any burden of racism in its beginning.

The book falls into two sections, of which the first, taking the Virginian story to the early eighteenth century, stands securely on its own merits, and if published separately would have made by itself the best account yet written of the character and development of the labour system of seventeenth-century Virginia. Professor Morgan writes with invariable clarity and with occasional touches of sympathetic humour; he is a historian with understanding and compassion for the past. Unlike predecessors who have written of the early development of slavery and race relations, he has taken account of the general problem of poverty in Britain during the centuries of American colonization. He begins by tracing the original plans of Sandys and Thorpe to found a biracial, Anglo-American Indian society and labour force in Virginia, the collapse of this concept, and the agricultural crisis resulting immediately in the desperate food shortage and the failure of the Virginia Company. While attributing these problems largely to the surplus of gentlemen who never expected to work and who refused to learn from the Indians even when survival was at stake, Professor Morgan reveals the beginnings of the attitude by which masters treated their servants as mere things. But he finds no evidence that distinctions in labour discipline were based on race. After the failure of the design for incorporating the Indians, and with perhaps no more than 500 Negroes in the colony as late as 1650, this is not surprising. Virginians, he points out, did not enslave their first Negroes, who were already slaves; but as these new-found servants had neither indentures nor contracts it still seems unlikely that they were released from bondage later. Virginians, however, could hardly have expected them to form the basis for economic growth, and Professor Morgan's careful exclusion of racial considerations from his account of the growth of the labour force may be thought to disprove a little too much. In committing himself to taking the labour problem as far as he can without admitting any distinction on lines of race he is of course carrying the attack—though it is an attack by silence—to Winthrop Jordan, who emphasized the racial, religious, aesthetic, and moral preconceptions which helped to shape European views of Africans and which appear to have made them peculiarly vulnerable to enslavement. There were other factors, of course. Indians were enslaved and destroyed by Spain and Portugal; but in Virginia they nearly destroyed the settlers, and after the massacre of 1622 the disadvantages of trying to coerce them were painfully obvious.

If slavery were to be contemplated, another possible candidate was the white servant, and Professor Morgan eloquently brings to light the slavish treatment to which servants were subjected. 'My master Atkins,' wrote one of them from Virginia in 1623, 'hath sold me for £150 sterling like a damnd slave' (p. 128). But it is doubtful whether legal enslavement of English people was ever in question; it would have been a moral anachronism which in any case, as Professor Morgan points out, the Crown, in the interests of further English settlement, would never have tolerated.

Professor Morgan thinks that until about 1660, Virginia was 'absorbing' Negroes and there was no particular reason to anticipate a racially divided society. His evidence for this view is slight and inconclusive; but the evidence for incipient racialism, though somewhat more impressive, is also necessarily thin. Any such development had to wait on events, which began to come after 1660. About that time began the rise of a better capitalized, richer, and more assured planter oligarchy—earlier noted, incidentally, by Bernard Bailyn.[11] Government office began to become an important source of income and status. Blacks began to be legally enslaved—and to be born into slavery.

Why, then, when actual enslavement began to form the basis of a labour force on which rich estates were to rise, was it blacks who were the victims? Morgan asserts that 'the actions that produced slavery in Virginia . . . had no necessary connection with race' (p.

11. Bernard Bailyn, 'Politics and Social Structure in Virginia' in James Morton Smith, ed., *Seventeenth Century America* (Chapel Hill, 1959).

314). Yet he has already noted differences in treatment—which could hardly be ignored in the light of Jordan's evidence that Negroes were regarded as both inferior and undesirable and were probably even enslaved, as reflected in laws and reports from New England to Barbados from as early as the 1630s[12]—and he is later to admit that 'a degree of racial prejudice was doubtless present in Virginia from the beginning' (p. 327). By an act of 1667 Virginia decided that conversion to Christianity did not alter slave status; an act of 1670 determined that Negroes shipped into the colony should be slaves for life—as opposed to Indians, who if brought in by land were to serve for twelve years; and an act of 1682 confirmed this trend by making slaves of all imported non-Christians. By that time slavery had been definitely set on a racial basis.

These policies, according to Morgan, were deliberately racial. The poverty of the mid-century years produced chronic disorders, and the problem of controlling the poor, which reached formidable proportions in Bacon's rising of 1676 was to be resolved by racism, an attitude which, once inculcated, steadily set the whites above the blacks, preserved even the poorest whites from the degradation of slavery, and gave them a sense of common identity with their superiors. Slavery meanwhile brought into existence a permanent, disciplined labour force of the kind the planters needed as the European demand for tobacco raised the prospects of the colonial economy.

The error of this ingenious attempt to extrude the racial factor from the motives for the original introduction of permanent slavery, while admitting it later under an economic motivation, is the exact corollary of the Whig interpretation of history. Just as Whig historians supposed that the great institutions must have great beginnings, and sought the intention to found the parliamentary system in such episodes as the 'Lancastrian experiment,' so Professor Morgan supposes that a great evil must have origins in evil motivation. The truth, clear in Morgan's pages although not the sub-

12. Jordan, *White Over Black*, pp. 44–98.

ject of his own emphasis, is that racial prejudice was already quite sufficient to mark the African off as a potential victim of hostile and degrading treatment; and that racial identification—quite simply, skin pigmentation and physiognomy—was sufficient to make him a convenient subject. Morgan seems to suppose that if the historical explanation of slavery lay in racism, it could only be because racism was as profound at the beginning as it later became, but this is not so. It was only necessary that racism should be sufficient, and that visible identification—already a cause of racial repugnance— should make slavery so easily practicable. It is not necessary to hold that racism was a profound or ineradicable social phenomenon which had already doomed America to its subsequent racial miseries. Small beginnings had deep and terrible consequences. The decisive factor, however, was not so much that these beginnings were small in the total context of their time, as that, in that context, they were sufficient. From that time forth, slavery would grow to become both enduring and massive, and racial prejudice would grow into the cruel but still more enduring phenomenon which Tocqueville noted when he attributed racial prejudice against Negroes to the enslavement of the Negro race.[13]

After a lucid account of the rise of the great Virginia families and their fortunes, which was accompanied by a marked increase in the sense of rank among whites, Professor Morgan embarks on the line that leads him to the final paradox, in which he attributes the ideology of liberty to the existence of a racially based slave system. He does this by tracing the reception of 'Commonwealth' and republican ideas in eighteenth-century America and tacking this theme rather crudely to his argument about the racial basis of the economy.

Professor Morgan's description of the 'republican' ideology of

13. Alexis de Tocqueville, *De la démocratie en Amérique*, ed. J.-P. Meyer (Paris, 1961), pp. 1, 357. These views are I think close to Jordan's concept of the 'unthinking decision' to institute racial slavery. Morgan consistently underrates the cumulative weight of Jordan's evidence for the sixteenth and seventeenth centuries.

Harrington and his circle is meant to lock neatly into the economic theory and provide a complete platform on which the Virginian leadership were able to affirm their faith in human rights, equality, and liberty precisely because the society they led was to so large an extent a society of freemen and even of freeholders, raised and consolidated on the enslavement of the labour force, all of which was made possible by the special element imported into the situation—racial contempt. 'Racism,' he concludes, 'became an essential, if unacknowledged, ingredient of the republican ideology that enabled Virginians to lead the nation.'

This account of the specific circumstances in which republican ideology took shape in Virginia commands particular attention because of the argument that racial contempt served even at this early period to unify the whites and to give them a sense of social equality which would otherwise have been out of keeping with their manifest differences. Professor Morgan also makes the point that the presence of slavery itself reinforced the whites' sense of the reality of such a condition, which played a powerful part in the colonists' anti-British rhetoric. People who held slaves felt they knew what it meant to be reduced to slavery. We also owe to Professor Morgan's explanation the comment that the stability of the state could be seen as threatened, not only by monarchs or oligarchs, but also by the existence of a large class of disaffected poor. But as an explanation of the necessary conditions—and he had used the word 'essential'—for the development of republican ideology, the argument appears to me to be flawed in structure and dangerous in its implications. It may help to explain the kind of republic that Virginia established when it eventually became independent; but it does not explain slavery and it does not explain the ideology of the new American Republic. If we were to follow the theory in reverse, it would be necessary to conclude that republican liberty would never have been possible in America *without* racial slavery. Yet everything that the leaders of Jefferson's generation had learnt from Harrington and the Commonwealth tradition taught them that liberty was safest in a republic of small and independent farmers; in no sense was a large, undifferentiated labour force essential to this view of the foundation of liberty. That in fact was one of Jefferson's deepest beliefs, and if he had not found himself in the circumstances of a great landowner and considerable slave-owner he would have had no theoretical difficulty whatever—though he would certainly have had much personal discomfort—in adapting his whole set of political beliefs to those of a small but independent farmer in a real republic of equals. Neither did Harrington himself believe that Oceana could or should rest on a force of serfs. His ideology was based in an Aristotelian distribution of land, and his famous dictum that power follows the distribution of property stood as a permanent warning to all his disciples in future generations against permitting the rise of the overmighty subject, of whom some of the planters of Virginia and South Carolina could well have served as examples.

It is true that the forms taken by the systems of representation in Virginia and other Southern states reflected the interests of the great proprietors, but even so they did not afford them specific constitutional status. It has been argued that the very fact that the labour force was so largely black had the effect of concealing from the ruling classes the true limitations of their republican theory[14] and permitted them by excluding the labour force from the boundaries of political society to congratulate themselves on having created a free republic. Morgan is clearly quite right, if not strikingly original, in claiming that the factor of race made it possible for the masters of Virginia to base their economy on a non-absorbable labour force; but it is an error to regard the society raised on this structure as the only available contemporary model for republican society, and still more erroneous to argue that slavery was indispensable to the ideology of the founders—that they were republicans because they were slave-owners.

It is worth reinforcing this objection by returning to Virginia it-

14. J. R. Pole, *Political Representation in England and the Origins of the American Republic* (New York and London, 1966), pp. 533–34.

self in the mid-seventeenth-century period which Professor Morgan recounts so well. In 1652 Virginia was not far from being an independent republic, yet in 1655 only for the first time did the assembly impose a property qualification for the suffrage (to be repealed the following year). Yet all this was before either the foundation of racial slavery or the rise of the 'Commonwealth' tradition—in fact before Harrington had published *Oceana*.

A curious feature of Morgan's reasoning is that, if logically pursued, it actually leads away from his own central thesis. Instead of making the republicanism of Virginia the archetypical ideology of the American Republic, his argument makes Virginia into a special and peculiar case. This case would have represented a sharp departure from Commonwealth principles, and calls for a far clearer disentanglement of Virginian circumstances, and by consequence of Virginian principles, from the old republican tradition. Morgan as I read him essentially runs them together. (Nor do I agree that eighteenth-century thinkers such as James Burgh or Fletcher of Saltoun, who suggested enslaving the disorderly poor as a form of social control, can be properly compared with the slavemasters of America, where slavery was a condition of birth.) Seventeenth-century English Commonwealthmen and Whigs had not learnt the principles of liberty from having a huge and unabsorbable mass of poor and vagrants; on the contrary (as Morgan notes in a different connection) poverty threatened the conditions of liberty. France did not learn the doctrine of liberty from slavery, and neither Rousseau nor such contributors to the *Encyclopédie* as the Chevalier de Jaucourt would have understood the suggestion that their ideas of liberty were founded in the very slavery they attacked. John Adams must remain silent in face of Professor Morgan's implied assertion that his political principles rested on the profits of Southern slavery. But New England, New York, and Pennsylvania had no need to acknowledge such foundations for their concept of the Republic. If they had, Adam Smith's ironies would have remained unwritten.

4

Property and Law
in the American Republic
(1978)

The Granary Burying Ground in Boston, which must be one of the oldest in English America, contains many tombs of interest from the historical point of view and that of mortuary iconography. The most curious, however, is a small obelisk, not much above four feet in height, which bears the plain inscription, THIS TOMB IS THE PROPERTY OF ELIZABETH PICKLING AND MARY HOOTEN, HEIRS OF DEAC. JOHN LEE.* Nothing beside remains. But if, as I suspect, this unusual monument dates from a rather more recent period than some of its neighbours, it may also stand as a memorial to a remark of Sir Henry Maine, who noticed that it was the United States that had attained the extreme form of the concept of private property in land.[1] The policy of making public land over into private property is a theme to which I shall return. Maine is more

---

*I am grateful to Bernard Bailyn for verifying this inscription.

1. Sir Henry Maine, *Ancient Law*. (London, 1888 ed.).

This essay is a revised and expanded version of a lecture delivered to the Anglo-American Conference of Historians at the Institute of Historical Research, London University, in July 1978. I would like to express appreciation to Mark Kaplanoff and William L. Letwin for their comments on the original text.

often remembered for having said that the tendency of progressive societies had been from status to contract; and a modern historian of the social effects of law, Professor Willard Hurst, has described the first three-quarters of the nineteenth century as pre-eminently the period of contract law in the United States.[2] It seems reasonable to follow by asking whether in fact the United States also achieved the extreme form of contract theory. To that question I will not now risk a specific answer, which would involve a wide-ranging review of comparative law, though I do suggest that the comparative view would have much to suggest about the relationship between the economics of capitalist development and the functions of law. Contract law clearly played a necessary and enabling role in all forms of capitalist development and we shall have to try to relate it to its American context.

The popular name of the type of capitalist economy that sprang up so rapidly in nineteenth-century America was a 'free labour' economy, perhaps because it was labour rather than capital that needed to be convinced of its freedom. In the third quarter of the century, Standard Oil's legal advisers began to devise the trust as a form of corporate government for multiple branches of business; within a few years, the increasingly monopolistic aspects of the corporate form of business became a matter of major public concern; but the more heavily concentrated and monopolistic the system became, the more firmly did its political and business spokesmen commit themselves and the nation to the conviction that the system incorporated all that was best of free private enterprise and of what came to be called economic—eventually 'rugged'—individualism. It followed in one of those logical sequences, which so often give retrospective symmetry to historical interpretations, that the American Revolution was essentially a free enterprise revolution, whose ideals and indeed—this was the more significant point—whose patriotism, could be plotted on a curve running from Adam Smith and Benjamin Franklin to Herbert Hoover, and if necessary beyond, as far as Robert A. Taft.

2. James Willard Hurst, *Law and the Conditions of Freedom in the Nineteenth Century United States* (Madison, 1956), p. 18.

In the aftermath of the New Deal these views were demolished, primarily by two important studies of Massachusetts and Pennsylvania, one by Oscar and Mary Handlin, the other by Louis Hartz.[3] They showed that the early American state governments were as mercantilist and as interventionist—in intention if not always in power—as the royal government they had overthrown. These monographs represented an important step in the liberation of historical interpretation from a particular nexus of political dogma. They are still indispensable to any study of early state history as well as to early national political economy. But the Handlins and Hartz did not nationalize the story they were telling, nor was it their task to pursue in detail the connections between law, public policy, and economic growth, which increasingly dominated both state and national development from the second quarter of the nineteenth century, and often earlier.

The American revolutionaries never claimed to be fighting for new principles. They asserted repeatedly that they were engaged in the defence of ancestral English rights and privileges; and when they fell back on the rights of man, they relied on rights which we must take to have been even older than those of Englishmen. In all these rights, nothing was more fundamental than the laws of property, in which not only their fortunes but their liberties were at stake. The Massachusetts Circular Letter of 1768[4] stated the issue clearly: 'It is an essential, unalterable right in nature, engrafted into the British Constitution, as a fundamental law, and ever held sacred and irrevocable by the Subjects within the Realm, that what a man has honestly acquired is absolutely his own, which he may freely give, but cannot be taken from him without his consent.'

In the concept of property rights, Britain's American subjects

3. Oscar Handlin and Mary Flug Handlin, *Commonwealth. A Study of the Role of Government in the American Economy: Massachusetts, 1774–1861* (revised ed., Cambridge, Mass., 1969); Louis Hartz, *Economic Policy and Democratic Thought: Pennsylvania, 1776–1860* (Cambridge, Mass., 1948).
4. Quoted in Richard Schlatter, *Private Property: The History of an Idea* (London, 1951), p. 174.

had nothing to add to the laws of their forebears. It is true that the states soon began to amend some of the existing distributive principles, where these were controlled by such usages as primogeniture and entail; but this was a legitimate exercise of legislative power, involving no change in the fundamental concept that ownership of property, and especially of real property—how clearly that designation reminds us of its character—was normally to be considered as a right of total dominion, of complete domination and possession, with which no one else, and no other power, could interfere. The abolition of entail actually increased the landlord's powers over his own land since it extended his freedom to decide when to dispose of parts of the estate. The legal rule of possession was expressed by the phrase 'quiet enjoyment.'[5] This principle did not survive the Revolution without some shocks, but it did survive, and for nearly another half-century it continued to be the governing principle as administered by American courts.

The rights of property were not confined to landowners. All forms of property, whether in land, goods, investments, or services, were held subject to an underlying concept which seems to have been open to very little question of principle, however it may have been stretched by the complexities of events. This is the idea, which held together the concept of property as dominion with the nature of property rights in objects, that the right of property consists in a direct relationship between a person and a thing. Whether the property is a landed estate (with or without women, children, slaves, or livestock) or a set of false teeth, the peculiar fact about the owner's relationship to it is that his claim is immediate and exclusive. The strength of this idea no doubt resides in its simplicity and apparent conformity not only with the obvious facts but with our proprietary sense of its rightness. The case was clearly put by James Wilson, a significant figure in any attempt to identify the revolutionary generation's ideas of law, because he

5. Morton J. Horwitz, *The Transformation of American Law, 1780–1860* (Cambridge, Mass., 1977), p. 174.

signed the Declaration of Independence, took a prominent part in the Constitutional Convention of 1787, and became a justice of the first bench of the Supreme Court of the United States. Wilson's Miscellaneous Papers contain a short essay 'On the History of Property,'[6] which begins: 'Property is the right or lawful power, which a person has to a thing. Of this right there are three different degrees. The lowest degree of this right is a right merely to possess a thing. The next degree of this right is a right to possess and use a thing. The next and highest degree of this right is a right to possess, to use, and to dispose of a thing.' (Which is why we may say that the abolition of entail enhanced the rights of property.) Wilson was well aware that there was more to the problem than that. In his lectures at the College of Philadelphia, delivered in 1790–91, he distinguished between things in possession and things in action, the latter extending to debts, rights of damages, and rights of action.[7] Since the owner of a particular piece of property was not the last authority on the question of what sort of rights he enjoyed in each case, and these might be controlled by such varied outside authorities as an entailment, or a will, or an act of parliament, it should be clear that even in the less complex jurisprudence of the period there was going to be some sort of trouble ahead for the view that the rights of property could all be explained in the simple relationship of person-to-thing. We shall need to bear these points in mind a little later when the concept of property comes up for reconsideration. For the moment, historically speaking, the important point is negative: the very distinct quickening of commercial activity in the later eighteenth century gave rise to an abundance of issues for litigation (that had been one of the reasons for the creation of vice-admiralty courts, which merchants liked because they despatched business without juries and without the interminable delays of the common law) but this quickening did not appear to give rise to any new principles of law.

6. Robert Green McCloskey, ed., *The Works of James Wilson*, 2 vols. (Cambridge, Mass., 1967), II, p. 711.
7. *Ibid.*, I, p. 95.

Neither as colonials nor as citizens of a new Republic were Americans quick to make any distinctive contributions to English common law theory. Even if new ideas had occurred, their diffusion and teaching would have been difficult in the absence of an organized profession with such attributes as professional schools, inns of court, law journals, or even formally reported judicial opinions. The very early years of the Republic witnessed a sharp reaction against lawyers, which affected their public standing even if it did not prevent them, as individuals, from continuing to take important parts in political leadership. But towards the close of the century the profession began to recover its confidence and to organize its forces—in fact, to emerge as a profession in the modern sense; and this process was so rapid and effective that by the 1830s, nearly every state provided for the publication of its own reports, and the views of the profession were treated with a respect accorded to no other established order. It was in this, and nowhere else, that Tocqueville discerned the traces of an aristocracy.[8] But this was not the work of the Revolution's generation of lawyers and was in no direct sense an outcome of the Revolution. The great work of transforming the common law into an instrument suitable for the transactions of a mercantile state was performed earlier, but it was performed in Britain, under the jurisdiction of Mansfield. Thomas Jefferson did not approve. Mansfield, in the Virginian's opinion, was corrupting the common law by introducing new meanings and usages, thus depriving it of the certainty to which he felt the citizen was entitled. Jefferson therefore suggested that Americans should cease to regard the common law of England as having any authority over them from the date of Mansfield's accession to the bench.[9]

In one important sense, Americans did construct their own law, a sense strongly consistent with Anglo-Saxon traditions. Most of the causes tried in the courts of the Northern colonies and states—

8. Alexis de Tocqueville, *Democracy in America*, tr. Henry Reeve, 2 vols. (London, 1835), II, p. 181.
9. Horwitz, *op. cit.*, p. 18.

I am not sure how far the same system applied through the South—were essentially tried by juries rather than by judges. The question on which the jury was called to decide would depend on the form of writ taken out by the plaintiff, and in principle the jury could do nothing beyond a determination as to whether the facts alleged in the writ were true or not. It then fell to the court, that is to the judge, to determine the legal consequences of this finding of fact. But in many cases the defendant adopted a procedure known as pleading 'the general issue,' which had the effect of placing the whole trial at the disposal of the jury. In many of these cases there devolved onto the jury the responsibility for deciding the law applying to the case as well as the facts of the case.[10]

These juries were far more representative of their local communities than came to be the case in later, more urban, and more impersonal generations. And the community was held together by a stronger, more adhesive, and at the same time more coercive cluster of moral values. This was particularly true in New England, where the town long remained the normal focus of public life and of much that the citizens held in common. A town's moral rules were indistinguishable from its civil and criminal laws. It was a moral unity, and its laws were enforced to maintain that unity. In cases of sabbath breaking, swearing, and breaches of sexual codes, but also in matters involving fairness in bargains, juries often found themselves transmitting the community's moral values. These duties did not call for the making of new law. The deeper responsibility of the jury, of which the legal verdict was only the form, was thus rather to uphold custom and the community sense of justice. It is significant in this connection, as we shall see a little later, that a jury adjudicating a dispute over a contract would be likely to take upon itself to determine whether the price was fair, whether it was the right price for the service, and would regard this as more important than determining whether the price had been fixed and agreed between the parties.

10. William E. Nelson, *The Americanization of the Common Law* (Cambridge, Mass., 1975), pp. 21–31.

The force of these customs sometimes made it remarkably difficult to govern in accordance with the objectives of government, and especially in Massachusetts, of the British government. In 1761 a Massachusetts jury virtually nullified an admiralty decree issued under the authority of the Navigation acts. A writ for trespass was brought by a shipowner against a revenue officer after his ship had been seized for smuggling. The judges of the Superior Court held unanimously that the admiralty decree, passed under the authority of the act, barred a civil action, and they so instructed the jury. These stout men, however, simply disregarded this judicial instruction and returned the vessel to its owner.[11] Judges in the county courts, although not locally appointed, were on the whole more likely than those of the Superior Court to be sensitive to local opinion; a jury sitting under a county court judge normally afforded a strongly community based system of justice. Altogether—and nowhere more so than in Massachusetts—the judicial system tended to reflect the mores and collectively felt interests of the people of the colonies.

Since property is defined as well as being maintained by law, I have passed from the concept of property to that of law without clearly marking the transition. By the time of independence, the Americans had been quietly making their own laws from a period dating from the first migrations, and in some cases they made laws that did not exist in England. These were not alterations to English common law but provincial statutes and regulations, a fair proportion of which were disallowed by the Privy Council. But it was only with the Revolution itself, and the newly felt need to assert the authority on which they took their stand, that they began to look seriously for different sources of law.

A law which emanated from the customs of the community was only very rarely in need of amendment or restatement. Readers of colonial statutes are bound to be struck, and sometimes entertained, by the order of the questions on which colonial legislators enlarged their powers of debate. Shall any person be allowed to

11. *Ibid.*, p. 31.

keep more than one dog? Shall the colony assist the diggers of clams this year? May a farmer have permission to hang a gate across a public road that passes through his field? Shall a certain lady have a divorce? These questions called forth the day-by-day operations of the legislative power, which often attracted less notice than the town meeting. The legislative power was superior to the collective mind of any one town or county and spoke with a constitutionally superior voice. But the position had never been codified until the appearance of Blackstone's *Commentaries* in and after 1765. Blackstone's authority quickly crossed the Atlantic to take root in American society.

Blackstone cleared up any doubts that might exist by declaring that law was the expression of the will of a superior to an inferior; and this superiority he located in the legislature. In other words Blackstone codified for all British jurisprudence what has been called a 'will theory of law.'[12] It was left to American commentators to counterpose a very strong theory of consent, based in part on natural law—for which they drew on Hooker, Locke, and the natural law theorists of the seventeenth and eighteenth centuries; and in part, perhaps in truth the stronger part, on the essential rightness of immemorial customs. Custom was itself regarded as the most convincing proof of the ratification of law by popular consent.

The tension is visible in Wilson's law lectures, to which we have referred. One of his main objects was to confute Blackstone, in whose theory of sovereignty he perceived the seeds of divine right. Professor Morton Horwitz has pointed out that in spite of this, Wilson was more under Blackstone's spell than he would have cared to admit, and actually stated that 'in every state, there must be somewhere a supreme power, arbitrary, absolute, uncontrollable.'[13] On the strength of this sentence, Professor Horwitz

12. Horwitz, *op. cit.*, pp. 22–26. Blackstone defined the relationship; Americans were obliged to reconsider the question of the course, which led towards law as majority will. In a technical sense the theories converge.

13. Wilson, *Works*, II, p. 506, quoted by Horwitz, *op. cit.*, p. 19.

assigns Wilson to the supporters of the will theory of law. But this certainly is not where Wilson wanted his own emphasis to fall. He gives many pages to building up a voluntarist view which at least reposes the supreme will in the acts and customs of the people and particularly goes to the trouble of denying legislatures any rightful claim on that supreme power.

Americans of the revolutionary generation were no newcomers to constitutional or legal theory. Their society had spent some hundred years absorbing the assumption that all political systems acquired legitimacy from conformity with the laws of nature. It was a standard item of Whig thought that property rights antedated those rights that were given by political society. The scheme worked well in England and it worked well in England's American colonies (and it was not until the outbreak of the quarrels that led to the Revolution that Americans began to take an interest in England's Irish dependency, where different principles seemed to prevail). It would have seemed fanciful, or merely perverse, to envisage a situation where the will of a lawful superior ran counter to the laws of nature. There would in fact have appeared to be little room for worry on this count even in theory; will, after all, normally dealt with matters requiring regulation and action, and there was no reason to suppose that the political will from which statute law flowed would be in any danger of running into conflict with the more fundamental principles of natural law; the political will was in the safe keeping of Parliament and the common law. It was therefore extraordinary that the political will should conflict with precepts which any British subject could regard as belonging to the province of natural law. James Otis could hardly believe what was happening and his first pamphlet against parliamentary taxation subscribed in almost fulsome language to the sovereignty of Parliament.[14]

It was easier to inveigh against specific acts of a misguided administration or a tyrannical king than to construct an alternative

14. Bernard Bailyn, ed., *Pamphlets of the American Revolution* (Cambridge, Mass., 1965), I, pp. 419–70.

theory of sovereignty. Americans, however, were very soon confronted by hard necessities which could be acted on only by the authority of their own local legislatures and of the Continental Congress. Where consent to these authorities was not willingly given it had to be forcibly extracted. Congress and state legislatures had to raise money, supply armies and militias, enforce severe restraints on economic liberties, and in certain cases to conscript men for military service and requisition property. Never had American assemblies assumed such authority to deal with prices, wage rates, imports, exports, the promotion of some products and the suppression of others, and perhaps above all, with the ownership and disposal of land.

When after several years of acrimonious disputes the states of New York and Virginia ceded their vast land claims in the Ohio Valley to the Continental Congress, they contributed to a situation which bore a certain affinity with a dictum of Locke's, and before him of others, who held that God gave the earth to men to enjoy in common.[15] It was an old theme on which there were many variants, but all of them rejected the claim of any man or class of men to engross more land than they could use for their own support.

In a new sense, the people of the United States did now hold the land in common, for their own benefit and that of their descendants. The governments of the United States both under the Confederation and under the Constitution clearly had on their hands an immense responsibility, which rival interests of speculators and settlers eagerly sought to help them discharge. Even before the close of the War of Independence, the Congress adopted the policy of making land grants in payment of debts to soldiers of the Continental army. Soon afterwards, vast tracts were chartered away to the Ohio and Scioto companies, while the famous Ordinance of 1787 created a system for the establishment of govern-

15. Peter Laslett, ed., *John Locke: Two Treatises of Government* (Cambridge, 1967), p. 309.

ment in Western territories that would eventually be admitted to the Union as new states.

During the long history of controversy over land policy, one school of thought steadily maintained that the price of land should ensure a source of income for the payment of government debts. But much more was possible. In the 1820s John Quincy Adams and Henry Clay advocated a policy of promoting great national objectives to which land sales would contribute a major source of revenue. These far-reaching aims, which lay beyond the scope of state governments, came under constant pressure from both speculators and settlers.

That story belongs to another theme in American history. But for our present purposes it is worth noticing that both these schemes envisaged the conversion of America's great holding of public lands into private property. These aims culminated in the Homestead Act of 1862 which, notwithstanding its defects, transmitted into law the old Jeffersonian aim of creating a nation of small, free, independent farmers. But this time, there were corporate forces that were better equipped to exploit the resources of the land than the small farmer with only private capital, and by this time also the city was beginning to gain over the countryside as the main centre of economic growth and population; but for all that, the Homestead legislation was by no means a trivial or wasted effort.

We must come back to the legislation that followed independence if we are to follow the developments that affected the basic principles already outlined.

I spoke of a conservative and protective concept of the rights of property. That concept came under acute political stress in the 1780s as a result of the economic crises that afflicted the new states in the immediate wake of the war. State governments met their difficulties in different ways, depending on the local formations of economic and political power. In most states there was pressure on the currency, and six of them exercised the prerogative of law as the will of the legislature by issuing various forms of paper money.

In doing so, of course, they were intervening to affect the value of property. State laws were also enacted to protect the properties of debtors through periods of emergency, or laws which allowed the payments of debts in almost worthless commodities.

None of this represented a legislative response to the economics of expansion. On the contrary, it was crisis legislation, protecting one set of interests against another, and in the process upholding one *morality* against another.

The series of necessities and crises that resulted directly from the Americans' decision to set up independent governments from Britain was thus responsible for bringing about the first distinct change in the system of values that had survived so long. Old, solid community values were breaking down. Bitter disagreements about the true meaning of those values now cut through town and country; creditors and debtors denounced each others' policies in the language of a presumed morality which they could no longer afford to share.

In the light of these disputes the Constitution itself, brought into existence by the Philadelphia Convention of 1787 and ratified in subsequent months by a series of remarkable state conventions, has often been seen as a conservative instrument. And it was assuredly true that many of the men who made it were concerned to protect the interests of the more substantial holders of property and credit against the levelling propensities of democratic hordes. This view moreover gains a measure of credibility from the early speeches of Edmund Randolph and Elbridge Gerry [16] and from the frequent interventions of Gouverneur Morris, among others. From this point of view I think we can regard the Constitution as a *defensive* instrument of government, embodying the protective concept of property that was felt to be under such dangerous attack by legislative majorities. It was no longer any good looking back to the old days of stable and dependable community values. On the continental scale the issue was too vast; and the communities

16. Max Farrand, ed., *Records of the Federal Convention,* 4 vols. (New Haven, 1937), vol. I.

themselves were too often fragmented by conflicts caused by economic hardship and economic ambition.

The desperate nature of the crisis was that people on all sides felt threatened—the small farmer, artisan, and debtor classes no less than the large landowners, slave-owners, and international merchants. The lesser livelihood of the poor and weak was often rendered precarious by the drainage of hard money and the absolute shortage of other forms of circulating currency, by taxation of an order they had never experienced under British rule, by trade stringencies, and for foreclosure for debt. On all sides there were those who would no doubt have appreciated a period of 'quiet enjoyment' and of direct and absolute possession of their own properties. Although the pressure was so acute, however, the old *concept* of property was not in question. Wilson's lectures, which I have quoted in this connection, were written after the adoption of the Constitution. It might be worth exploring the possibility that later changes in the fundamental concept governing the rights of property were anticipated in the economic debates of the 1780s and that Wilson, who was to some extent *parti pris* in those debates, was marking out conservative lines to law students for the benefit of future generations. But no formulation of such changes seems to have appeared.

The new Constitution, however, did far more than provide a protective cover for formal ideas of property rights derived from the old Whig tradition. It also provided cover for the release of the energies that transformed the continent in the nineteenth century. And that was at least a latent objective of some of the men who made it. I do not suggest that they were looking into the distant future; their immediate objective was to gain security for their own activities. But a very large-scale transition was already beginning to affect the character of the American economy. That transition can be suggested by using successively the expressions 'intercolonial,' 'interstate,' and 'continental.' Without a constitution of federal or national character this transition could never have taken place.

Not only in its generally federal character but in much of its specific language, the Constitution, as I have suggested, provided the necessary cover for the energies and ambitions that were to transform the face of the continent within a century. To that great transformation—much the most rapid and dramatic of the Western world's industrial revolutions—the adaptations of American law made a distinct contribution. In his immensely influential book, *Law and the Conditions of Freedom*,[17] Professor Willard Hurst has styled this the 'release of energy' principle. Hurst's interpretation treats the law itself as an agency of economic growth, to be compared in its effects to steam power and the development of communications.

Professor Hurst laid foundations for a pragmatic interpretation of the role of law. In his early work, done in Wisconsin (from whose laws he has always been fond of taking his evidence), he showed the interplay between legislation, judge-made law, and economic development. More recently we have further studies which follow these processes in great depth and detail, concentrating principally on the Eastern states. Professor Horwitz's *The Transformation of American Law, 1780–1860* is entirely different in tone and emphasis from Hurst and bears little trace of indebtedness to his example. I think we may soon see why. But its outlines and many of its evidential details are consistent with Hurst's basic themes. Professor William E. Nelson's misleadingly titled monograph *The Americanization of the Common Law*, concentrates on Massachusetts; and in a different vein, Professor Bruce Ackerman's *Private Property and the Constitution*[18] suggests a framework for the analysis of public policy. We are thus suddenly in possession of a rich new field of ideas and information, from all of which I think we can plot the outlines and supply much of the substantial detail of certain profound changes in those concepts which I sketched earlier in this lecture.

17. Hurst, *op. cit.*, pp. 1–32.
18. Horwitz, *op. cit.*; Nelson, *op. cit.*; Bruce Ackerman, *Private Property and the Constitution* (New Haven and London, 1977).

All the principles and concepts discussed began—at first very gradually—to come under pressure early in the nineteenth century. The pressures arose from two different types of expansion. It is easiest to think of American expansion as geographical, and that began when the Americans took control of the lands lying to their west. But the other type, economic expansion, actually began to suggest reformulations of common law rules taking place at first in New York and Massachusetts, where the open-ended kind of western expansion was rapidly ceasing to be available. In the next half-century or so both the processes and the concepts of law underwent profound changes, brought about almost entirely by new kinds of conflict of interest, and all of these involved the rights of property.

The transformation of the American economy and the transformation of American law were related processes. An earlier, slow-moving, agrarian society, served but in no way dominated by movements of commerce, rapidly transformed itself into a society whose pace and rhythm, and whose very sense of needs, were dictated by the rising pulse of commerce and manufactures. Everyone will at once think of the rapidly spreading networks of waterways and railroads as the instruments of this transformation; it has been Willard Hurst's central claim that the law itself, and particularly the inventive adaptation of the law of contracts, was instrumental to the process.

In the colonial economy, very few people did any sort of business with persons whom they did not actually know or see. Such transactions were in fact indispensable to the Anglo-American system but they were conducted by comparatively small numbers of individuals, who themselves operated through factors or merchants whom, as a rule, they did know. But as the economy itself reached out over immense distances and as the amount of business multiplied, so that transactions came as a matter of course to be conducted among parties who were unknown to each other, it was no longer possible to rely on community consensus or the sense of fairness. Complex and anonymous transactions called for highly standardized forms and for a high level of certainty and predictability in agreements.

This process was facilitated by changes in the way the law was given. Perhaps the most conspicuous shift came in the locus of power in the court itself. About the end of the eighteenth century, judges began to take power from juries. The problem was stated by a judge in Pennsylvania in 1792 in a way that threw light on the dangers to commerce from uncertainties in the law. The question was whether to allow juries to interpret questions of law, as they had so often done in the past, but now, on the contrary, this discretion 'would vest the interpretation and declaring of laws, in bodies so constituted, without permanence, or previous means of information, and thus render laws, which ought to be an uniform rule of conduct, uncertain, fluctuating with every change of passion and opinion of jurors, and impossible to be known until pronounced.'[19]

Judges seem to have been gaining more confidence in their status. As late as 1808 Judge Hugh Henry Brackenridge of the Supreme Court of Pennsylvania argued for the abolition of the common law and its replacement by statutory codification; but six years later he had changed his views and deplored the timidity of English judges for the narrowness of the construction they gave to their own powers and their deference to precedent![20] Brackenridge was arguing the case for the new school of American judges, who increasingly took it upon themselves to limit the issues on which the jury was to decide, and in the process enlarged their own powers of deciding the legal merits of the cases before them. It was undoubtedly this powerful new code of judge-made law that opened the way for the reinterpretation of contract and of the many other issues that soon arose from conflicts caused by economic development.

The American legal profession was entering into that process of professionalization which made it into the nation's only really pow-

19. Horwitz, *op. cit.*, p. 28.
20. *Ibid.*, p. 34.

erful professional body and occasioned Tocqueville's much-quoted comment on the influence of lawyers. With the rising tide of commercial issues before the courts, members of the judiciary, reflecting this growing professional pride and confidence, showed marked resistance to admitting any interference from other sources of law or even of arbitration. They rejected agreements reached by arbitration and asserted their own exclusive competence in all disputes. By the 1830s these trends had been firmly established. It may be noticed also that judges were quietly extending the scope of the theory that law emanated from will. In theory, the will might be that of the popular majority; but as the judiciary came increasingly to reflect and sympathize with the needs of merchants and entrepreneurs, it became difficult to disentangle the will that now ruled through the common law itself from the will of the judges. The judiciary was taking upon itself the responsibility of interpreting the dominant mood and future needs of American society.

We have been accustomed to recognize the role of state legislatures in promoting economic enterprise, chiefly by the procedure of conferring charters on corporations for specified purposes and often with special or even exclusive privileges. Many of these were for various forms of transport—turnpikes, canals with locks, quays and rights of way, and then railroads. It is rather less common to think of the contribution of the judiciary in the same connection. The central issue can be stated as a matter of risk. Wherever development took place, wherever the existing distribution of property was disturbed, damage or depreciation was likely to result for someone. Who, then, was to bear the risk? The fundamental contribution of the courts was to alter the balance of the laws of property to favour the forces of development—or progress, as it was generally called until recently.

The courts did not always take the first step. In Massachusetts in the early nineteenth century the legislature passed a number of acts to encourage the use of water mills. This encouragement included indemnification when the operation of the mill flooded a neighbour's lands. The courts could have restricted the effects of these measures by applying a strict interpretation of eighteenth-century concepts of property, and notably that of 'quiet enjoyment.' But instead the judiciary willingly followed the intentions of the legislature, accepted the principle that the economic interests of the Commonwealth demanded an increase of its manufactures, and threw the burden of risk onto the passive recipient of the effects of change rather than its active agent. In 1827 the Supreme Judicial Court added a touch of doctrinal decoration which can hardly have alleviated the plaintiff's feelings when it resolved an action for damages by finding entirely in the mill owner's favour, observing that the plaintiff had received benefits by irrigation which outweighed the injury, leading Professor Horwitz to comment that 'this marked the final break with the eighteenth century's conception of property, which regarded the flooding of land as a fundamental invasion of right regardless of actual damage.'[21] The nature of the right conferred by ownership had changed. Property, as Professor Horwitz says, was now 'an instrumental value in the service of the paramount goal of economic growth.'[22]

In former days the law equated property and property rights with the preservation of liberty. That was the core of the colonial defence against Britain. It was a corollary to this concept that when two property owners clashed over the same natural resource, the courts would invariably find in favour of the original owner. It was the newcomer's act which disturbed the peace and constituted an invasion of established right and therefore, in a strict sense of the word, an established liberty. When these clashes occurred over water rights it was because an upstream landowner had done something to affect the natural flow of the water, and in these cases the courts protected the downstream owner's existing interests. We can see the shift in the locus of public interest taking place in a case in Boston in 1823.[23] The value of a private house has been

21. *Ibid.*, pp. 50–51.
22. *Ibid.*, p. 53.
23. *Ibid.*, p. 72.

depreciated by the regrading of a nearby highway. The house-holder takes an action against the surveyor of the highways, complaining that the damage amounts to taking property without due compensation, and loses. The Constitution of Massachusetts provides that compensation must be paid when private property is taken for public use, but the court will not now interpret this clause as meaning that compensation is payable for depreciation resulting from a public improvement. In the earlier dispensation, the public as a whole could have no higher interest than that of property owners in the absolute possession of their estates. But a new kind of public now exists; its will is represented in the legislature and its agents are the officers appointed to carry out improvements in the public interest. So we can see two profoundly significant changes reflected in this one case. The one is that development now takes precedence over mere possession; and the other and related change is that the public interest in improvement of facilities takes precedence over the private owner's interest in remaining undisturbed by whatever may be going on outside.

A handful of court cases would hardly have struck the ordinary citizen as a portent of revolution. But the issue was dramatized as never before by the advent of the railroads, which were already on order in America within two years of George Stephenson's first demonstration of The Rocket in 1826. The railroad forced the pace of judicial thinking just as it forced the pace of transport, and farmers whose crops were set on fire or whose lands were taken found again and again that they were obliged to bear the costs of the overriding public interest in faster (if not cleaner) transport both for goods and people. But the cluster of issues dramatized in the railroad cases had already begun to form through the growing spirit of economic competition. We can trace them to the case of *Palmer v. Mulligan*,[24] decided by the New York Supreme Court as early as 1805. This case affected water rights, and it was the first in

24. *Ibid.*, pp. 37–38.

which a court decided that an upper riparian owner could legitimately obstruct the flow of water for mill purposes; it was here that the passive condition of mere original ownership began to yield to business development; in 1818 the same court went so far as to permit an upstream owner to hold back the supply of water for a few days at a time.[25] Each owner had an equal right to the resources provided by nature, and when one made use of them it did not infringe the property rights of the other.

The doctrine we can see entering into American law through these cases is that legally permissible injury will depend, not on prior rights of possession, but on the relative efficiencies of conflicting uses of property. An owner could now suffer severe private loss without being able to claim redress through the courts for legally recognized injury.

It would be a mistake to try to trace an unbroken line, particularly with Joseph Story on the bench of the Supreme Court. But the most conservative legal reasoning had to answer the new doctrines in something resembling their own language; and when trying in the case of *Tyler v. Wilkinson* (1827)[26] to perpetuate the traditional doctrine which preserved water's natural flow, even Story invoked the doctrine of 'reasonable use,' which already carried utilitarian overtones. New large mills were soon going up, whose multiple and complex operations required great power, hence bigger dams; and by the early 1840s the courts were holding that these could be built without incurring risks of indemnification. In a comparable connection the New York Supreme Court overthrew the doctrine of 'ancient lights' when it permitted a building that blocked off the plaintiff's sunlight.[27]

Enterprise involved risk and a consequent obligation to ensure that others were not injured by mere negligence. But in 1833 Chief Justice Gibson of Pennsylvania heard a case arising from the destruction of a bridge resulting from a break in an upstream dam.

25. *Ibid.*, p. 37.
26. *Ibid.*, pp. 38–39.
27. *Ibid.*, p. 46. I doubt whether this was the first instance.

There was no evidence that the dam owner had been guilty of carelessness, and the chief justice therefore held that he was not liable for damages. As Horwitz comments, 'injury brought about by risk-producing activity was itself no ground for imposing legal liability.'[28]

A shift of this scale in the balance of risk in the ownership of property was likely to be accompanied by at least an undercurrent of political feeling. On the other hand the changes were gradual, they were often merely local in effect, and by most people, most of the time, they were hardly perceived at all. Yet the conflict was dramatized in the celebrated case of the Charles River Bridge,[29] whose exemplary character should now be easier to understand.

The Charles River Bridge, which displaced the old ferry between Boston and Charlestown, was built under a legislative charter given in 1785, which prescribed certain conditions and even laid down the tolls to be charged. The bridge was to revert to the Commonwealth after forty years, a period soon afterwards extended to seventy years. Other bridges were later constructed to connect Boston with other shores, and it was in response to the implied challenge of the first of these that the Charles River Bridge proprietors secured the additional period for their own charter, but it is clear that no one contemplated two bridges between Boston and Charlestown. The bridge was a great success and soon constituted a source of sustained profit for its stockholders. But in 1785 Boston had a population of only 17,000, Charlestown of 1200; by 1827, when the legislature, after much deliberation and controversy, at last authorized the Warren Company to build a second bridge, the relative populations were 80,000 and 6000, and on a total outlay of some $70,000 the Charles River Bridge Company was collecting some $30,000 a year. The

28. *Ibid.*, p. 97.
29. *Charles River Bridge v. Warren Bridge*, XI Peters 419–650 (1837). For this passage I have drawn on Horwitz, *op. cit.*; Stanley I. Kutler, *Privilege and Creative Destruction* (Philadelphia, 1971); Carl B. Swisher, *The Taney Period, 1836–1864* (New York and London, 1974) in *History of the Supreme Court of the United States*, Paul Freund, ed.

Warren Bridge by its charter was to revert to the Commonwealth after only six years; but since it would be toll free after the initial outlay had been cleared, it would therefore not merely compete, but stood to deprive the old bridge of all its traffic; and the threatened company bitterly declared that the chartering of the new bridge was nothing less than an act of confiscation.

By the time it was finally settled in 1837, by a Court on which five members, including the new Chief Justice, Roger B. Taney, who had been appointed by Andrew Jackson, the case had been a subject of legislative, judicial, and political debate for some ten years. Unlike any previous case in the Supreme Court's history, and unlike any succeeding case until that of Dred Scott twenty years later, it set the Court in the centre of the political process. Jacksonian politicians and newspapers denounced the Charles River Bridge Company and its stockholders as a privileged and exclusive aristocracy, seeking to gain an unearned living from the needs of the people. Simon Greenleaf, as counsel for the Warren Company, was careful to avoid all such rhetoric; and Chief Justice Taney's opinion for the Court offered no leverage to party sympathies.[30] But this did not inhibit Democratic editors from hailing the outcome as a political victory. If the political implications of the case were exaggerated, however, the responsibility was not exclusively that of the publicists who politicized the issue at the time, and who bragged of or lamented their consequences; the plea of Daniel Webster for the old company, and the long dissenting opinion of Joseph Story, quivered with distress at the threat to time-honoured values and old laws.

The technical question at issue was whether the original charter was to be construed as exclusive. For the plaintiffs it was argued, and maintained by Story in his dissent, that the grant was exclusive by implication, and that no explicit provision was included merely because no company would ever have embarked on such a venture if the exclusive nature of their privilege had been in

30. XI Peters 461–72; 535–53; Kutler, *op. cit.*, p. 80.

doubt. It followed that all risk capital was now in jeopardy; who would subscribe to new ventures if mere temporary legislative majorities were free to destroy the value of the investment? But Taney held, with good English as well as American precedents, that the language of gifts by the public was always to be narrowly construed; and he added that if this plea were upheld, old turnpike companies would 'awaken from their sleep' and claim the value of improvements made under new grants by their successors. The public interest turned both on the hope of future improvements and on the immense masses of capital already invested.[31]

In spite of all the political rhetoric and passionate feeling aroused by the case, the judgement for the Warren Bridge portended no threat to property and carried no explicit attack on wealth. Joseph Story,[32] who felt deeply that moral issues of the highest importance were at stake, stiffened his plea for moral values by posing one form of utilitarian argument against another. Story 'could conceive of no surer plan to arrest all public improvements, founded on private capital and enterprise, than to make the outlay of that capital uncertain, and questionable both as to security, and as to productiveness.' Taney also introduced an appeal to general principles, insisting that the public's interest in improvements could not be obstructed by claims which did not expressly appear in the words of the grant. In the last resort the issue was compensation; and Massachusetts did make some small payment a few years later, though only enough to absolve it of outright confiscation.

Any study we make of the relationship between law and property must take account of Story's passionate belief that 'the old law' was passing. 'I am the last of the old race of judges,' he wrote in deep depression.[33] The Court's position was in tune with the general demand for improvement, and similar positions were being taken in Britain. Within a few years, American legislatures would

31. XI Peters 551.
32. XI Peters 583–650.
33. Kutler, *op. cit.*, p. 3.

charter railroads on terms of far broader discretion than had been granted in 1785. The public interest in transport has been a particularly plain and sometimes heedless demonstration of the general principle that private property has few rights that can stand against legislative determination. In recent years the decision to concentrate traffic in airlines has destroyed massive property in railroads, and innumerable decisions to build new highways have destroyed the businesses of motor mechanics and small restaurants. Usually the gains have been made by powerful organizations and the losses have been borne by family firms. That was not a consequence anticipated by Jacksonians but it was a logical outcome of the determination. In subsequent decisions the Supreme Court reassured those who feared the onset of democratic mobs and the overthrow of property. But Story, though overwrought about the consequences, was right in believing that the law had shifted its bias. If it had always been true that property was subject to the overriding interests of the crown or commonwealth, that interest now more clearly than ever before was subject to the determination of legislative majorities. And the forming of a legislative majority in any particular case had more to do with the arts of lobbying and committee management than with the disinterested interpretation of the will of the people.

In the adaptation of legal principles to the needs of capitalist development there could be no more important field than that of contract. Professor Hurst says that contract law was the main field of the creative energy of the judges,[34] and the dominant policy was to work for the release of private energy. In the eighteenth century a contract was an agreement which gave two parties a title to certain items of property on terms that reflected a generally understood fair price, and as I remarked earlier, an unfair bargain would have stood little chance if contested in the courts.

This may be called a 'title' theory of contract.[35] Its main feature, as Horwitz points out, was to subordinate contractual agreements

34. Hurst, *op. cit.*, p. 43.
35. Horwitz, *op. cit.*, pp. 160–72.

to the general laws of property; 'Exchange,' he remarks, 'was not conceived of in terms of future monetary return, and as a result one finds that expectation damages were not recognized by eighteenth century courts.' During the first half of the nineteenth century the rise of impersonal relations over wide markets in transactions based increasingly on expectations of future returns made it necessary to liberate contract law from the nexus of conventional mores and seat it firmly in the *intentions* of the contracting parties. These intentions were to be judged not by local conditions but by objective criteria applicable to all cases where similar forms were used and similar principles involved. The role of the court had changed. Since it was assumed that the contracting parties had free and independent wills, the court, after ascertaining the facts of the case, had to determine whether a genuine 'meeting of minds' had taken place—that is, not whether the argeement was fair by conventional standards, but whether both parties had actually understood it and freely consented to its terms. This constituted a 'will' theory of contract which reflected the strenuous and competitive individualism of maturing capitalist development.

Legal theory followed the interests of economic enterprise by making the assumption that the economy—and therefore the public interest—was best served by permitting the execution of contracts among parties of free will. On the face of the matter this liberated contract law from the constraints of political opinion. But the face of the matter was not always the whole of it, since objective standards were susceptible of narrow definition, and a party who had not been literally coerced was normally held to be free. This might operate with relative fairness among persons of approximately equal economic or educational status engaged in commercial transactions; but when the system attributed to the labourer with nothing to bring to the market but his labour, the same freedom as to his prospective employer, the effect could be to ally the courts with the employing classes. This is a familiar charge against the judiciary of the period, which was certainly stiffened by the use of the injunction to break strikes and jail their leaders and a

propensity for invalidating reformist and regulatory legislation. But
it does not reflect an unmixed picture. Even at the height of the
conflict between labour and capital the courts had before them the
recent guidance of Chief Justice Waite in *Munn v. Illinois* (1877)
that 'every statute is presumed to be constitutional' and that a statute could be invalidated only if it were 'clearly' unconstitutional.
The degree of clarity could vary with a judge's political convictions;
but in 1898 the Supreme Court actually upheld a Utah statute
limiting mineworkers to eight hours a day and stated, through Mr.
Justice Brown, that the legislators of Utah recognized 'that the proprietors of these establishments and their operatives do not stand
upon an equality. . . . In other words, the proprietors lay down
the rules and the labourers are practically constrained to obey
them.'[36]

The most celebrated case of supposed doctrinaire laisser-faire
principles determining the constitutional powers of legislative
intervention is *Lochner v. New York* (1905),[37] which resulted
from a challenge to a statute regulating the hours of work in
bakeries. Mr. Justice Holmes's famous dissenting opinion has
given currency to the belief that the case was decided on grounds
of economic theory—a theory which, as he pointedly remarked,
the majority of the country did not hold; and it would be difficult
to say how far such prepossessions may have entered into the
minds of the majority of the Court. But the question at issue was
whether the State had abused its police powers to regulate health
in order to place an outright labour law on the statute book. In the
outcome this may appear to have been a fine distinction, but it did
not leave the question of contractual freedom as completely at the
mercy of employers as has often been supposed.

It was wholly consistent with the formation of the harder and
more individualistic values that the old ideas of the 'fair price' rap-

36. For this and for my remarks on *Lochner* I am indebted to William L. Letwin's
   unpublished paper, 'Economic Due Process in the American Constitution, and
   the Rule of Law.' I very much appreciate his permission to use these remarks.
37. *Lochner v. New York*, 198 U.S. 45 (1905).

idly gave way in the early nineteenth century to the hard but more formalistic doctrine of *caveat emptor*.[38] A party to a bargain was not a prospective object of judicial pity; he was solely responsible for knowing and understanding the terms to which he agreed. In its early form, the courts made the value of the items at issue depend wholly on the intentions and wills of the parties; but by the early 1850s they had already begun to shift to a softer view, under which they would ascertain whether the contracting parties had in fact enjoyed equal opportunities to learn the objective market price of the commodity. This seems to have reflected a leaning back to the older view that the courts themselves had some obligation to recognize a public interest in fair or objective prices; but it did not restore the fair price as an end in itself. The individual seller could still outbid or undersell or in other ways ignore the community norm, and the full burden, on both sides, remained an individual burden. It was part of a larger process by which the market economy separated the individual from the community and, in the same process, liberated him from its constraints and its protection.

Professor Horwitz, to whom much of this information is due, has charted these developments with a great wealth of learning. But an objective reader, influenced no doubt by vague and insubstantial notions of the fair price, and viewing this contribution in light of the recent development of the subject, will perhaps be surprised by the absence of any explicit recognition of the powerful continuities with the fundamental work of Willard Hurst. It is not altogether surprising that one reviewer[39] has been critical of what seems a reluctance to acknowledge an obvious intellectual debt. I promised a little while ago that I would come back to this question, which I now do.

The difference between the two writers appears when we take account of Horwitz's concern not only with the process but with

---

38. Horwitz, *op. cit.*, pp. 58–62.

39. Harry N. Scheiber, 'Back to "The Legal Mind"? Doctrinal Analysis and the History of Law,' *Reviews in American History* V, 4 (December 1977), 459, 462.

the consequences of economic development, and therefore of the legal processes which contributed so heavily to that development. Hurst appears at times to be celebrating an achievement; Horwitz accepts the achievement—at least he does not openly deplore it—but his attention is directed to a highly critical analysis of the social costs. Wherever land values altered for the worse, where lands were seized for railroad building, where new methods of transport and communication overtook the old, where a farmer's crops were reduced to cinders by flying sparks, or where existing buildings were superseded or even undermined by new ones, the cost had to be met by those whom Horwitz sympathetically describes as the 'inactive' members of the community. The burden of paying for an important share in the development costs, in other words, fell on those who had no money invested in the development and were least able to bear it; and these were costs that would otherwise have been met, either by the developers themselves or, if there were a major public interest (as there was always said to be), then by taxation. Horwitz virtually maintains that there was a sort of conspiracy between courts and legislatures to protect enterprise from the risks of actions for damage and negligence, and he wants to remind us that, while these costs had to be borne somewhere in the system, their actual distribution was a result not of chance nor of some natural working of economic law, but of decisions made by the strong at the expense of the weak.

I should say here that the argument, so far as it has been presented, does not yet entirely convince me. The *Charles River Bridge Case*, which might be described as the exemplary case for the relationship between law and economic development, can hardly be offered as a contest between the unoffending but productive weak, as represented by the corporation's stockholders (who included Harvard College), and on the other side the demons of rapacious capitalism. In fact the politics of the case were an exact reverse of this view. But even if the effect of this were simply to depose that case from its exemplary position (which I am not sure should follow), the undertone of class war in Professor Horwitz's thesis does not seem to have been substantiated by the necessary research into the comparative resources available to the rival parties. Yet it is clear that his substantive inference is right. The costs had to be borne, as he is right to insist, and they were certainly not borne by the public in the form of taxation or by the enterprisers in the form of damages. It might on the other hand be useful if we could have a counterfactual analysis of what these costs would have amounted to and what the effect on investment, or of public promotional policies, would have been if they had been differently distributed.

It is quite possible that such an analysis would show that such a procedure would have kept economic development closer to ascertained needs and would have meant a more equitable distribution of the burdens. It is in any case a tribute to the power of Professor Horwitz's exposition that he should have raised the discussion to this level. His tone if of course entirely different from that of Professor Hurst, who constantly uses the plural of the personal pronoun to describe the achievements of the Americans through the agency of their legal system. For Horwitz, one feels, the Americans are divided into 'we' and 'they'; for Hurst, they are always 'we,' and there is a strong sense that the whole community gained fairly distributed benefits from economic progress. Yet how close they are in certain substantial points can be seen from the key words they use. Hurst calls the phase of legal inventiveness 'pragmatism,' Horwitz calls it 'instrumentalism.'

We can now come back to a point of definition that I first raised when I introduced the concept of property. I suggested that James Wilson's definition of property as a direct and exclusive relationship between a person and a thing was not likely to hold up under the growing complexities of the nineteenth century's extended market economy. Professor Bruce Ackerman,[40] who comments on this problem under the heading of 'Scientific Property Talk,' observes that 'Instead of defining the relationship between a person and "his" things, property law discusses the relationships

40. Ackerman, *op. cit.*, p. 37.

that arise between people with respect to things. . . ." Modern American legal usage has made these relationships extremely complex. The best that can be said about the claims of the owner of a piece of property is that he possesses a bundle of rights, with respect to that object, which contains a range of entitlements more numerous or more valuable than those held by any other person with respect to the object in question. But these bundles and their values can be changed from time to time, with changing social circumstances, by legislatures and by courts.

In principle all this was already true in the eighteenth century. After all, legislatures laid taxes and appropriated resources while courts adjudicated between conflicting claims to property. But the scale of public intervention since that time has been so immense as to transform the problem and to call for refinement of definitions. This seems to me another tranformation that can be attributed to the rise of the extended market economy.

The market economy meant large-scale impersonal economics and required standardized methods of control as well as reliable protections for the interests of shareholders. In response to these needs, the corporation became the preferred method of company organization. By the 1830s this pattern had clearly emerged under the authority of numerous state legislatures, which granted charters to corporations for specified purposes on the basis of individual petitions. These purposes could be narrow, but they could be so extensive that in certain cases the charter would confer on the corporation the right to take possession of land by eminent domain.

Corporations endorsed with—or as in the case of the Charles River Bridge Company, claiming—exclusive privileges, came under heavy attack in the Jacksonian period on the charge that their privileges were monopolistic and therefore 'aristocratic.' It entered very strongly into American political ideas at this period that monopolies were offensive to the democratic spirit; in the *Slaughter House Cases* of 1873,[41] the first to arise under the Four-

41. *Slaughter House Cases*, 83 Wall. 16.

teenth Amendment, counsel for the plaintiffs ransacked English history for attacks on the abuses of monopoly and linked these with republican principles in America. But these charges did not prevent the development of the corporate form of business organization for the simple reason that the corporate form took care of the general needs of business activity, and could be adapted to those of both management and investor. This began to happen in the 1830s, but only became general after the Civil War.

It is a commonplace of the subject that the principle of limited liability played a crucial role, without which the corporation could not have assumed its general importance. It therefore seems worth noting two things. One is that in working out the limited liability principle, British law preceded that of the United States (which is by no means surprising considering the timing of capitalist development in the two countries). The other is that as early as 1810, American courts began to recognize limitations on the liability of individual investors. It was after about 1850 that the judicial presumption in favour of limited liability was supported by statutes in a phase of legislation completed about 1880.[42] Here then is another instance in which the courts took a formative hand.

As one reviews the developments that I have touched on, there seems to be one unexpectedly negative aspect that calls for comment. American economic growth became extremely rapid towards the middle of the nineteenth century; in some respects much earlier. It was made possible by a variety of forces which began to converge perhaps some two generations after the American Revolution. How much, then, did all this owe to the Revolution or even to the constitutional guarantee of a republican form of government?

To ask this question is to set the whole process in a comparative dimension. Other countries forged industrial economies serving extended markets in the same period, and most of the devices developed by American courts and legislatures had their counterparts

42. Willard Hurst, *The Legitimacy of Business Corporations in the United States, 1780–1970* (Charlottesville, 1970), pp. 6, 27.

in Europe. No doubt it would have been difficult to carry out all these modern developments within the legal system of the old British Empire, but since comparable developments were carried out when they were needed in Britain, it is only in a very indirect sense that American independence can be described as a pre-condition of the specifically American contributions to the laws of property.

The Constitution, nevertheless, was indispensable to that process. It was John Marshall who moulded the Constitution so as to lay the foundations for the nationalization of the economy; once again the process began long after the Revolution, and in the third decade of the Constitution itself; and after his time, formally until the passage of the Sherman Anti-Trust Act of 1890, the law stood aside to permit the business corporation to run its lines of communication across the states and to build and supply a national market.

The keynote of the new economy was individualism—a word which increasingly dominated the description of economic and legal relationships in the later nineteenth century. If this emphasis on individualism was set over against the obvious corollary of the rise of corporate power, that contrast suggests that in concluding this lecture I may be about to begin another one. From this, without threatening to keep you longer, we may at least get a glimpse of how the concept of property could lead into an appreciation of a society's wider aspirations—or its more pervasive and serviceable myths.

The later nineteenth century produced a spate of learned and speculative studies in primitive and ancient law, of which Sir Henry Maine's is the most famous. The impulse behind much of this work was a desire to confute the claim that individualism in private property preceded civil society and lay at the root of all recognized social relations and political forms. Ancient and primitive law, as Maine argued, knew collective property long before the recognized beginnings of private claims to ownership of external objects.

Another keynote, less easily recognized and seldom publicly admitted, was a very intense concentration on the present. Buildings were thrown up and torn down; farmers gouged their lands and moved on. In the presence of these drives it was not easy to keep the public interest in sight, except of course in the Smithian sense in which the public interest was supposed to be fulfilled through the operations of the market; and it was still less easy to keep in view the public interest of the future. That interest was never a signatory to agreements reached under the 'will' theory of contract. I want to conclude by suggesting that it was only when a much more powerful concept of overriding public interest could be revived that this dimension could be served. And it was with respect to land and natural resources that the issue was most vital.

The land, as I have suggested, had once belonged to the people. With the beginnings of the conservationist movement, promoted by Theodore Roosevelt and one wing of the Progressives, the interest of the American people of the future began to raise its claim to political attention, against the dynamic but fierce individualism of whatever, at any one time, constituted the present.

Section Two

5

Abraham Lincoln
and the Working Classes of Britain
(1959)

The outbreak of Civil War in the United States did not take the people of Britain by surprise, nor did it seem to lie wholly within the province of foreign affairs. In the fifteen years ending in 1860, nearly two and a half million of them, nearly all workers or Irish peasants, had crossed the Atlantic. Allowing for those who returned, and for the duplication of family relationships, at least an equal number, out of a British population of less than thirty million, must have had family ties with America going back not more than fifteen years. Besides this bond of kinship, and of greater importance, was the fact that too many in Britain, of all classes, were likely to be affected economically if not emotionally, to have ignored the portents of danger in the West.

The feelings of the British working classes about America, however, were not well represented in the press or publications of that period. The elements of crudeness in American society, the notorious 'Yankee brag,' which helped to sustain the better educated observers, writing largely for middle- and upper-class readers, in

This essay was originally published by the English Speaking Union, London, 1959.

their ingrained sense of British superiority, were matters of little importance to the workers. They, much more than their employers and social superiors, were ready to accept the American view of America. Unenfranchised in their own country, they knew that their American counterparts—sometimes their American kin—exercised the suffrage franchise under the protection of the ballot. No single factor could draw more sharply to their eyes, the distinction between the two nations: the American was indeed a citizen, but the great bulk of the British people were ruled by politicians over whom they exercised no constitutional control. Thus the British constitution perpetuated the distinction between the 'two nations' within Britain, between the few rich and the many poor, the few privileged and the many who were denied the power of personal representation; and the inferior 'nation' needed little encouragement to identify its interests with those of the English-speaking Republic in which political equality was a matter of both fact and law.

The suffrage, though of basic importance, was not the only thing to count. It was commonly said that in America 'a man might better himself.' The absence of a hereditary aristocracy, of unearned but inalienable privilege, attracted the British workers in precise measure as it repelled the aristocracy. Whatever admitted defects American society might have, no observer on the spot, no reader of published accounts of the letters of emigrants, could miss the tang of a very real and direct man-to-man equality. Not all those so affected were workers, for Dissenters still suffered some of the disabilities of religious discrimination. Only in London, or in Scotland, could they receive a university education. Their sects were represented in vast numbers in the United States, where church and state were separated by the constitutions both of the Federal Union and of the individual states.

This grand conception of the United States, rough and ready no doubt, but right where it was important to be right, was not in fact a representation of the whole American Republic. It was a picture of the North. It was the North whose social institutions appealed to

the free labour of Europe; it was the North to which British workers were allied by interest and kinship. For as a speaker remarked
at a public meeting in London in 1863, 'No one ever emigrates
from England, to a slave state.' No worker wanted to compete with
slave labour or to transplant himself to a society in which all labour
suffered from the stigma of an implied relationship to that of
slaves.

This working class interest in the defence of freedom as against
slavery went some way to counter-balance their direct economic
interest in the supply of raw cotton from the Southern states to the
textile mills of Lancashire. Moreover the North, whose cause
might have been endangered if hostile or indifferent feelings
among the British masses had encouraged the government to risk
intervention, was fortunate in the timing of the Civil War; for
while they pursued their own struggle for enfranchisement, the
British workers became unusually sympathetic to foreign causes of
a liberal character. Italy had enlisted their support, Poland in turn
would do so. Working class opinion had advanced beyond the
crude nationalism of the Crimean War.

It was not difficult to see, for some years before the election of
Lincoln in November 1860, that a crisis portended in the United
States, and that slavery was in some way responsible. In 1857 British cotton manufacturers showed alarm at the dependence of their
vast industrial superstructure on 'the treacherous foundation of restricted slave labour.'[1] But British opinion, whichever side it
might take, was poorly served with information. Among those who
favoured the North, a simple enthusiasm for the struggle against
slavery far outran their understanding of either the constitutional
problems of the Union or the political problems facing the Republican Party which had elected its first President.

The vast shadow of slavery clouded every other aspect of the
contest. Practically all pro-Northern sentiment proceeded from the
assumption stated soon after the election by the Freethinkers'

1. Clapham, *Economic History of Britain*, p. 140.

newspaper, *The National Reformer*, which confessed its bewilderment and ignorance at American parties, affirming that it knew only two parties, slave and abolition.[2] In August 1861 the same paper discussing Federal policy after the defeat in the battle of Bull Run remarked of the abolition of slavery,[3] 'We have all along contended that it was the only principle in the struggle worth fighting for.'

In August 1861 also, *The Working Man*, aiming at a far more working-class readership, commented optimistically that the orders given to Federal troops for the reception of fugitives tended towards anti-slavery, and a week later showed marked interest in the development of anti-slavery feeling in America. Of Abraham Lincoln himself, so little was known that he emerged not as an individual but only as the leader of the party that was opposed to any further extension of slavery. Where Lincoln's conservatism was noted, it was noted with disappointment; and the Union cause was upheld because it was believed to be the anti-slavery cause.

Lincoln, however, was far from being unknown in his own country. In 1856 he was already prominent enough to contend strongly for the nomination as Republican candidate for vice-president. In 1858 he attracted the attention of the nation by holding his own in an exciting series of debates, held at his challenge as part of a contest for an Illinois seat in the United States Senate, with the incumbent, Senator Stephen A. Douglas. Douglas won the seat but at the cost of taking positions which were to weaken his claims to the presidency in 1860. Four years previously, in 1854, Douglas, as chairman of the Senate Committee on Territories, had introduced the bill for the organization of the Territory of Nebraska (later divided into Kansas and Nebraska), which introduced the principle of popular sovereignty in place of the existing rule of Congressional control of slavery in the territories—regions under American government not yet admitted to the Union as states. This event aroused intense anxiety among those in all parties who

2. *National Reformer*, December 15, 1860.
3. *National Reformer*, August 17, 1861.

had hoped that the slavery question would remain at rest. For although slavery was not expected by Douglas or his supporters to spread into the North-West, the actual Congressional restraint on such a development had been withdrawn; and the danger seemed to grow worse when in 1857 the Supreme Court declared that Congress had no power, under the Constitution, to exclude slavery from any territory of the United States. The thought that slavery, instead of dying gradually in the confines of its existing limits, might actually spread with the growth of the Union, and come eventually to dominate instead of decline, though too terrible to contemplate, was not too terrible to be believed. The governing principle which brought the Republican Party into being and brought Lincoln into its fold was determination to prevent any further expansion of slavery. Lincoln plainly stated his position in a famous speech in 1858 when he said:

> 'A house divided against itself cannot stand.' I believe this government cannot endure permanently half slave and half free. I do not expect the Union to be dissolved—I do not expect the house to fall—but I do expect it will cease to be divided. It will become all one thing or all the other. Either the opponents of slavery, will arrest the further spread of it, and place it where the public mind shall rest in the belief that it is in the course of ultimate extinction; or its advocates will push it forward, till it shall become alike lawful in all the states, old as well as new, North as well as South.

Lincoln was convinced that the Federal government possessed no constitutional power to intervene against slavery in the states which permitted it in their own constitutions. To reassure the South he, in his first inaugural address, offered to accept an amendment to the Constitution which would forever protect slavery, where it already existed, from federal interference. Believing slavery to be protected under the Constitution, he was offering no real concession of principle. But Lincoln also believed that if slavery were bottled up it would die. He belonged to the contemporary school, among whom were certainly included some energetic advocates of slavery, which held that slavery must expand in order to survive. To Lincoln it was therefore of fundamental importance that the Federal government should exert every constitutional power to check the spread of slavery. When he came to power, however, his immediate care was neither the preservation nor the abolition of slavery, but the preservation of the Union. Seven Southern states (four more were to join them) had already declared their secession and had joined to form an independent government, styling themselves the Confederate States of America— a conception which Lincoln perforce regarded as a mere pretence. In order to hold the loyalty of those 'border states' (slave states adjoining free states) which might prove of decisive strategic importance, Lincoln proceeded with extreme caution, hoping, even after the war had broken out in April 1861, that the Unionists in the South might regain their influence. His object, first and last, was to save the Union; it was not only his duty, it was his mission.

All this, and especially the limitations of the power of the Federal government, were very imperfectly appreciated in Britain, as was also the fact that much pro-slavery sentiment existed in Northern and border areas which it was essential for Lincoln to hold. In the absence of understanding, the supporters of 'the Federals' and opponents of slavery were free to indulge the most extravagant expectations; which, in the first six months or so of war, were destined to collapse in a commensurate degree of bitter disappointment. In July 1861 Lincoln sent to the special session of Congress a message in which all the emphasis was placed on the preservation of the Union, and British supporters were dismayed at his failure to proclaim a crusade against slavery. In this session, moreover, the Congress expressly disclaimed any intention of subjugating or interfering with 'established institutions.' In October the President had the disagreeable task of countermanding an emancipation proclamation, issued entirely without authority, by General Frémont, who proposed to free the slaves of disloyal owners in his command area. This measure, if endorsed, would not only split the North but would impair presidential authority. By countermanding it, however, Lincoln enraged the radical anti-slavery wing of his own supporters and decimated the ranks of Northern supporters in Britain.

The conservative press in Britain, led by *The Times*, had firmly taken the position that the North was motivated by ambitions of empire, the South by a legitimate desire for independence; Lincoln, by this stroke, seemed to have deprived the North of the moral sanction of its cause. 'Now that it is clear,' said *The Working Man*, 'that the Northerners are not fighting for the emancipation of the slaves, we are relieved from any moral consideration in their favour; and as the Southerners are not worse than they, why should we not get cotton?'[4] It went on to demand the raising of the blockade which the Federal navy was attempting to enforce against Southern ports.

The cause of the North in this troubled early period was weakened by a more material consideration. It was generally believed, even among its friends, that a Northern reconquest of the South was hopelessly impracticable. However it might be deplored, the dissolution of the Union was very widely regarded, by the time of Lincoln's inauguration, as an accomplished fact. And a war of invasion followed by subjugation, even if it had seemed possible, was a prospect that aroused scant enthusiasm. The Northern humiliation in the battle of Bull Run in July 1861 merely confirmed the general impression.

The difficulties of the Union cause in Britain were in no way lightened by the strikingly hostile attitude of many of the older generation of labour leaders, particularly those who controlled the labour press.[5] Before the Emancipation Proclamation of 1st January, 1863 the tone of this press was generally and often stridently unfriendly to the North. Even after that date, there remained some antipathy or reserve among editors claiming to represent and to address the organized interests of labour. *The British Miner* (also called *The Miner* and *The Miner and Workmen's Advocate*)

4. *Working Man*, October 5, 1861.
5. Harrison, 'British Labour and the Confederacy.'

remained sympathetic to the South until 1865, when it changed hands. Reynolds, the editor of *Reynolds Weekly*, though representing no working-class body, associated himself strongly with the working classes and maintained a quite virulent antagonism to the North. Most striking, because most influential, was the case of *The Beehive*, founded in 1862 by George Potter and managed by George Troup. Potter, later the organizer of the London Working Men's Association, was an energetic and at times a militant leader of working-class interests. His long and often bitter struggle with the powerful group of trade-union leaders who came to be known as the 'Junta' detracted from his reputation and no doubt diminished his influence; but that influence could not be ignored in this period.[6] He did nothing to restrain his editor, Troup, who pointedly drew attention to the inferior position of the Negro in the North and maintained that secession would result in the extinction of slavery. Troup showed the kind of consideration that weighted his attitude when he attacked the Yankees for taking up arms to fight for high tariffs. Close to Potter stood T. J. Dunning, Secretary of the Bookbinders, who had been called the 'father of London trade unionism.' Dunning was not uniformly sympathetic to the Confederacy. He attacked, in the pages of *The Beehive*, the insolence and cruelty of Southern manners, but also sneered at Northern education and character.[7] In the light of this diatribe it is interesting that something of Lincoln's quality had made its way through to Dunning, who remarked that Lincoln, 'with all his faults . . . has too much good sense and thorough honesty of purpose ever to be their truly chosen representative.' (He did not ask himself how, in that case, Lincoln had in fact been chosen.) Dunning later got his society to withdraw from the London Trades Council because it had taken sides with the Emancipation Society and the friends of Lincoln.

The attitude was duplicated in the country, and in Scotland too. Alexander Campbell, more than thirty years a Scottish labour

6. A contrary opinion is expressed by the Webbs, *History of Trade Unionism*.

7. *Bee-Hive*, March 28 and July 11, 1863.

leader, was closely associated with the *Glasgow Sentinel*, which accused the North of desiring territorial aggrandizement and described the Emancipation programme as 'petty and abortive spite.' Similar views were maintained in many newspapers addressed to working-class readers throughout the industrial north of England. The foundations of these views lay partly in the history of British labour over the previous thirty years. Some of these man were old Chartists; they had not come to terms with industrial capitalism or forgiven the manufacturing middle class for enlisting the support of the workers to gain its own ends in the Reform agitation of 1832. In the United States they saw only a repetition of the same system, competitive, cruel, and intensely self-interested. The Morrill tariff, adopted on the very eve of the Civil War, warned them that American capitalism would stick at nothing in the international race and had no interest in the aspirations of British workers. They believed they saw in the American manufacturers an alarming duplication of their own master class which they had fought so long and bitterly; and was not John Bright, the old opponent of the British factory acts, now enlisted in the cause of the North? Bright, a mill owner himself, was not their man. Though they of course opposed slavery, they were inclined to minimize this aspect of the struggle; they failed to appreciate the open character of American society or the significance of the fact that the American worker already possessed the suffrage franchise. They seem also to have been increasingly out of touch with their following, of which, on this issue, they may have been aware, for they very seldom took the risk of adopting the usual procedure of the time by calling public meetings in support of their stand.

Upper-class Britain on the whole had little difficulty in making up its mind. The desperate ordeal of the world's leading experiment in republican government was observed without dismay. Secession, moreover, was regarded as so clearly accomplished that *The Times* could speak in the midst of the war of 'the late United States.' The government, however, had little inclination for risking ventures in the West. Neutrality was proclaimed early in the war, and from thence forth it seemed to Russell and Palmerston to be little more than a matter of time until the defeat of the North should make recognition of the Confederacy a diplomatic necessity. If Russell, as Foreign Secretary, desired to hasten this process, it was only insofar as he felt that by so doing he might help to curtail the carnage. A warlike mood flared up over the *Trent* affair, in which two Confederate agents were removed by a United States naval vessel from a British ship, in the autumn of 1861; but after Lincoln had ordered the release of the men there was no further overt excuse for intervention. For another year Russell nursed a plan for mediation, which, however, gained no opportunity to mature. The Emancipation Proclamation, at the beginning of 1863, and the Union victories at Gettysburg and Vicksburg in July, between them ended any possibility of British mediation. News from the front always had the last word in the determination of British policy.[8]

Meanwhile a new leadership was taking shape among the organized craftsmen of London and the provinces. In July 1860 the newly formed London Trades Council held its first meeting. From a modest beginning this body rapidly became the leading representative of British trade unions (Trade Union Congress being yet unborn), increasing its organizational membership, and directing labour policy in trades disputes. It did not act alone. Trade councils in many industrial cities were soon in correspondence and close co-operation with it. Together they agitated for repeal of the master-and-servant law, under which employers enjoyed gross advantages over their workers in actions arising from breaches of contract, and they were associated in the renewed drive for parliamentary reform. The London Council took the lead in organizing the workers' welcome to Garibaldi in April 1864, and by that time had already promoted massive working-class demonstrations against Negro slavery and in support of the North. Before the formation of the London Trades Council, the trades had proved cool

8. Cf. Allen, *Great Britain and the United States*, p. 479.

to attempts to use their organizations towards the general political betterment of the working class, but the new Council avowed its political objects from the beginning. It came into existence in the aftermath of a builders' strike in 1859, and the building trades continued to be the centre of industrial unrest. But the control in London passed increasingly into the hands of a small group of able men whose likeness of mind and variety of trades gave exceptional power to the central direction of the trade-union movement.

It was this group which was known as the Junta. The most prominent member was George Odger, a shoemaker, who became secretary of the London Trades Council in 1862. William Allan, an engineer, devoted great labour to building his own trade society into an efficient and reliably financed organization and brought keen judgement and integrity to the Council. Robert Applegarth, a carpenter, who had emigrated to the United States in 1855 but returned for family reasons was especially persuasive in the advancement of political causes and a leading member of the first 'International.' Edwin Coulson guided the rise and expansion of the London bricklayers, while Daniel Guile was general secretary of the long-established iron-founders. By the beginning of 1864, the Junta had gained almost complete control of the London Trades Council. A year earlier, towards the close of 1862, they had ousted George Potter from the control of *The Beehive*, had dismissed Troup, and had brought about a revolution in that paper's policy towards the American Civil War.

The men of the Junta were firmly on the side of the North, whose cause was becoming ever more clearly linked with the abolition of slavery. But abolition no longer stood alone as the only moral principle in the struggle that seemed worthy of British attention. In an article in January 1863 a pseudonymous contributor, in line with editorial policy, denounced *The Times* for leading the upper classes in attempting to create a 'retrograde opinion' in Britain on the subject of slavery. Who, he asked, were these sympathizers with slavery? They were millionaire aristocrats, venal politicians, and some of the press, led by the great bully, *The Times*.

'The motive' (said the writer) 'is hatred to freedom, jealousy of the growing power of the United States, and a desire to see democratic or republican institutions overthrown or brought into disrepute.'' *The Beehive* was at last propagating the conviction that the domestic interest of the British workers was tied to the Northern cause. The interest of labour was one. The existence of Negro slavery in America was held to be an affront to the dignity of free labour in Britain—and, should the South be victorious, it might in some distant way prove even to be a threat to it. Throughout the Civil War, British labour pronouncements on the subject not only deplored slavery but assumed a certain degree of identity of interest with its opponents. In earlier phases, when the labour press was unfriendly to the North, this identity was not denied, nor was slavery defended: rather it was argued that the North was not honestly opposed to slavery or sympathetic to Negro freedom. *The Working Man*, when denouncing Lincoln's countermand of Frémont's emancipation proclamation in October 1861, spoke of the slaves as 'our African co-workers.' The absence of racial feeling, of any conception of colour as factor dividing worker from worker or man from man, was distinctive throughout the whole period.

The Junta not only promoted the cause of the North, but came to take the attitudes of other trade unionists towards the Civil War as a test of their radicalism in domestic affairs. But the Lincoln administration moved slowly, almost, it seemed to observers, with reluctance, towards the great objective of emancipation. Neither did the steps publicly taken to that objective go far to strengthen the hands of Northern supporters abroad. In August 1862 Lincoln stated his cause unequivocally in reply to the demand of Horace Greeley, editor of the *New York Tribune,* who had urged that the loyal millions of the North insisted on decisive action against slavery.

> 'My paramount object in this struggle' (Lincoln wrote) 'is to save the Union, and is not either to save or destroy slavery. If I could save the Union without freeing any slave, I would do it, and if I could save it by freeing all slaves I would do it . . .'

He did not fail to add his 'oft-expressed personal wish that all men every where could be free.'

Greeley did not know that when he wrote, a decision had already been taken. Earlier in the summer, Lincoln, whose party in Congress was increasingly under the influence of its radical, anti-slavery wing, had made up his mind that the Union cause would be promoted both at home and abroad by a great public step towards emancipation. He was deterred from an immediate proclamation by the sound advice of his Secretary of State, Seward, who warned him in a cabinet meeting that in view of the low state of Northern military fortunes at that time, the gesture would be taken as one of mere despair. It was decided to await a military success. The battle of Antietam (17th September 1862), though far from decisive, had perforce to be considered adequate for the occasion, and the President promulgated his preliminary Emancipation Proclamation. This he did, not in his capacity as Chief Magistrate, but as Commander-in-Chief. The Proclamation itself did not emancipate, it merely promised, or threatened. The pronouncement said that on and after 1st January 1863, all slaves in any state still in a state of rebellion, or in any part of such a state as the President might designate, would then be declared free; and the military power of the United States would be used to ensure this freedom.

There were some both in America and in Britain who regarded this Proclamation as carrying to the South a threat of servile war; and clearly both this danger and the emancipation of the slaves could be averted by a peaceful return to the fold of the Union. The policy met with little immediate favour. Radicals regarded it as inadequate; conservatives, especially among the Democratic opposition, feared its social consequences. The Northern armies failed to gain further ground. A wave of disquiet troubled the country and weakened the Republicans at the November 1862 congressional elections. In Britain the Proclamation was in general received with derision. It seemed to lack the quality of definitive action. Indeed, *The Bee-Hive*, still under Troup, in a contemptuous account of the

Proclamation, sailed perilously near to an apology for slavery.[9] *The British Miner*[10] reported, truthfully enough, that American opinion was divided, while printing the Proclamation in full. *The Bee-hive* proceeded, in November, to attack the Northern tariff policies and to express its fear of a North American zollverein; to make a bitter attack on the political record of Bright; to advertise evidences of Northern hostility to the Negroes; and to explain Lincoln's dismissal of McClellan from military command on grounds of political jealousy.[11] Yet before the end of December the same paper corrected an error in *The Times* by pointing out that the measure was military and not legislative.[12] It also printed an account of a method of torturing slaves.

On 1st January 1863, Lincoln duly promulgated the Emancipation Proclamation. Critics on both sides of the ocean pointed out, with incredulity or derision as suited their temper, that it could not free a single slave, since it applied only to territory still outside the control of the Federal government; and, of course, that it made no move to free the slaves within that control. 'The principle,' remarked *The Spectator*, 'is not that a human being cannot justly own another, but that he cannot own him unless he is loyal to the United States.' But this argument took little account of the movement of events. Lincoln and his administration intended to press on the war until the whole South should be restored to the Union. So with every Northern advance the Proclamation would extend its field of force. Moreover, this great act of policy pointed a general direction. Whatever means might be adopted towards eventual emancipation, it was hardly to be conceived that anything, other than a complete Northern defeat, could now reverse the movement towards that final object. The war from this time forth was bound to assume an increasingly anti-slavery character, a conclu-

9. *Bee-Hive*, October 18, 1862.
10. *Miner*, October 11, 1862.
11. *Bee-Hive*, November 8, 29, 1862.
12. *Bee-Hive*, December 20, 1862.

sion that did not escape the spokesmen of the British workers in their own movement for parliamentary reform.

The entire logic of Lincoln's thought about the origins of the Civil War demanded that Northern victory, when it came to pass, should make certain the ultimate extinction of slavery. He believed, as he had said in 1858, that 'ultimate extinction' lay in the future, so long as slavery was not allowed to grow with the growth of the Union. Lincoln himself, felt profoundly that events moved in currents beyond individual control. 'I claim not to have controlled events,' he remarked in 1864, 'but confess plainly that events have controlled me.' Though to observers who pressed upon him their urgent policies he often seemed wearily, unresponsively patient, patient of evil, patient of events beyond any hope of effective action, yet he was in fact extremely sensitive to the forces behind such policies; as to their ultimate significance he was philosophically understanding, as to their political implications he was canny. He deeply believed that American government was the world's testing ground of the principle—the 'proposition,' as he called it at Gettysburg—that all men are created equal; the principle that what government owes to individuals is the opportunity to rise by merit and to control their public affairs by majority rule; that republican institutions could prove to the world that public order might be combined with private opportunity. He believed himself to be the incarnation of this principle. The American Republic, then, was proving the doctrines announced in the Declaration of Independence. Yet Lincoln, always so self-consciously one of the common people, always at once honestly yet deliberately humble, derived his practical outlook on affairs from the country with which he grew up—from the Middle-Western borderlands between frontier settlement and farmer's civilization. Of this region he was a superb representative, because it was in his bones, and because his enlarged and penetrating vision enabled him, while looking in the same direction as his fellows, to see farther than they.

Lincoln had little taste for speculative thought, but of practical questions, of institutional principles, his judgement was keen. When, in 1854, he turned his attention in earnest to the problem of slavery (many had done so at an earlier date) he perceived with greater analytical acumen than most of his contemporaries the incompatibility of slavery with democracy. In a private memorandum entitled 'Fragment on Slavery' in 1854, he argued that anyone who defends the institution of slavery on moral grounds creates an ethic under which he may himself be enslaved. To a friend he observed that the exclusion of social groups from the enjoyment of social rights might spread, and indeed with the rise of virulent anti-alien and especially anti-Catholic politics, seemed to be spreading; though such a spread might be opposed on arguments of expediency, it could never, given the assumptions of slavery, be stopped on principle.[13] In so fluid a society as that of Lincoln's America this argument was particularly serious. Historians looking back on the whole course of events have not always appreciated that the sudden rise of xenophobia and religious intolerance on the one side together with the restlessness of the slavery issue on the other threatened the future of that open society, that combination of order with opportunity, which Lincoln believed to be the special purpose of the American experiment.

Yet his insight did not entirely free him of the limitations, the prejudices of the region he felt called to represent. Freedom he believed, due to all; but the freedom that concerned him, whose danger brought him to contest with Douglas the leadership of the great North-West, was not so much that of the Negro, (whether slave or not) as that of the independent farmer, the mechanic, the small business man—the typical white settler of the West. The antipathy of these masses to slavery was based overwhelmingly on their fear and hatred of slave competition, but it extended to an almost equal dislike of competition with the labour of, or society that

13. Richard Hofstadter, chapter on Lincoln in *American Political Tradition*.

offered hospitality to, the free Negro. Lincoln, before 1861, though a man of unusual compassion, does not seem to have been more than ordinarily sensitive to the feelings of Negroes in their social situation. There is little evidence that he was ever ready to accept the full implications of social equality. The war, however, and the great services of Negroes to the Union cause, enlarged his vision and softened his feelings. As he learnt to take a wider and more national view of events, so also, characteristically, he learnt to take a wider view of the peoples of America, and was privately urging that at least some of the freed men be granted the right to vote.

But the aversion of the free white masses to the prospect of Negro social equality was a fact which no one aspiring to lead those masses could ignore, even had Lincoln been disposed to ignore it. Lincoln's arguments appealed with striking success to the free settler's fear of slavery extension, and believing slavery to be unjust and a denial of the foundations of American republicanism, he was able to enlist the eager support of the rising body of genuine opponents of slavery itself. He did not, like Douglas, have to try to keep the loyalty of a Southern wing in his party. He won the party battle; but when he did so, the mere fact of his election to the presidency was held, by seven Southern states, to be sufficient reason to secede from the Union.

The problem of emancipation had always been complicated by the problem of the future relations of the freed slaves with the white majority, and for many years the majority of those who favoured liberation had hoped to combine it with some form of colonization. Bands of volunteer free Negroes did in fact sail for Liberia, Haiti, and other outlying spots; but none of these projects ever had much chance of attracting more than a fraction of the American Negro population. Yet Lincoln, in his very pratical concern for the American future, clung to these schemes long after their inadequacy was all too plain. There was little in his experience of political life to modify the conviction that the white and

Negro peoples would be unable to live side by side in complete harmony or mutual respect; but he saw with consternation that their relations would be frightfully embittered if emancipation were to be achieved suddenly, by force and without compensation. As it became clear during the summer of 1862 that emancipation must be embarked on, Lincoln became occupied with the great problem of achieving emancipation without exacerbating the relations between the races.

As early as March 1862 he recommended to Congress a joint resolution offering financial aid to any state that would take steps towards gradual emancipation with compensation to the owners who gave up their slaves. He went so far as personally to draft two bills for this object for Delaware. Then he summoned the congressional representatives of the border states, whose institutions were the crux of the problem, and urged on them the wisdom of his policy. To a senator and to the editor of *The New York Times,* who opposed these measures, he wrote a letter pointing out that one million dollars or less than half of one day's cost of the war would buy all the slaves in Delaware at $400 a head; $174,000,000, or less than eighty-seven days' cost of war would buy all the slaves in the border states and the District of Columbia; and he argued that this step would shorten the war by more than eighty-seven days. In March the Congress passed the resolution, but without support from the border states. Next month it went on to pass a bill for gradual and compensated emancipation in the District of Columbia, over which the Federal government had full jurisdiction. Voluntary colonization in Liberia and Haiti was provided for. Soon afterwards, however, Lincoln was faced with another unauthorized military emancipation order, applying to the slaves of Georgia, South Carolina, and Florida, and this, like Frémont's, he countermanded. The order had been brought forth partly because of the problem presented by the fugitive slaves who came into Union lines; and with this problem Congress dealt by a law forbidding military commanders to return fugitives to disloyal owners. In the same act slavery was abolished in the territories, in defiance of the judgement of the Supreme Court given in 1857. The Federal government further showed its goodwill by negotiating with Great Britain a treaty for the joint suppression of the slave trade.

Near the end of the Congressional session of 1861–62 Lincoln returned to the theme of voluntary and compensated emancipation. If the border states would but accept it then a great blow would have been struck in the war and, he felt, much of the poison that threatened the future would be drained away. In his annual message to Congress in December, Lincoln proposed a Constitutional amendment offering remuneration by government bonds to all states abolishing slavery before 1900 (here was gradualness indeed!) granting freedom to all slaves liberated by the war and—once again—authorizing Congress to provide for the colonization of freed Negroes. There was a further appeal, made with passionate and persuasive sincerity, for compensated emancipation. Without doubt it was one of the major objects of Lincoln's presidency, and without doubt his almost complete failure to impress the border states with the urgency of the project boded ill for the future. Yet, emancipation by voluntary action having failed, Lincoln knew that he could not go back; if the states would not act for themselves, then the last expedient remained the only alternative: total emancipation by Constitutional amendment.

It was in the face of this situation that Lincoln began to promote that Thirteenth Amendment to the Constitution of the United States by which slavery was finally abolished and the unfinished work of the Emancipation Proclamation completed. The amendment passed the Senate by the necessary two-thirds majority in April 1864 but failed in the House of Representatives. In December, Lincoln asked the House to reconsider its vote. Behind the scenes he exerted every influence, every means of pressure at his command, with threats and promises of patronage, to ensure success. In January 1865, amid great excitement, the amendment passed, and the ratification by state legislatures afterwards completed the process. Less than four years earlier, Lincoln had been ready to accept another thirteenth amendment.

The Emancipation Proclamation alone, however, was the decisive weapon that friends of the North in Britain needed to let in the stemmed tide of Northern sympathy. On 13th December 1863 a meeting, reported to have been largely attended by working men, was held in Lambeth, under the auspices of the Emancipation Society. (Confederate President Jefferson Davis's coachman, an escaped slave, was present, and subsequently addressed a number of similar audiences.) *The Bee-Hive*'s change of direction was manifest in a review of the old year which declared that the frightful loss of life had not been in vain and that the slaves would be freed as a result of the war. The first three months of the new year saw a truly extraordinary spate of working-class activity, the product of an enthusiasm, a directing intelligence, and a unity of purpose that the parliamentarians of either party would not long be able to ignore.

On the eve of Emancipation, 31st December 1862, large meetings in London and Manchester hailed the new era and heard rousing expressions of enthusiasm for Anglo-American understanding. Cheers were given for Emancipation and for Lincoln. The spokesmen of the workers' interest, both at public meetings and in the press, now became more explicit than ever before about the connection between their cause and that of the Union. But where Lincoln had moved first to save the Union, and had said that he would, if necessary, have achieved this end without freeing a single slave, the British enthusiasts ignored the refinements which seemed to belong to the strategy rather than to the meaning of the war. To them the war was not really comprehensible unless the abolition of slavery were envisaged as its principal object. By the inexorable course of events, to which Lincoln bowed, and which he had foreseen, the strategy of the war was brought into collaboration with the principles of the abolitionists. Neither in America nor in Britain could this collaboration be long resisted.

The programme of meetings became more ambitious; on 31st January a major gathering was held in the Exeter Hall in London, while three others were held in London and yet more in Leeds and Bath. Resolutions carried at Leeds avowed the object of strengthening President Lincoln's hands. In these activities the Nonconformist ministers were prominent, appearing at a large number of the meetings addressed by radical and by artisan leaders. C. H. Spurgeon led a huge congregation in his tabernacle to pray for the strengthening of Northern arms. The press gives little impression of Lincoln as an individual, however; nor does his personality or history seem yet to have excited much curiosity. What did interest people was the simple fact of his humble origins. Professor E. S. Beesly,[14] who, though not a member of the Junta, had become the most cogent political contributor to *The Bee-Hive,* remarked in an editorial review of the Exeter Hall meeting that working men, wonderful as it might seem, did not think any better of the South because it was led—or driven—by 'gentlemen.' 'A state of society in which a rail-splitter can rise to the highest dignities is not to them so obviously intolerable.' It was quite clear, he observed, that this vast assemblage, both within and without the walls of Exeter Hall, was anxious to express its zeal, not only for emancipation, but for the triumph of republican principles and institutions over the aristocracy of the South. Three cheers were given for President Lincoln. Manchester workers were forming an 'Emancipation and Union Society.' '*The Times,*' Beesly pointedly remarked, 'thinks it prudent to call attention to the fact that "there was not a single man of influence on the platform." So much the worse for the "men of influence" . . . To prudent people it will perhaps occur that when, on a grand moral and political question the line is so very sharply drawn between the upper and the lower classes, we must be on the eve, or rather in the first stage, of a revolution. In the meantime the people will not fail to perceive its superiority to the wealthy and refined classes. The very fact that the wealthy are refined has, it seems, depraved their conscience. In the face of this scandalous revelation, it will be difficult to show why they should retain the exclusive direction of society . . .' He

14. Beesly was professor of history at University College, London.

predicted that the calm of late years was about to be disturbed, for the American war had made apparent the profound chasm between the upper and lower classes; and he claimed that the British workers would move forward in their own struggle for enfranchisement with the immense advantage of their demonstrated moral superiority over the class 'which now monopolises political privilege.' The political lesson was driven home with almost brutal insistence:

> 'If not a single county member' (Beesly said) 'has raised his voice for emancipation, what do we gain by having a constitution which secures the government of England to country gentlemen? If the peers one and all have stood aloof from the cause of justice and freedom as though it would defile them, why should we keep up a separate branch of the legislature for the express purpose of enabling them to control the national policy?'

The trade societies were in general barred by their constitutions from taking part in political agitation. But the members of the Junta, working in close consultation with Marx, were anxious to use the organization of the societies to call together a great meeting on the American question—a distinctively working-class demonstration of solidarity with the North, avowedly, if not technically held under the auspices of the trade unions. They also had in view another object: though the meeting would be of the workers, they wanted to achieve a reconciliation with John Bright, the staunchest champion of the North in Parliament and long an advocate of the extension of the suffrage at home. They well knew Bright's fearless integrity. They clearly understood that Bright's powerful leadership inside the House of Commons, backed by the massive following of the organized though disfranchised workers without, would prove the most potent engine of reform to be seen in their whole generation. While crowded meetings in favour of Emancipation continued to be held, the Junta went ahead with plans to bring Bright down to address their rally to be held in St. James' Hall on 26th March. Bright agreed to take the chair. Tickets were distributed free by the trade societies among their members. The demand was tremendous.

The great night came and went. But when it had gone the reformers knew in their hearts that their power was irresistible. Nor did they miss the opportunity to weld together two great shafts of their argument—for Northern victory and parliamentary reform. Bright said:

> 'Privilege has beheld an afflicting spectacle for many years past. It has beheld thirty millions of men happy and prosperous, without emperor, without king' (cheers) 'without the surroundings of a court' (renewed cheers) 'without nobles, except such as are made by eminence in intellect and virtue—without State bishops and State priests—those vendors of the love that works salvation' (cheers) 'without great armies and great navies—without a great debt and great taxes—and privilege has shuddered at what might happen to old Europe if this great experiment should succeed.' (Loud cheers).

He dwelt on the Southern philosophy of labour and emphasized the right of the trade societies to maintain the rights of industry. In the Southern philosophy, he declared, it was not only black men who were to be slaves: their specific for the labour problem was to make labour capital.

Odger drew attention to discrimination in England against the Irish. Other craft leaders spoke. Late in the proceedings came the cogent Beesly. The cause of labour, he declared, was one all over the world. The British ruling classes were united in defence of their order—the gentlemen of the South. 'Well,' said Beesly, 'stand by yours.' He concluded by stating that they were met not merely as the friends of Emancipation but as the friends of Reform; it was the first time the trade unions had met on a political subject but it would not be the last.

The orderliness of the proceedings were pointed out in later comment for the benefit of those who feared working-class riots. Meanwhile similar motions were on foot throughout the industrial north. W. E. Forster, the radical Member of Parliament, claimed at Bradford that his prophecy that the war would steadily acquire an anti-slavery character had been vindicated. At a Newcastle emancipation meeting cheers were given for Lincoln, the American Union, and the Poles, then in rebellion against foreign domination. Manchester was also the scene of anti-slavery demonstrations; in Liverpool a committee was established 'to inform the public mind.'

Despite the jeers with which Bright was greeted in the Commons when he referred to the London meeting, no one, least of all those who hoped to direct the political life of Britain in the coming generation, could ignore the significance of these massive demonstrations of quiet, disciplined power.

In the north country, however, and especially in Lancashire, the industrial workers had already for more than a year shown their capacity for discipline under conditions of hardship unknown to the skilled craftsmen of London. In 1860 some half a million persons were employed as operatives in the cotton mills of Lancashire and its neighbourhood, and it was stated by *The Times* in 1861, that one-fifth of the whole population of England was held to be dependent in some way on the prosperity of the cotton industry.[15] Nearly 80 percent of the raw cotton consumed by this industry came from the southern United States and was therefore immediately affected by the war. The overwhelming dependence of the British economy on this single commodity was well known, indeed too well known, in the South, whose political diagnosticians had for some years nurtured an overweening sense of Southern indispensability. It was confidently believed that the mere threat to withhold cotton would force Britain to intervene decisively in the interest of the South. This reasoning foundered on three rocks, two lying in the economic and political situation in Britain and one in the argument itself.

The fact was that the increase in Southern cotton production had already overloaded the market; in 1860 itself the South sent to Lancashire nearly half a million more bales than in any previous year. The manufacturers' long-term fear of a famine due to some

15. Adams, *Great Britain and the American Civil War*, Vol. II, p. 7.

crisis in slavery had given way to an immediate fear of an over-production crisis due to glut. Consumer prices were already falling, and the threat of a stoppage of supplies had no immediate terror. But when the shortage began to be felt, not before October 1861, the South discovered that British policies were not to be determined by single factors, however potent, and that the general lack of sympathy for Southern institutions among the British workers was to be a non-economic determinant. The war continuing, the South desperately needed to raise funds in Europe; but here her reasoning collapsed—for the greatest source of Southern wealth was, of course, cotton, and in the check to overseas trade the South now had the co-operation of the blockade imposed by the Union navy!

By December 1861, supplies to Britain had stopped. In the ensuing six months, the bales received amounted to less than one per cent of those received in the same period of the previous year. The distress of the Lancashire workers was deep and prevailing, and though alleviated by occasional fluctuations, and by some development of alternative sources of supply, it was not until the spring of 1864, after the North had renewed supplies by occupation of Southern soil, that employment returned to normality. The disorganized industry suffered further crisis later in 1864 and again in 1866. In ordinary periods some 48,000 persons in the textile districts appear to have received poor relief; by March 1862 the number had risen to 113,000. In December 1862 the nadir of unemployment was reached, with some 284,000 in receipt of relief. These distresses were the more acute in that the population affected had previously known a fairly wholesome level of activity and had begun to have some share in the improvements earned by a prosperous industry. The most grievous loss was that of the older people whose working life was closing and whose savings were ravaged. But grave as was the cotton famine, it never threatened to reduce the population to the verge of starvation. The need for relief threw upon the poor law system the greatest crisis of its history; and the poor law was amended in 1862 to strengthen the resources of the localities most directly affected. Private relief was gradually organized, and by the end of 1862 was reaching 236,000 people. Some manufacturers owning property remitted the rents of their unemployed workers and gave other forms of aid. Others did not. The whole country was drawn into the effort, not least the trade societies, and the columns of *The Bee-Hive* and of other working-class journals repeatedly carried appeals for funds and announcements of relief organization. Another source of timely aid was New York, from which three well publicized grain ships reached Liverpool early in 1863.

The chief victims of the cotton famine were the working people of the north country. If any demonstrations for breaking the blockade were to be expected it was certainly to Lancashire that any observer would look for the first signs of unrest. There were some disorders, but remarkably few; and it was here that the quietness of the workers must first have communicated its muffled warning to the South's agents and British partisans. One keen commentator, Karl Marx, after writing in December 1861 of the 'indestructible excellence' of the British working class, expressed disappointment, a year later, with the mildness and inactivity of the men of Lancashire. He was soon reassured of their soundness—despite, as he noted, the workers' renegade press. While Southern sympathizers in Parliament based their appeal for recognition of the South and British intervention to end the blockade on the plight of their suffering fellow-countrymen, the sufferers stubbornly refused to support them. And in Lancashire as elsewhere, the Emancipation Proclamation freed and clarified the whole flood of long-restrained emotion. The stroke was not sudden, since the preliminary Proclamation had given one hundred days' notice; and it took even the radicals some time to overcome their doubts as to the intent of this policy and its consequences. But the London working men's meeting of 31st December 1862 approved an address to the President, which was presented to the American minister in London. The address declared that as Englishmen and workers the subscribers prized free labour on free soil; they approved emancipation and prayed, on the eve of the Proclamation, 'to strengthen the President's hands and confirm his noble purpose.' Lincoln, in his reply, emphasized the importance of free institutions and their place in the struggle. On 1st January a great meeting in Manchester, presided over by the Mayor, adopted an address to Lincoln warmly approving his work and declaring that slavery was the only thing that had lessened the people's sympathy with the United States. Lincoln was well aware of the importance of these expressions of sympathy, as he was evidently moved by the patient support which he had already received from the workers of Britain. To the working men of Manchester he made a memorable reply.

> 'I know' (Lincoln wrote to them) 'and deeply deplore the sufferings which the working men at Manchester, and in all Europe, are called to endure in this crisis. It has been often and studiously represented that the attempt to overthrow this government, which was built on the foundation of human rights, and to substitute for it one which would rest exclusively on the basis of human slavery, was likely to obtain the favour of Europe. Through the action of our disloyal citizens, the working men of Europe have been subjected to severe trials, for the purpose of forcing their sanction to that attempt. Under the circumstances, I cannot but regard your decisive utterances upon the question as an example of sublime Christian heroism which has not been surpassed in any age or in any country.'

He concluded by hailing the interchange of sentiment as an augury that,

> '. . . whatever misfortune may befall your country or my own, the peace and friendship which now exist between the two nations will be, as it shall be my desire to make them, perpetual.'

Lincoln had always believed that the general fate of free government was involved in that of the American experiment. His expressions at Gettysburg were no mere rhetoric, but stated the essence, distilled into the briefest form, of his doctrine that it was the mission of the American Union to vindicate popular government. For Lincoln, therefore, the solid, deliberate sympathy of British workers, prepared to suffer in the American cause, must have come as a peculiarly warm and gratifying gift.

Yet one of the steadiest fires of Lincoln's political mind did not light up the British workers' image of America. For Lincoln, the American Union was much more than a significant political experiment. Lincoln, and many of his countrymen—and not least in the South—had made of this experiment an act of faith which drew together the strong bands of natural patriotism, a fervent belief in justice understood in terms of political equality, and a singularly American dedication to the future: others might imagine themselves judged by their ancestors, Americans would be judged by their heirs. All this was at stake. If the Union were destroyed, whatever else might follow, all this would irretrievably be lost. Lincoln was sustained by a strong sense of divine providence; not of a providence which takes affairs out of the hands of men, nor yet of the sort that submits them to the caprice of human control, but rather of a providence which demands of men their most arduous exertion in its cause. The fate of the Union seems for Lincoln to have had a meaning of almost mystical character. But this passion, which British people may find easier to understand when they think of the year 1940, does not seem to have inspired the North's British supporters in the Civil War. Their feelings indeed were strong and their thinking clear. They stood on the rights of labour—which involved their full status as human beings; on democracy, political and economic. Because they were disfranchised, excluded from complete recognition in their own country, they were able to transfer some perhaps of their native patriotism, as many indeed transferred their persons, to America. But the touch of mystique is missing. It would have been a little too much to ask.

The dignified conduct of the working folk of Lancashire made its impression on the most important political mind of the coming generation of leaders, Gladstone's. In May 1864 he gave his opinion that this conduct deserved to be considered when the suffrage franchise came to be reformed. And it was in the course of the same speech that he made the famous declaration that everyone not morally incapacitated ought to come within the pale of the constitution.

Meanwhile, however, it was possible for a British worker to feel that the President of the United States was nearer and more accessible than the member of parliament for whom he had no vote. Intending emigrants sometimes wrote personally to Lincoln, sometimes to Seward, expressing their aspirations and asking for help. In 1865 some handloom weavers of Scotland collectively sent a representation on their problems and hopes of emigration.

The political consequence of working-class sympathy was far too great to escape Lincoln's attention. It is likely that the Liverpool conference of January 1863, from which sprang a committee 'to inform the public mind,' was arranged by Peter Sinclair, who in 1862 had written a book, *Freedom or Slavery in the United States*, to prove that the choice between the two was the real issue, and in it had favourably compared the conditions of American workers with those of British. He was working for the North in Lancashire early in 1863, by speaking in public and organizing societies. Lincoln himself took the trouble to show the way he wanted the case to be presented when he drew up a resolution to be presented for adoption at British meetings. This argued that, whereas formerly slavery had sometimes been merely tolerated, the establishment of the Confederacy was now attempted with the fundamental object of perpetuating slavery; and that 'no such embryo State should ever be recognized by, or admitted into, the family of Christian and civilized nations . . .' This emphasis on slavery did not appear before 1863.

The wave of demonstrations died down in the spring of 1863. There was no longer the slightest doubt of the sympathies of the British masses and no longer any material danger that a British government—even had it wished to do so—would risk any form of intervention. In the *Alabama* case (the British built Southern sea-raider which destroyed many U.S. merchant vessels) the government's position was purely legalistic and in the cases of the rams later built by the Lairds the government leaned, nervously and undecidedly it is true, towards the restraint even of private transactions that might lead to Confederate purchase. (The legal problems here were not so simple as Northern sympathizers thought, but they could have been more vigorously tackled.)

While American war news continued to be amply reported after mid-1863, the main editorial attention of the British working-class press turned to domestic problems. The terrible slaughter and negative results of the actions through the dreary summer of 1864 gave little cause for anyone to rejoice; and in the late summer Lincoln became convinced that his own re-election in November was exceedingly unlikely. Lincoln's re-election, however, was assured in good time by the news of Union successes, particularly of Sherman's march through Georgia. The election campaign attracted little British attention. But as soon as the election was over a very important moral was drawn. *The Bee-Hive* [16] editorially pointed out the extraordinary nature of what had happened, and printed a letter from Goldwin Smith, formerly Regius Professor of History at Oxford and now in the United States, treating the matter in detail. A great democracy, in the midst of a terrible civil war, had quietly gone through the whole complex procedure of a general election with hardly a sign of disorder or even of bad organization. A northern paper [17] proclaimed the magic influence of success and noted that Disraeli in the House of Commons had conceded 'sagacity' to the people of the United States. 'The Americans,' said an editorial, 'have shown that they can govern themselves, suppress a fearful rebellion, and conduct a general and most exciting election in the midst of civil war, with perfect tranquility. Hence the antagonism which prevails amongst the aristocracy against America.' Proponents of the Northern cause and domestic reform already had in their hands the weapon of Emancipation; now they could point to the orderliness and efficiency of the electoral process; within a few

16. *Bee-Hive*, November 26, 1864.
17. *Newcastle Weekly Chronicle*, March 18, 1865.

months they would be reinforced by the decisive argument: victory.

The foundation of a new Reform League, in February 1865, was of more immediate interest than the news from America, which seemed to assure imminent Southern defeat. The League, whose leadership included several of the Junta, received the support of the recently former International Working Men's Association. The interest of the international working class in Northern victory was firmly asserted, and it is not without instruction that one finds the signature of 'Carl Marx' subscribed to the declaration that 'From the commencement of the titanic American strife, the working men of Europe felt instinctively that the star-spangled banner carried the destiny of their class.'[18]

The final triumph of Northern arms was joyously claimed as a victory by the reform interests in Britain. The case was put with his usual pungency by Beesley in *The Bee-Hive*.

> 'Our opponents' (he wrote) 'had told us that republicanism was on its trial. They insisted on our watching what they called its breakdown. They told us plainly that it was forever discredited in England. Well, we accepted the challenge. We staked our hopes boldly on the result . . . Under such a strain as no monarchy, no aristocracy, no empire could have supported, Republican institutions have stood firm. It is we, now, who call on the privileged classes to mark the result. They may rely upon it that a vast impetus has been given to Republican sentiments in England . . .'[19]

Everywhere the spokesmen of the working class and reformist side proclaimed their profound satisfaction with the result. *The National Reformer*,[20] a genuinely liberal though not a working-class paper, summarized the democratic case in a leading article. The valour of Northern troops had vindicated popular government, and 'opened the more fertile states of the American Union to the

18. *Bee-Hive*, January 7, 1865.
19. *Bee-Hive*, April 29, 1865.
20. *National Reformer*, April 30, 1865.

European emigrant and established at a stroke the rights and dignity of labour. The cause of the North,' it concluded, 'was our cause; its triumph is our triumph.' *The Beehive* [21] called upon the toiling millions to sign a congratulatory address to Lincoln and to the American people on the extinction of slavery, and announced that a committee to carry out this object had been formed in London.

When these words were written Lincoln was dead. The news of his assassination, at first pathetically disbelieved in some quarters, gave the whole British nation a convulsive shock. The Queen wrote a letter of condolence to Mrs. Lincoln. Kind words, and by Disraeli moving words, were spoken by the parliamentary leaders. *Punch*, not without magnanimity, apologized publicly for its former criticisms. But to the working people of Britain the loss was personal and extreme. Huge crowds gathered in meetings of tribute and heard Lincoln's praises in deep silence broken by loud bursts of cheers. It was then, in this posthumous phase, that the sense of Lincoln's personality, suddenly withdrawn, became apparent and vital.

Most of the wartime caricatures of Lincoln had been hostile. (For which reason they were bad; Lincoln, whatever his shortcomings, had no malice in his countenance.) The labour press carried no portraits, and the press as a whole did not cater to personal curiosity. His strong presence had presided, literally and symbolically, over the destinies of America and had become the image in which his country was seen. But it was not, as later with Woodrow Wilson and Franklin D. Roosevelt, a clearly depicted visual image. Late in 1862 *The Bee-Hive* [22] reprinted W. H. Russell's rather genial description of Lincoln's personal appearance, but such accounts were rare. His qualities, however, had emerged, slowly, with the progress of the war.

At the mass meetings of sympathy the many speakers took advantage of the opportunity to demonstrate the unity of the Ameri-

21. *Bee-Hive*, April 22, 1865.
22. *Bee-Hive*, December 27, 1862.

can cause with their own. A 'monster meeting' in St. Martin's Hall on 4th May was told by Thomas Potter, Cobden's successor as M.P. for Rochdale, that Lincoln's programme had been Union and Emancipation—and that they in England also held to a programme of Union and Emancipation—unanimity among themselves and emancipation from the vestiges of feudalism. 'The working men of London feel the deepest sympathy with labour in America,' he said. 'The cause of the one is the cause of the other; and at this meeting they extended the right hand of friendship to their fellow-men on the other side of the Atlantic, and wish this meeting to be the scene of everlasting friendship between the two peoples. (Loud and continued cheering).' The meeting was then addressed by trades' leaders, the report in each case naming the craft of the speaker.[23] And the glassmakers and plasterers and stone-masons of London made clear that republican institutions had stood their test and that to their eyes the place occupied by Lincoln was equal to that of 'the greatest monarch on earth.'

Later speakers, including Beesly, reminded the audience of a forthcoming first public meeting of the National Reform League and appealed for its support.

The circumstances of the assassination lent themselves to a quotation from *Macbeth,* which appeared in many articles and speeches,

> Besides, this Duncan
> Hath borne his faculties so meek, hath been
> So clear in his great office, that his virtues
> Will plead like angels, trumpet-tongu'd against
> The deep damnation of his taking-off . . .

Duncan was a king. Nothing could more vividly exemplify the profound feeling of working people and of reformers everywhere, that Lincoln, a man of humble birth and beginnings, a manual labourer risen by merit and the choice of the people to the highest elective office in the world, was truly and personally their own

23. *Miner and Workmen's Advocate,* May 6, 1865.

honoured representative, than the repeated use of language drawn from the repertoire of royalty. Again and again working-class audiences cheered the declaration that his position and his example were kingly. A minister, the Rev. J. C. Street, was loudly applauded by a northern audience when he struck the note which, at once rhetorical and entirely sincere, expressed the deep conviction of the British working people.[24]

> 'There have been great rulers in time past . . . and there are some great rulers today; but the kingliest of them all—greater than any of the past, greater than any living today—was Abraham Lincoln.'

Bibliographical note on the materials which have been found useful in this essay:

Newspapers.   The following were consulted.
The Working Man.
The British Miner: also called *The Miner and Workmen's Advocate.*
The Bee-Hive.
The London American.
The National Reformer.
The Newcastle Weekly Chronicle and Northern Counties Advertiser.

Printed documents.
Abraham Lincoln: The Complete Works (Six vols. ed.).
Karl Marx and Frederick Engels: *The Civil War in the United States.* Ed. Richard Enmale, n.d. London, Lawrence and Wishart.

Articles.
Joseph H. Park, 'The English Workingmen and the American Civil War,' *Political Science Quarterly,* vol. 39, 1924, pp. 432–57.
Royden Harrison, 'British Labour and the Confederacy,' *International Review of Social History,* Vol. II, 1951, pp. 78–105.

24. *Newcastle Weekly Chronicle*, May 6, 1865.

Other studies, special and general.

E. D. Adams, *Great Britain and the American Civil War* (New York, 1924).

H. C. Allen, *Great Britain and the United States* (London, 1954).

R. A. Arnold, *History of the Cotton Famine* (London, 1864).

J. H. Clapham, *An Economic History of Britain* (Cambridge, 1926).

Dr. Charlotte Erickson of the London School of Economics kindly let me use her notes of correspondence in the State Department archives.

Frances Elma Gillespie, *Labor and Politics in England, 1850–1867* (Durham, North Carolina, 1927).

W. O. Henderson, *The Lancashire Cotton Famine 1861–1865.* Univ. of Manchester Economic History Series, No. 9 (Manchester, 1934).

Richard Hofstadter, *The American Political Tradition and the Men Who Made It* (New York, 1951).

S. Maccoby, *British Radicalism 1853–1886* (London, 1938).

Henry Pelling, *America and the British Left* (London, 1956).

J. G. Randall, *Lincoln the President,* vols. I and II (London, 1945).

B. C. Roberts, *The Trade Union Congress* (London, 1958).

Benjamin P. Thomas, *Abraham Lincoln* (New York, 1952).

G. M. Trevelyan, *The Life of John Bright* (London, 1913).

Sidney and Beatrice Webb, *The History of Trade Unionism* (London, 1894).

For findings subsequent to the date of this essay, see Mary Ellison *Support for Secession: Lancashire and the American Civil War* (Chicago, 1972).

6

Abraham Lincoln and the American Commitment
(1965)

Abraham Lincoln died on April 15, 1865. The centenary of his death seems a proper moment for commemoration, provided always that one undertakes the task while recognizing that the only commemoration worthy of the subject or the occasion will be an honest attempt at appraisal.

When Lincoln died, the United States had reached the end of a civil war, but was in the middle of a new crisis. In 1863 Lincoln had set forth a plan for the reorganization of the governments of the first two Southern states to have been reconquered—Louisiana and Arkansas. But at the close of 1864, Congress had refused to seat the first representatives elected under Lincoln's plan. Thus the President, who was intent on returning to a normal relationship with the states of the former Confederacy as speedily as possible, was already at loggerheads with the Congress.

The assassination of the President, on Good Friday, 1865, was an event whose symbolic and sacrifical implication was obvious to all, except perhaps to the assassin. It may well have hardened

This essay was first a lecture delivered in the University of Cambridge to mark the centenary of the death of Abraham Lincoln.

Northern feeling and thus have influenced the course of events; but it would be superfluous to attribute any specific consequences to the quasi-religious symbolism of Lincoln's death. That, however, does not remove from us some responsibility for trying to estimate its historical significance.

The death of the President has relieved historians of the obligation to judge his policy for Reconstruction beyond the limited steps he had already taken. The problems were extraordinarily difficult, and as one can see no clear line through them to a complete resolution, it seems almost certain that the record of Lincoln's second administration was bound to have been one of partial failure.

Lincoln's wartime leadership was crowned with ultimate, though costly, success: he won the war. Historians who venerate Lincoln for his achievement in saving the Union are absolved, by his death, from the disagreeable necessity for admitting his incomplete success in Reconstruction; but historians who dislike the Radical Republicans can take comfort from the conviction that Lincoln would have opposed the imposition of a root-and-branch solution on the South. On the other hand, those who venerate Lincoln both for saving the Union and for improving the condition of the Negroes, find themselves freed from the still more disagreeable necessity for actually condemning him, on account of any subsequent opposition he might have offered to the Radicals.

But all this is speculation. We do not know what would have been the history of Lincoln's second administration. Yet we can hardly deny that his assassination was an event; and as such it affected the course of subsequent events: so that if we are to make any attempts to appraise its significance, I do not think we can simply dodge the questions that were left unanswered. I feel that those who presume to speak about Lincoln have some duty (to themselves among others) to decide in what way the course of events was affected by the removal of the wartime President. If the problem can be neither fully resolved, nor fairly evaded, that does at least leave us with a residue of responsibility for thinking about it, and I therefore propose to return to it.

That promise cannot be properly redeemed until one has reconsidered the analysis which Lincoln brought to bear on the crisis of his time, and the way in which events took shape under the relentless pressure of his extraordinary combination of inflexible determination and flexible tactics. He once remarked, 'I claim not to have controlled events, but confess plainly that events have controlled me.' Perhaps, in shrugging off the credit for Union successes, he was also diminishing his personal responsibility for the war itself. At all events the disclaimer is a shade too modest. From 1854, when he returned to active political life, there had at least been a fair measure of give-and-take between Lincoln and the events that controlled him.

Some of Lincoln's principal biographers have been troubled by the contrast they have noticed between Lincoln in the period of political struggle between 1854 and 1860, and Lincoln the President. Committed to the task of revealing Lincoln's greatness, they found themselves tracing the manoeuvres of an ambitious state politician whose calibre never seemed to rise above the second-rate and who did not always get the better of the argument with his rival, Stephen A. Douglas. Yet Lincoln did gain the supreme prize, and did prove himself a supreme leader. And so his wartime leadership cast a sort of retrospective vindication over his earlier struggles and ambitions.

The rise of Lincoln from origins of such profound obscurity has seemed to many Americans to have been providential. Even Lord Charnwood declined to set aside all possibility of some form of divine intervention; but if this took place I fear that it must be considered at least as a Constitutional impropriety. Others have fallen back on the explanation that Lincoln disclosed exceptional powers of growth—powers barely discernible in earlier years.

These views do not seem to me satisfactory. When a man exercises presidential powers he works with great materials, and when his decisions affect the movement of nations or of armies, then his successes acquire the aura of what the world chooses to regard as 'greatness.' As President, Lincoln was in a position to make—and made—mistakes which cost many thousands of lives. He also achieved success which held together the factions in his Cabinet, maintained the basic unity of his party, kept up the will of the North to win the war, and attained ultimate victory. There was no other position in which he could have revealed these powers to the full. Yet his activity as a state politician does not, in my opinion, stand in contrast, but rather in broad continuity, with his later development.

There was nothing providential in the rise of an Illinois politician to national leadership. Lincoln grew up in the north-west at the period when that region was growing rapidly in wealth and population; the political centre of gravity was beginning to shift into the Mississippi Valley. In the 1850s, Illinois itself was the most rapidly growing state in the Union. It leaped ahead of its neighbours in agricultural production, competed with them in industry, and advanced in railroad mileage. It was altogether probable that the north-west would soon give the nation a President. The case can be seen in clearer perspective when it is pointed out that Lincoln's most serious rival in the presidential election was Douglas, his personal rival in their home state of Illinois.

In 1852, Lincoln's old party, the Whig party of Clay and Webster, began to crumble. But when Douglas split the Democratic party by introducing the Nebraska bill and pressing through the repeal of the Missouri Compromise, the Whigs experienced a temporary revival, especially in Illinois. During the next two years Lincoln came to realize that the old party could not be held together; and at the same time he felt the most serious alarm about the rise of a new and menacing group, the so-called 'Know-Nothings,' who held themselves bound by pledges of secrecy, and whose nativist prejudices threatened the precepts of equality which in Lincoln's view lay at the source of the American Republic.

In these extremely dangerous and fast-moving currents, Lincoln proceeded to take a leading part in forming, in Illinois, a branch of the new Republican party. He moved with such dexterity and ef-

fect that by 1856 he was already regarded in his own state as a potential national figure, and his name was put forward as a possible
candidate for the Vice-Presidency. Nothing came of that particular
move. In the next two years, while the territory of Kansas provided a microcosm of the coming civil war, Lincoln worked to hold
his party together and to challenge Douglas for the United States
Senate in 1858. The campaign of that autumn showed that he
could deal damaging blows against a rival of undisputed national
stature, and, although Lincoln lost the fight for the Senate, it was
not very long afterwards that his supporters began to broach the
prospect of the presidency.

These were years of tense struggle whose outcome was always in
doubt. But the errors and the triumphs of the President were in
character with those of the aspirant. Lincoln certainly did grow
with his office. He became more authoritative in his style, more
comprehensive in his vision, and more compassionate in his feelings. He also revealed an increasing appreciation of the problems
and aspirations of Negroes. But all of these developments had
sources in his earlier life. Assuredly the support of his huge following in Illinois, and the intense loyalty of his political friends, were
the result of qualities already perceived in the state long before
they had had the opportunity to appear before the nation.

In Illinois, as later in the Union, the outcome, as I remarked,
was in doubt. I also remarked that Lincoln did not always get the
better of his argument with Douglas in 1858. Yet Lincoln did see
farther than Douglas. Douglas knew the passions and energies of
his section, and represented them with energy and ability. Lincoln, who was no less a product of that rough and turbulent western society, shared most of the same passions and many of the
same prejudices. Yet, if he looked in the same direction, he saw
beyond the outlines visible to his opponents and beyond what was
visible, I think, to many of his supporters. The penetration of Lincoln's vision owed its depth to his very personal combination of
three general characteristics.

First, Lincoln was a nationalist. There was nothing unusual

about being a nationalist in the middle of the nineteenth century. But in the United States, at a period of vast and rapid sectional growth, and of rival interpretations of the Constitution, the specific applications of nationalist attitudes could sometimes be difficult to state and unpopular to propose.

Secondly, Lincoln believed that the American dedication to democracy was an act of will and purpose. He was far more subtle than Douglas in his appreciation of the complexity of the problems raised by simply believing in democracy. The meaning of human quality was for him inextricably involved in the problem. Democracy was the only method of government which offered the chance to find out the fullest possible meaning of equality; the quest for the meaning of equality was the purpose of the American experiment; and certainly, in Lincoln's mind, that purpose would not be simply shoved to one side by the triumphal march of the popular majority, right or wrong. Democracy therefore required leadership, and, in face of crisis, that leadership must be informed by a sense of national purpose. In the 1850s these views could only mean that the survival of the Union and the survival of slavery were, at the least, related problems. Their relationship to each other helped to identify the national problem, though it did not offer clear solutions.

Thirdly, was Lincoln's sense of history. The American sense of history in the years of the formation and expansion of the Republic generally took the rather alarming form of a sense of destiny (a form which some people think it has not entirely outgrown). But Lincoln's view of American destiny was linked with his convictions both of American nationalism and of the very special American responsibility—a responsibility held before the world—for the progress of democracy.

I doubt whether any major political leader in the nineteenth century was possessed by a more compelling sense of responsibility to history than Lincoln. I do not mean this in the ordinary sense of being 'judged' by history. The complexity of the problem lay in the fact that the United States, at its inception as a nation,

had undertaken and avowed before the world a permanent commitment; but that in actual historical fact the country had always
been, and remained, deeply and perilously divided over the meaning of this commitment. The division was made all the more per-
plexing by the fact that this original meaning had never been fully
worked out. Perhaps not many understood its full implications of
racial equality. Many of Lincoln's own Republican supporters
would not have been willing to see it through to its full extent; not
even Lincoln himself.

Lincoln's sense of the special character of American history, and
of the special responsibility it imposed, involved him in trying to
explain that theme to the American people and in trying to persuade them to accept that responsibility. If they failed in that task,
then American History would lose its exceptional meaning. It
would become that of other countries and would cease to be essentially American. He brought out this sense of historically conscious
responsibility at its clearest when in 1862 he tried to persuade
Congress to accept his plan for the voluntary and compensated
emancipation of the slaves in the loyal states:

> Fellow-citizens, *we* cannot escape history. We of this
> Congress and this administration, will be remembered in
> spite of ourselves. No personal significance, or insignificance,
> can spare one or another of us. The fiery trial through which
> we pass, will light us down, in honor or dishonor, to the latest
> generation. We *say* we are for the Union. The world will not
> forget that we say this. We know how to save the Union. The
> world knows we do know how to save it. We—even *we here*—
> hold the power, and bear the responsibility. In *giving* free-
> dom to the slave, we *assure* freedom to the free, honorable
> alike in what we give, and what we preserve. We shall nobly
> save, or meanly lose, the last, best hope of earth. Other
> means may succeed; this could not fail. The way is plain,
> peaceful, generous, just—a way which, if followed, the world
> will forever applaud, and God must forever bless.

Lincoln's conception of American history, and his strong and
very western form of nationalism, were two sides of the same

thing. They blended together to control his judgement of the major events of his life; all of the three factors that I have mentioned influenced his response to the crisis caused by the repeal of the Missouri Compromise and by the resurgent threat of the extension of slavery.

I have said that Lincoln was a nationalist. But a flamboyant and often ruthless nationalism was so much part of the texture of the American democracy that the attribution can hardly, in itself, be taken as either complimentary or original. What seems to me significant about Lincoln's view of national development is that it constantly embraced the whole complex and diverse picture, allowing for the differentness of the South without allowing separatism to be the right of the South; and at the same time that it never flinched from affirming the powers of the central government.

In Lincoln's politically formative years it was especially difficult to keep track of what was happening, and to anticipate what was going to happen, because in fact America was moving in different directions at the same time. One of the difficulties of giving a satisfactory account of American history in the period after about 1815 lies in that fact. One is continually tempted to impose on the subject a unity in which contemporary Americans did not seem to share. American history was a large number of local and regional histories somewhat loosely knit together—and held together by ties that were often too tenuous and too remote to be firmly felt. This local diversification has to be broadly classed as the rise of 'sectionalism.' But each section had its own brand, and the progress of sectionalism did not correspond to the progress of any one movement.

Sections stand in obvious contrast to the nation. To many inhabitants of the newer areas of settlement it would have seemed reasonable to say that the nation grew as a result of the growth of sections rather than sections grew as a result of the growth of the nation.

Yet sections were not necessarily anti-national either in tendency or in sentiment. It is often pointed out that the West tended to be strongly nationalist; that new states owed their existence to the provisions of the federal government, whereas the old ones did not. The mid-century was a period of slackness in the energy of the central government, a phase during which the energy came from the regions; but it was in the nature of the case a temporary phase. Railroads, waterways, and the telegraph, inter-state commerce and international trade, the increasing extent and sophistication of industrial production, and eventually the commitment of the United States to its foreign interests, all these things were the relentless driving forces of a powerful, underlying nationalism. The problem was to ride out the strains and conflicts of the period while maintaining the authority of the Constitution. The fundamental conditions of this national unity, the requirements for the maintenance of peace and order over the continent, were the integrity of the Constitution combined with the recognized authority of the federal government.

But the sectionalism of the South was significantly different from that of other regions. Southern sectionalism, especially as a result of the Mexican War, did begin to assume an anti-national character. One can reconcile this particular brand of Southern sectionalism to the more general character of its counterparts in the nineteenth century by calling it a form of nationalism. Southern nationalism, on that view, was bound to pose questions for American nationalism.

Lincoln went into Illinois politics at the time when these larger strains were becoming clear. His choice of political affiliation gave a significant mark of his future nationalism on broader issues; because Lincoln joined the Whig party. This was by no means an obvious thing to do. The Democrats enjoyed what seemed to be a more or less stable majority in the north-west and their chieftain was President of the United States. An ambitious young politician would probably have been better advised to join the Democrats than the Whigs.

The fact, however, is that a deep difference of principle divided the two parties. This difference is in some danger of being discounted because of the influence of Professor Lee Benson's study of the political sociology of the state of New York. Studies of state politics will not tend to bring out the major division because it did not apply with particular force to state government. The serious ideological division was over the powers of the federal government.

Lincoln never seems to have doubted the rightfulness of effective government at whatever level it was required. During Lincoln's apprenticeship in the Illinois legislature, the Democrats showed themselves wedded to the antiquated dogma of limited government, as it had been preached by Jefferson. Jackson's show of strength over South Carolina no doubt gave the states' rightists a salutary reminder of the power that remained in the federal government, but it did not increase that power. Jackson did little to add to the actual institutional authority of the federal government as opposed to the state governments, and his supposedly forceful administration concealed a quiet drift of effective authority out towards the states.

When Lincoln accepted Clay's so-called 'American System,' he put himself on the side of a much wider range of federal powers than his opponents were prepared for. He adopted the view that government—even the American one—had a duty to co-ordinate the different impulses and to harmonize the divergent interests of the nation, to lay down lines of national policy and to lead the people in that policy. Lincoln was not a man much given to speculation. But his papers contain a well-known fragment on government, apparently written in 1854, in which he states that 'Government is a combination of the people of a country to effect certain objects by joint effort.' He went on to remark that the best framed and best administered governments were 'necessarily expensive.' Errors and mal-administration led to oppression: why then did people need government? The answer was that the people needed many things done that they could not do by themselves. 'The legitimate object of government is to do for the people what needs to be done, but which they cannot, by individual ef-

fort, do at all, or do so well, for themselves.' Some of these needs
arose, he noted, from natural causes, but 'by far the larger class of
objects springs from the injustice of men.'

Lincoln's whole conception of government therefore implied the
legitimacy of social policy. He belonged in the tradition of strong
executive leadership that had been marked out by the Federalists
but had very largely lapsed since, if not before, the retirement of
Jackson. The leaders of this tradition were never afraid of power.

The authority of the central government was confronted with a
particularly serious, because popular and insidious, challenge by
the doctrine of 'popular sovereignty.' The national Democratic
party, with its tremendous strength in the West, was committed to
the doctrine of popular sovereignty during, and after, the election
of 1848. Stephen Douglas, Senator from Illinois and dominating
leader of the section, took over the doctrine and made it his own.
It had obvious attractions both for the territories, which had not
yet been incorporated as states, and for the politician who aimed to
get to the top in the central government, and must avoid alienating
too many sensitive feelings in the jarring sections. To allow the
people of the territories to determine all their own laws and local
customs was in an obvious sense a democratic thing to do; and to
allow them to make the final decisions on troublesome and nationally divisive questions, such as slavery, was a way of relieving
the federal authorities of the responsibility. Thus the issue which
most seriously threatened the tranquillity of the nation could perhaps be withdrawn from the federal arena: and it was there that
the rival sections had in the past worked out their differences.

Douglas hoped, and persistently argued, that the entire issue of
slavery could be side-stepped by leaving it to the final determination of popular sovereignty. But Lincoln rejected popular sovereignty as a theory of government. Behind its plausible political attractiveness lay very great dangers. The greatest danger lay in that
very attractiveness; it seemed to offer a 'solution' to the most divisive issue in the country by taking it out of the purview of national
politics. Since the earliest years of the Constitution, and in fact

before the Constitution, Congress had exercised full powers over slavery in the territories. Popular sovereignty in this historical context was not just one among a choice of methods for determining this fundamental question; coming forward as it did in the middle of the nineteenth century it threatened to withdraw from Congress a power that Congress had always exercised. The long-term effect of adopting such a policy in place of that of congressional supremacy could only be to impair the authority of the general government.

Lincoln's nationalism was a morally conscious nationalism. It was based not only on a rudimentary pride of country but on pride in the country's founding principles. The Declaration of Independence was to him a statement without whose inspiration the Constitution would have had little value. As a matter of fact he came rather late to a serious contemplation of the political implications of slavery, though he had loyally voted for the Wilmot Proviso when he was in Congress during the Mexican War. Lincoln recoiled from the Abolitionists, who formed a sort of C.N.D. of the opposition to slavery, because he thought they could do the slaves no good and because they endangered the Union. But he did believe that the principles on which the great Republic was founded were ultimately incompatible with slavery; that the Declaration of Independence was itself a death warrant made out against slavery and signed by the founders. This was an arguable case: but it was not cut-and-dried. The Southern colonies which subscribed to the Declaration had certainly not read it in that light.

But Lincoln's understanding of the history of his country did not stop short at a particular interpretation of its basic documents. His view of American history involved a subtle relationship between doctrines, events, and human will. In the Gettysburg Address, he was to say that America had been 'dedicated to the proposition that all men are created equal.' As Dr. Roy Basler has pointed out, 'proposition' was a very unusual word to use in this context. It had probably never been so used before. A proposition—a term Lincoln may well have got from the prolonged study of Euclid with which he had indulged his leisure hours in Congress—technically means a theory which remains to be demonstrated.

That is not what Jefferson had said. He, and the subscribers to the Declaration of Independence, had called the truths that it proclaimed 'self-evident.' And it is certainly very odd to hold that a self-evident truth requires to be demonstrated. But it was equally plain to Lincoln that the truth of human equality had not actually been demonstrated at the time of the Declaration of Independence. American history was the process of proving those truths. It was by way of being a demonstration: but the result of that demonstration was not a foregone conclusion.

By the middle of the 1850s that conclusion was in the gravest doubt. Douglas, in opening up the vast Kansas–Nebraska territory to settlement, had allowed the doctrine of popular sovereignty to dictate the repeal of the Missouri Compromise; in consequence Congress voluntarily withdrew its hand from the control of slavery in the territories. In 1857 the Supreme Court endeavoured to settle this issue by declaring that Congress had never rightly had such a power. Not only did Southern leaders proclaim the right of slave-owners to take their slave property with them into the territories owned by the nation, but other developments in American politics raised new threats to the American national commitment to personal equality under Constitutional safeguards. The Know-Nothings, who poised their antagonism against Catholic immigrants from Ireland and Germany, looked for a time like the most serious contenders for the succession to the Whigs. It was not only slavery but this new brand of nativist extremism and religious intolerance that made the 1850s into a period of crisis which put the avowed commitments of American nationhood to their most serious test.

The doctrine of popular sovereignty could offer no guidance whatever on the grave problems of principle raised by these developments. All it could say was that the majority was always right. Lincoln—and this was the crux of his difference with Douglas—did not accept the view that the majority in the South was right about slavery.

Yet Douglas was a formidable opponent and had a powerful case. He based it on the geographical determinism that had been the theme of Webster's famous speech of March 7, 1850. According to this thesis, the limits of slavery were predetermined not by human inclinations but by climate and soil; its boundaries were marked out by the Great Plains; it could flourish only under the Southern plantation system and therefore constituted no practical threat to freedom in the North and north-west. The people of these regions, if left to determine the issue by their own local legislation, would see to that. Popular sovereignty thus offered a means by which slavery could be effectively excluded from most of the areas remaining for settlement without antagonizing the South, and without reversing the Supreme Court by attempting to enact a new ban on slavery in the territories.

Senator Douglas was fighting a brave fight for his own political life. By 1858 he had quarrelled with President Buchanan over the actual application of popular sovereignty in Kansas. Northern colonization of the territory, at the cost of a bitter struggle which furnished a sort of preliminary sketch for the Civil War, had built up an anti-slavery majority; but the constitution approved by a convention at Lecompton, in Kansas, sanctioned slavery, and Buchanan agreed to accept that constitution. Douglas read the signs in the huge volume of anti-slavery protest in his own section: he had once said that he 'did not care whether slavery was voted up or voted down' in Kansas, but events forced him to dig in against the Lecompton constitution and against the administration of his own party in Washington.

In this situation Douglas had begun to flirt with the Republicans in Congress. The future of the newly formed Republican party was by no means assured and, if Douglas could have attracted an appreciable Republican element into his own camp, he would have re-established his leadership in the west and strengthened his claim to the Presidency in 1860. His movements were full of danger for the Republican organization and constituted a grave personal threat to the burning ambitions of Lincoln.

Douglas was also fighting to hold the Democratic party

together—and with it to hold up the bridge between North and South. But his position was weak. Southern leaders saw clearly enough that popular sovereignty meant the exclusion of slavery from the western territories and regarded it as a deliberate rejection of their Constitutional right to carry slaves with them in all of the unincorporated areas of the United States. Popular sovereignty was not a doctrine with which Douglas could retain the support of the South.

Lincoln hammered on Douglas's weaknesses. In his most famous speech of the period, delivered on June 16, 1858, when he accepted the Republican nomination for the Senate, Lincoln accused Douglas of being a party to a conspiracy to spread slavery, first throughout the territories, and eventually throughout the Northern states where it was forbidden by state laws. It was reasonable to see in the highly fluid and unsettled situation that had developed in the last four years a source of danger to freedom and instability to the Union. 'A house divided against itself cannot stand,' Lincoln declared, in a phrase that was becoming current at the time. But it was a misrepresentation to charge Douglas with being on the slavery side of the conspiracy when Douglas's difficulties arose largely from the fact that he was upholding the verdict of the anti-slavery forces in Kansas itself.

The two-sided burden of Lincoln's task in the great public contest for the Illinois seat in the United States Senate of the fall of 1858, was that of exposing dialectical weaknesses in Douglas's position while advocating a positive policy of opposition to all further slavery extension. In taking the measure of this debate we must give the fullest possible credit to Douglas's standpoint. It seems probable that his policy could have allowed for the completion of territorial settlement without a disproportionate addition to the power of slavery, and that if he had achieved this and been elected President in 1860, there would have been no civil war *at that time*. Lincoln did not believe that such a result would put an end to the threat of slavery expansion. On the contrary, it would have had the effect of grievously impairing the federal government's power to resist further demands from the South.

To grasp the problems that confronted Lincoln and Douglas we need first of all to exclude from our minds our knowledge of how the story ended, and to try to look straight at the situation that flowed from the repeal of the Missouri Compromise and the organization of Kansas on the expectation that it would come in as a slave state. We know that the attempt to make Kansas into a slave state failed and that it eventually voted to come in as a free state. This has oddly led some historians to feel that the free-soilers were responsible for greatly exaggerating the real danger from slavery. But as Professor Fehrenbacher has pointed out, this is to read history the wrong way round. There was nothing 'natural' about the exclusion of slavery from Kansas. Slavery was kept out of Kansas because Northern anti-slavery forces were prepared to mount a tremendous struggle and fight it out on the ground.

The popular sovereignty which Douglas determined to defend in Kansas was popular sovereignty with a difference. The truth was that 'bleeding Kansas' provided a microcosm of the coming civil war. If the issue were going to be left to be determined by popular sovereignty of the Kansas style, then you accepted the fact that a series of local civil wars could take the place of the authority of Congress. You had to accept the verdict of a physical conflict fought out between infiltrators from both sides. And it is to be remembered that even at that, the South was thoroughly opposed to popular sovereignty!

It was quite conceivable that the struggle might be renewed. The greatest danger that Lincoln perceived in Douglas's leadership was its total omission of any moral standpoint on slavery itself. When Douglas said that geography would exclude slavery from the north-west he affirmed, in effect, that the future inhabitants of those regions would never tolerate slavery. He was counting on the effect of convictions which he did not care, or could not afford, to affirm as his own. He could not allow himself the luxury of denouncing slavery as a wrong. Douglas's geographical determinism extended to morals as well as to laws and accepted the inference that slavery was wrong in the North but right in the South.

Slavery was actually proving itself to be a highly adaptable institution. It could be used on small farms and on great plantations; it could be used for a variety of skilled crafts; it could be used in raising all manner of crops that were not confined to the South. Slavery—though Lincoln may not have known this fact—had persisted in the Ohio Valley long after the Ordinance of 1787 had banned it there, and there had been strong local resistance to its extinction. In the end the people had indeed rejected it. But Douglas's professed indifference to the right and wrong of the issue threatened to undermine the strongest possible reason for the future rejection of slavery.

Lincoln had once written 'If slavery is not wrong, nothing is wrong.' The statement might be glossed for political purposes as 'If slavery is not a moral issue, nothing is a moral issue.' The force of moral issues in politics depends on—may perhaps even be equated with—the force of people's feelings. Douglas's standpoint on slavery accepted the existence of anti-slavery feelings but at the same time denied the need for them. If the majority should change their minds, the majority would still be right. It was an abdication of moral leadership on the one really urgent issue of the time.

Lincoln rejected in its entirety Douglas's comfortable view that slavery was wrong in the North but right in the South and had no room for the geographical determination of principles. But Lincoln observed not only the moral scandal of slavery but also the historical depth of the institution and the appalling complexity of the problem it presented. He never condemned the Southern people and regarded them as the victims of their own history. He knew that no Constitutional offensive against slavery was either lawful or practicable. So he confined himself to opposing the further spread of slavery in the belief that, once that line had been finally drawn, the evil institution would be placed, as he put it, 'where the public mind shall rest in the belief that it is in the course of ultimate extinction.'

Lincoln believed that, once a decision had been constitutionally arrived at, the Southern threats of disunion would recede. He badly misjudged the earnestness of Southern intentions, and in the winter of 1860 he greatly overrated the political effectiveness of Southern Unionist feelings. But civil war was a risk inherent in his policy. He was certainly not prepared to go to war to abolish slavery and he would have agreed to retaining it in the Union under permanent restrictions. But he would go to war to preserve the Union. And it was essential to the character of the Union, in which he was elected to the Presidency, that its peculiar institution of slavery must be placed under permanent restriction.

The tragedy of the Civil War has aroused the horror of all its historians. Consequently they have insistently asked why it came about, by what steps it could have been averted, by what better judgement, superior tolerance, more skilful negotiation, the divisive issues could have been brought to compromise. Practically all historians of the subject are agreed that the Civil War represented the greatest and most tragic failure in American history.

For these understandable reasons they have not asked themselves another question. Bear in mind that the Civil War made it possible to complete the unification of the continent, and to abolish slavery while ultimately maintaining the whole country under one government. Instead of attributing the Civil War to a catastrophic failure of intelligence, one may well ask how it was that these gigantic achievements were brought about at the cost of *only one* civil war?

An important part of the answer to this question lies in Lincoln's own policy. Both sides accepted a risk of civil war. Once Lincoln had been elected, the issue put constitutional government to the test. To make concessions under the threat of secession was to place all future governments in jeopardy. For secession, as Lincoln said, in his first Inaugural, was 'the essence of anarchy.' And when the war had been accepted as the necessary degree of force required to preserve the Union, Lincoln's relentless determination to fight it to a conclusion made it sure that, once the victory had been gained, there would be no further attempts at secession and no further warfare between the regions or sections of the United States.

The Civil War was therefore the supreme test of the American people's capacity for constitutional government. Lincoln had always been aware of the untractability of the problem of slavery, though he was keenly aware of the intimate relationship between slavery and the constitutional issues which brought the conflict to a head. The basic conditions controlling slavery and limiting the power of action were changed by the war. Its effect was to open a wider range of possible courses of action. Moving slowly at first, with great caution and perhaps some uncertainty, Lincoln took advantage of this opening. Before the end of his first term as President he had not only proclaimed the emancipation of the slaves of disloyal owners but had done much more: he had exerted his full powers to obtain the passage of a constitutional amendment to abolish slavery for ever.

Although the war provided this brief, much needed opening up of the range of solutions available for the problems which beset the Republic, it did not by itself resolve them. If the war had been short it would not have led to emancipation; it was not the mere fact of the war, but its prolonged continuation, which brought the policy of emancipation forward as an indispensable necessity to the pacification of the country.

In his second Inaugural, Lincoln, who seemed to be seeking for some religious explanation of the whole conflict, used language that reminds one more of the seventeenth century than of the age of electricity and evolution. I am attracted by the idea of a certain elemental resemblance between Abraham Lincoln and Oliver Cromwell—although Lincoln had the better sense of humour and some of the things that amused Lincoln would certainly not have amused Cromwell. I think that one can illuminate the relationship of slavery to the American Civil War by changing a single word in one of Cromwell's most familiar pronouncements and attributing it to Lincoln. Can we not with some considerable accuracy make Lincoln say?—

> For slavery was not the thing at the first contested for; but God brought it to that issue at last; and gave it unto us by way

of redundancy; and at last it proved to be that which was most dear to us.

The redundancy, one may add, is still with us in our own time.

I have suggested that Lincoln was a nationalist, in a stronger and more intellectually serious sense than most of his opponents, and I want to add now that I think this explains both his analysis of the drift of events before the war and his anxiety for a peace of conciliation.

As early as 1855 he had written to a law professor in Kentucky:

> Our political problem now is 'Can we, as a nation, continue together *permanently—forever*—half slave, and half free?' The problem is too mighty for me. May God, in his mercy, superintend the solution.

In June 1858 he was to restate this question in the speech which went much further by anticipating that the United States would become 'all one thing, or all the other.' Many things have been said about the meaning of the 'house divided' speech. The only addition that I want to suggest now is this: that this was the speech of a man who had grasped the essentials of the process of nationalization that was overtaking the main institutions of American life; what Lincoln had grasped was the fact that the United States was in the process of *becoming* a nation; that in spite of all the sectional forces, of all the diverse centres of economic and political power which made regional affairs seem to preponderate over national ones, the deeper tendency was towards an ultimate unification. And this explains why Lincoln felt ready by that time to say that the country could not remain, indefinitely, one country, half slave and half free. For passions had been aroused on both sides; and national institutions required some measure of national consensus on fundamental principles.

The war inevitably strengthened the hand of the federal government. Victory for the Union would advance the process of national unification. Moreover, the whole nation would be obliged to live with the consequences of the war. Lincoln earnestly hoped to mitigate the consequences by persuading slave-owners in the loyal border states to accept voluntary, compensated emancipation, and even tried to get his Cabinet to accept a plan to compensate Southern slave-owners who should agree to abandon slavery of their own will. Despite his passionate eloquence, these appeals completely failed; and it was this failure that led Lincoln to the Thirteenth Amendment, the real act of Abolition that was far more important than the celebrated Proclamation.

Reasons of humanity and reasons of state combined to make Lincoln seek a peace of conciliation rather than an imposed settlement. His work was left unfinished, hardly begun, and as it was left incomplete it cannot be judged. But I return now to the problem that I posed at the beginning: that of asking what difference Lincoln's death made?

The limited plans for the reconstruction of Southern government that Lincoln had already put into operation rested on a nucleus of a loyal 10 per cent of the population of each state to which it was applied. President Andrew Johnson continued the broad outlines of the programme initiated by Lincoln. But Johnson's policy does not justify historians in talking of a 'Lincoln–Johnson Plan,' because there had never been a hard-and-fast Lincoln plan. The point emerges more clearly from Lincoln's treatment of the Wade–Davis bill.

This bill, passed in July 1864, imposed more rigorous conditions for the renewed participation in government of Southern citizens than those offered by Lincoln. Qualifications for voting and for office were retrospective and more severe. Lincoln would not sign the bill, but in giving his reasons he admitted that it contained 'one very proper plan for the loyal people of any state choosing to adopt it.' This observation had two levels. The suggestion that the people of any Southern state might 'choose' to adopt the plan appears to have been quietly ironical; but yet it was, on its merits, a 'very proper plan.' On the other hand, reconstructed governments had been set up in Louisiana and Arkansas under his own plan and he did not want them set aside. Lincoln plainly disliked the Wade–

Davis plan—perhaps he disliked it more than he at heart disapproved of it; but his fundamental objection lay against its uniform procedure rather than its substance.

Lincoln was himself an experimentalist, by experience and by instinct. He had developed through the exercise of power a remarkable subtlety in his response to problems as they arose; he possessed an almost tactile sense of the realities and possibilities of politics. At the very end, on April 11, 1865, Lincoln clearly indicated that if his plans were not going to work he would try others. But certainly, given all the possible different needs of various states, the different contingencies that might unexpectedly arise, he was not prepared in 1864 to commit the government to one uniform programme.

It is important to bear all this in mind when turning to the question of whether Johnson's later policy carried with it the implied endorsement of the assassinated President. The defence Lincoln gave on April 11 of his conduct on Reconstruction, together with his hints as to future policies, suggest that he would have given up any attempt to override the majority in Congress and the extremely large public behind it. Everything that we know of Lincoln's methods should teach us to suppose that he would have sought ways of moving with rather than against a powerful majority in his own party, especially when that party dominated Congress.

There remains a further and more important point. Feeling against the South was high. But Dr. Brock has shown us that the overwhelming strength attained by the Radicals in the latter part of 1865 and 1866 was the product of a new wave of feeling, and that feeling was provoked by new developments in the South. Under Johnson's Reconstruction, the ex-Confederate states took advantage of their new governments to write the notorious Black Codes which practically destroyed the liberties of the freedmen and substituted peonage for slavery. When the peoples of the South openly rejected what the North regarded as the legitimate result of the Civil War, the North rose in a massive wave of indignation that swept the Radicals into power.

During the war, Lincoln himself had gradually moved closer to the Radicals for two reasons. One was tactical. The other was that his analysis of the causes of the war led him to encompass aims similar to theirs. He also gave signs of moving closer to the Negroes in his political, and even his personal, sympathies. Negro soldiers had made a very great contribution to winning the war.

It seems to me implausible to suppose that Lincoln would have stood out, almost alone, against his party and against the great tide of Northern opinion. The likelihood is that Lincoln would have shared the ordinary Northerner's reaction to Southern state policies; and in any case Lincoln would have treated that mass reaction as a *fact*—as one of the events which 'controlled' him. He would have moved with it, even if his pace had been slower, not against it. The struggle between the executive and Congress which disfigured political life and distorted the process of Reconstruction would then have been avoided. It is therefore by no means fanciful to believe that something closely resembling Radical Reconstruction would have been enacted under presidential leadership.

If this is so, then the death of Lincoln was exactly what it seemed at the time—a disaster for America and a cause of sorrow for the world: though not, from all points of view, for the same reasons.

Although Lincoln was a man of burning ambition, his nature lacked one of the more ordinary characteristics of ambition: after attaining power (not perhaps before) he was devoid of malice or vindictiveness, and singularly free from everyday resentments and desires for recrimination. He had never blamed the slave-owners for their historical predicament, and never having blamed them he felt no desire to punish them. The weakness of his plans for Reconstruction, so far as they went, was the lack of an economic analysis of the Southern situation and the failure to provide an economic base for the security of the freedmen. The mainspring and the strength of these plans were the conviction that the South could not be ruled against itself; that the interests of all would be served by a leniency that would spare the South from humiliation and bitterness in the future. These problems were not resolved, and were not capable of being resolved, in a few years or a lifetime: they have not been settled one hundred years later.

At the time of his second Inauguration, Lincoln still hoped for a peace without malice. The attitude expressed in the familiar closing passage of his Second Inaugural was not mere sentiment. It was an attitude which Lincoln hoped, by communicating, to translate into policy. If he could succeed in that, then he might still hope to bind up the nation's wounds, he might still hope to achieve and cherish that just and lasting peace for which he had worked, and for which, in at least one sense, he was very soon to give his life.

A note of works referred to in the text

Abraham Lincoln, *Speeches and Letters,* ed. Paul M. Angle, Everyman edn. (no. 206).

Godfrey Rathbone Benson, Lord Charnwood, *Abraham Lincoln* (1916); Pocket Book edn., 1948.

Lee Benson, *The Concept of Jacksonian Democracy*, Princeton, 1961.

Don E. Fehrenbacher, *Prelude to Greatness: Lincoln in the 1850's,* Stanford, 1962.

W. R. Brock, *An American Crisis: Congress and Reconstruction 1865–1867*, London, 1963.

The remark quoted from Dr. Roy P. Basler was made in a paper read to the American History seminar in the University of London.

7

Of Mr. Booker T. Washington and Others
(1974)

When Abraham Lincoln spoke on slavery at Peoria in October 1854, he opened with a remarkable disclaimer. 'Before proceeding,' he told an audience whom he intended to rally against slavery expansion,

> let me say that I think I have no prejudice against the southern people. They are just what we would be in their situation.
> . . . When southern people tell us that they are no more

It happened that the first two volumes of *The Booker T. Washington Papers*, edited by Louis R. Harlan and the same author's biography of Washington appeared about the same time as Robert Manson Myers's extraordinary collection, *The Children of Pride*. A request to review these books gave me an opportunity to see what could be gained by juxtaposition. The Jones family of Georgia would not have thanked me for this experiment; but I think it was worth making.

Books referred to: *The Children of Pride: A True Story of Georgia and the Civil War*, ed. Robert Manson Myers (New Haven: Yale University Press, 1972).
The Booker T. Washington Papers, vol. I, *The Autobiographical Writings*, vol. II, *Papers, 1860–1889*, ed. Louis R. Harlan (Urbana: University of Illinois Press, 1972).
Booker T. Washington: The Making of a Black Leader, 1856–1901 by Louis R. Harlan (New York: Oxford University Press, 1972).

This essay was first published in *The Historical Journal*, vol. XVII, No. 4 (1974).

> responsible for the origin of slavery than we are, I acknowledge the fact. When it is said that the institution exists, and that it is very difficult to get rid of it in any satisfactory way, I can understand and appreciate the saying. I surely will not blame them for not doing what I would not know how to do myself. If all earthly power were given to me, I would not know what to do as to the existing institution.

Some six years later, after Lincoln's election, but a month before Georgia's secession, the young mayor of Savannah wrote to his father:

> I have long since believed that in this country have arisen two races which, although claiming a common parentage, have been so entirely separated by climate, by morals, by religion, and by estimates so wholly opposite of all that constitutes honor, truth, and manliness, that they cannot longer coexist under the same government. Oil and water will not commingle. We are the land of the rulers; fanaticism has no home here. The sooner we separate the better.

The writer of this statement was Charles Colcock Jones, Jr., soon to become a Confederate army officer and, later in life, the leading historian of the State of Georgia. His father, the Reverend Charles Colcock Jones, was a retired Presbyterian minister who owned three plantations in Liberty County in coastal Georgia, and also, according to the Census of 1860, one hundred and twenty-nine slaves. When Dr. Robert Manson Myers first came across the extraordinary collections of the family's letters, he embarked on a work that was to take seventeen years to complete. By his own researches he has rescued and reconstructed from the past the lives and fortunes of a widely dispersed but closely knit family, and of many of their friends and relations, whom we can follow in their passage through the central crisis of Southern history. 'The Principal Characters' listed by the editor, scattered over twelve plantations and as many towns, include over sixty names. But the minister and his wife Mary provide the central thread. It would be difficult to immerse oneself in this mass of letters written over fifteen years of rising tension, military crisis, and eventual ruin, without becoming in some sense a guest of the family, conscious of and perhaps sharing their anxieties, if not their convictions.

The Joneses were well known for their high standards, particularly in their care of slaves. Mrs. Jones remarked at one point that a slave-owner's responsibilities extended to their immortal souls, and it was in that spirit that her husband had assumed a personal ministry to the Negroes. But the letters are crowded with the ordinary matter of life, and it is this which gives such authenticity to the picture of the past that they re-create. To Mrs. Jones and her kin, a plantation was a community whose members, free and slave, shared each others' pleasures, excitements and griefs as a sort of collective experience. Disease and death were near neighbours for these semi-tropical Europeans and no less for their slaves; the frequent comings and goings of doctors made little difference, though they sometimes managed to accentuate the sufferings of the sick. Yet these records also tell of much satisfaction in daily life, of days well spent and duties accomplished. All these writers were well educated and every one of them wrote better prose than is at all common among their compatriots of a later century. Mrs. Jones tended to be flowery, but had a gift for evoking place and scene; her husband was firm if not eloquent; their son Charles was inclined to strong feelings, vigorous but correct, and occasionally moving. One of his army camp letters (pp. 777–78) is a superb evocation of atmosphere through exact description. Conventional formalities of style do not detract from the force of feelings; these were people who deeply loved and respected each other and whose letters were among the vital channels of their lives. They seldom withheld their ideas or concealed their feelings and the subject matter encompasses gaiety and business, duty and despair. The young Charles knew despair in the summer of 1861, not through war but when his seventeen months' old daughter and then his wife died within a few days of each other. 'Oh, my dear parents,' he afterwards wrote from his stricken home, 'what voices dwell in these vacant chairs, this silent piano, this desolate bed, these folded garments, these unused jewels, these neglected toys, these noiseless rooms!'

This remarkable young man was elected mayor of Savannah at twenty-five, and his descriptions of the responsibilities of that office add incidental information about slavery and race relations in that city. Many Negroes whose labour was on hire enjoyed a degree of independence that led to lax conduct in the streets, where Charles even overheard them discussing politics; it was a state of affairs of which he could not approve. But, as Professor Richard C. Wade has shown, it could not be stopped, either. Nor, however, could Charles or his father approve the sentiment in favour of reviving the African slave trade, which cropped up during the federal trial of a slave captain. Mayor Jones thought the federal government should deal with such cases with a severity that would stop the practice by making it unprofitable. He took a firm line on all matters of law and order, deprecated mob action, and maintained, somewhat prematurely, that the South was the home of orderly rule. His parents worried constantly about the most important thing of all—his lack of clear Christian faith. They came back repeatedly to the needs of his soul. Charles did his best to reassure them by general expressions of a religious character; carefully, but not convincingly, he avoided direct discussion of the evidences of Christianity. On one occasion his father told him that he believed God had taken his wife and daughter to draw the young man to him—a course that does not seem to have made the Creator a more endearing figure.

Without doubt, these people, religious, educated, kindly, and intensely conscientious, felt free to make their own moral choices. As early as 1854 the young Charles wrote from Harvard that he began to harbour disunionist sentiments. This was his angry reaction to the excitement in Boston over the trial of the fugitive slave Anthony Burns. By 1856 his sentiments were hardening in the direction of Southern nationalism and in 1860 he had few doubts about secession or about the Confederacy's ability to win—if war came. Not one member of the family recorded a flicker of doubt about the basic issue of slavery. Towards their slaves they were attentive, responsible and kind; slaves' illnesses occupy a surprising amount of space in Mary Jones's letters, and their deaths, though sometimes noted as pecuniary losses, were treated as deaths in the family. The letters frequently bore friendly greetings for the servants on other plantations. On the one occasion when the senior Joneses felt compelled to dispose of an incessantly troublesome slave family, the incident weighed on them as an example of grievous failure. Even so, they took great care to ensure that the family was not broken up. But in spite of their precautions, news reached them that they had been deceived, that the family had fallen into the hands of traders, and soon afterwards that Jane herself, the chief trouble-maker, was dead. The minister reflected sadly on the consequences of their rebellious and unhealthy attitude. But however much he regretted these things, it did not occur to him to question the system in which such mischances might happen.

When the war turned for the worse, with Union warships lying off the coast and federal patrols inciting desertion, the Negroes began to appear in another light. Many letters from the summer of 1862 reveal anxieties about slave loyalties.

> The temptation of change, the promise of freedom and pay for labor, is more than most can stand; and no reliance can be placed *certainly* upon any. The safest plan is to put them beyond reach of temptation . . . by leaving no boats in the water and by keeping guards along the rivers.

This was the Rev. C. C. Jones's opinion in July 1862. A few days later he was back at the theme: 'The temptation of cheap goods, freedom, and paid labor cannot be withstood,' he told his son, now a Confederate lieutenant. In the same letter came an ominous note: 'They are traitors who may pilot an enemy into your *bedchamber*! They know every road and swamp and creek and plantation in the county, and are the worst of spies. If the absconding is not stopped, the Negro property of the county will be of little value.'

From this time onwards, the slave-owners knew no peace of

mind. The minister, after prolonged illness, died in March 1863, after which his widow revealed remarkable powers of management and great presence of mind through many hardships. With every-thing crumbling round her she still worried about the health and happiness of slaves whom she yet resolutely regarded as her right-ful property. When emancipation came, the family had no dif-ficulty in agreeing that it was an act of brazen robbery. By this time, Mrs. Jones had begun to reveal some bitterness about the fickleness of her Negroes, though she could still regard them as misguided children. 'My heart is pained and sickened by their vileness and falsehood in every way,' she declared in December 1865; 'I long to be delivered from the race.' Charles meanwhile took the first opportunity after the war to accept a partnership in a New York law firm. From this distance ('The Eighth Avenue cars pass every five minutes within one square of the dwelling, and the time from the house to my office is just one hour') he reflected:

> The transition in the status of the Negro has been such a marked and violent one that we cannot wonder that he does not adapt himself rationally and intelligently to the change. He has always been a child in intellect—improvident, incapa-ble of appreciating the obligations of a contract, ignorant of the operation of any law other than the will of his master, careless of the future, and without the most distant concep-tion of the duties of life and labor now devolving upon him. Time alone can impart the necessary intelligence; and the fear of the law, as well as kindness and instruction, must unite in compelling an appreciation and discharge of the novel duties and responsibilities now resting upon him.

The intellectual confusions of this passage are as revealing about the minds of the masters as about the problems of the freedmen. After all, it does not seem altogether astonishing that 250 years of slavery should have failed to inculcate into the Negro the obliga-tions of contract or the force of any law 'other than the will of his master.' Jones belonged to a race, and a class, which had never questioned their assumptions; it was experience, not reason, that had blown them to bits. Experience soon showed—Jones's letters reveal it—that despite many difficulties and shortcomings in the new system, Negroes could indeed work under contract, but that—as he rightly remarked—they needed time to learn. But in October 1867 he was gloomy about the South. He now wanted to sell the whole property, but there were no buyers, none at all. 'I must confess my heart is very heavy when I think of the present and future of the South,' he told his mother. 'I have no doubt but that Reason, at present dethroned, will eventually resume her sway; but intermediately what commotions may come before the white race regains its suspended supremacy?' That statement so exactly reflected the frame of mind of the large, only temporarily submerged majority of whites that Jones's opinions assume a representative character. Meanwhile his mother had undergone the ordeal of federal military occupation. Unrebuked by their officers, the soldiers had many times searched the house, robbing both masters and Negroes. There are telling comments on the ill-treatment of the blacks at the hands of Northern soldiers. In the end, everything fell into ruin and decay. Mary Jones was living in what she called 'a skeleton country.' After her departure to live with her daughter in New Orleans in 1868 (where she lived but little more than a year longer) the semi-tropical vegetation of the coast took hold of its own, and the editor tells us that the remains of the great Montevideo estate, where Mary spent her last years in Georgia, once the centre of a luxurious and self-satisfied civilization, are now hardly traceable in the undergrowth.

Both Dr. Myers and Yale University Press are to be congratulated on this magnificent production. These letters, amplified by hundreds of pages of notes, provide masses of information about slavery, land, prices, and styles of life. But they do much more. No work of history could so minutely and brilliantly light up the texture and quality of the lives lived by these many ordinary, and in a few cases exceptional, people, in their different places and stations, over such a period of fantastic change.

The Jones family were superior, but not extraordinary, examples of their class. Their great strength lay in the completeness and self-consistency of their views—or at any rate of those views, and those facts, which they allowed themselves to contemplate. When the slave Jane slipped away to hire herself under false pretences in Savannah, she was severely blamed, but blamed as a naughty and rebellious child; when her family had to go, the fault lay in their conduct. Examples of Negro courage and presence of mind were recorded with high appreciation—but were considered exceptional. Never were slaves expected to be other than children; their cleverness, or humour, or loyalty, were taken by their masters as manifestations of the better qualities of basically childlike characters. When freedom found them helpless before the novelties of contracts and the unfamiliar need for thinking about the future, the immemorial convictions of the master class were thus confirmed. Only gradually and with some reluctance did they recognize that blacks could understand any problem beyond the immediate present. These pages contain much evidence to confirm Professor Genovese's views about the paternalism of the planter class; the masters genuinely believed that slavery protected the Negroes from the weaknesses of their own natures. The intellectual system was self-supporting, for when slaves proved themselves to be stubborn, resourceful, and rebellious, these things were duly observed as evidence of delusion and disrespect for constituted authority. Professor Genovese is well aware that 'paternalism' could be severe. Assuredly these people had the time, the intellectual abilities, and access to the information they needed to judge their situation. On the evidence, as they saw it, on their vision of the right, as it was given to them to see the right, they fought to defend their own civilization. Assuredly also they were not wrong in perceiving that it was in many ways different from the North's. They would have been repelled by the suggestion that, allowing always for the inscrutable will of God, they were anything less than the free and voluntary makers of their own fortunes. Yet their great enemy, Abraham Lincoln, had expressed a conviction that they were victims of their own history and circumstances; with a vision extraordinary among contestants for power, he seemed to absolve them from blame. The Joneses would not have agreed, and historians seeking to find and apportion responsibility have by implication rejected Lincoln's fatalism. Yet there is a sense in which his view gains in subtlety and substance from this massive collection. It is not wholly fanciful to think of the Jones family and their contemporaries as falling into a Greek pattern of having been guilty of bringing upon themselves a previously determined fate.

Some two years after these records begin, in April 1856, a slave child named Bowker was born on the farm of James Burroughs in Virginia. He made his first recorded appearance in an inventory which placed his value at $400. His mother always called him Booker, to which spelling the name was soon changed. His surname was taken later from his stepfather (slaves of course did not need surnames). It would certainly have astonished any member of the Jones family to have been told that, before the end of the century, a mulatto born in slavery would have gained a bigger following, both North and South, than any single white Southerner. Yet, on reflection, Booker T. Washington would undoubtedly have been the black man to whom they could be most easily reconciled in that unexpected exaltation. Washington as the archetypical collaborator has long been the victim of a cloudy reputation, based on his known career and public statements but on an inevitably partial knowledge of the hidden and more complicated facts. From Professor Harlan's long-awaited biography, Washington emerges as many characters, public and private. Collaborationist and resistance leader, master and servant maintained among themselves the complex balance of his character.

In this first volume Professor Harlan takes the pursuit of Washington's various personalities down to 1901, by which time his leadership was conceded with more reluctance and skepticism by some Negroes than among American whites. No American black leader, before or since, has owed his pre-eminence so heavily to white patronage as Booker Washington. (And this does not overlook the importance of white support to the N.A.A.C.P. and even to DuBois.) It does not belittle Washington's achievements both in building the school at Tuskegee and in maintaining his delicate relationship with the white community, to recognize that his reputation outside Alabama resulted from white men's initiatives. White legislators took him along with them to help them persuade a House of Representatives Committee to recommend an appropriation in aid of the Atlanta Exposition of 1895, and the white promoters of that Exposition made the daring decision to invite him to speak at its opening ceremonies. They proved to have been shrewd judges of their man.

Booker Washington's 'Atlanta Compromise' speech was a rhetorical masterpiece of time and circumstances. It shot him to national prominence because it offered a programme of racial co-operation and harmony combined with the withdrawal of Negro demands for social equality. In a phrase that he had polished over the years, and which came to characterize his entire social policy, he told his astonished audience, 'In all things purely social we can be separate as the fingers, yet one as the hand in all things essential to mutual progress.' He also insisted that the Southern people, white and black, must solve their own problems rather than renewing their appeals for national intervention. Coupled with his message, the dominating immediate fact about the success of the speech was Washington's immense personal presence and dignity; it is hard to understand the rapture of his audience without appreciating these qualities, while recognizing that when they were joined to a message that relieved the whites of their own worst anxieties, they could acclaim the speaker as a kind of black messiah. Negroes, for their part, wept with joy and thundered applause, not only in Atlanta but, as reports spread, from all over the country. They might have reservations about some of Washington's sentiments; and his deprecatory if amusing remarks about his own people's shortcomings were even resented. But there was authority in the voice, and both races caught the note. The young W. E. B. DuBois himself welcomed the speech. It was not until 1903 that he saw and exposed the flaw in Washington's position.

When he published his famous essay, 'Of Mr. Booker T. Washington and Others,'[1] DuBois did not fail to pay tribute to Washington's extraordinary achievements in the South. But when he called the Atlanta Compromise 'by all odds the most notable thing in Mr Washington's career' he did not mean it as an unalloyed compliment. In the South, he observed, both radicals and conservatives approved it; and it seemed to release the whole country from the burden of responsibility for the rights of the Negro. 'If that is all you and your race ask, take it,' was the attitude that DuBois discerned in white public opinion.

The gravamen of DuBois's charge against Washington's leadership fell in the matter of timing. Washington's policy, he complained, represented nothing more than 'the old attitude of adjustment and submission; but adjustment at such a peculiar time as to make his programme unique.' Race prejudice was increasing, partly as a result of the contact of the more advanced races with the less developed ones; 'and Mr Washington's programme practically accepts the alleged inferiority of the Negro races.' The situation called for an assertion of self-respect. But in the interests of his programme, Washington was willing to sacrifice three crucial demands: political power (by abandoning the franchise); civil rights; and higher education for Negro youth. His Compromise came during a period of Negro disfranchisement, of the creation of a distinct status of civil inferiority for Negroes, and of withdrawal of aid for institutions of higher learning. Without attributing these trends to Washington's influence, DuBois blamed him for compromising with them.

Professor Harlan is in tune with DuBois in his emphasis on Washington's debt to white patronage, and leaves little room for doubt that, in his view, white patronage shaped Washington's principles. He ventures a psychological theory that Washington (whose real, but unknown, father was a white man) was unconsciously seeking for a white father. General Armstrong of Hampton filled this role until his death, by which time Washington's position

1. W. E. B. DuBois, *The Souls of Black Folk* (Chicago, 1903).

was established. The idea will have occurred to many students of Washington's career, but Washington's own instinctive caution and sense of self-preservation also played their part in defining the limits of his aims.

Negro leaders always occupied a slightly peculiar position in regard to their race. They did not emerge from the struggles of trade unions, which were inveterately antagonistic to black membership; only a few of them rose through the ordinary operations of party politics, and the more prominent of these had already been banished from political life in the South. A very high proportion of the opportunities for local political activity as well as social and religious life was provided by the churches, but the black ministry offered little political leadership in Washington's era. He expressed unusually scornful views of the moral and intellectual calibre of the ministry (*Papers, II,* 448–49) and also deplored the effects of religious preoccupations on the practical purposes of Negro action. Personal and racial self-advancement were deflected by hopes which he clearly regarded as little better than superstition. The blacks were thus deprived of these more usual sources for the discovery of leaders and those who took it upon themselves to speak for their race were usually intellectuals, most of them living and writing firmly in the North. It is interesting to find in Professor Harlan's pages that Timothy Thomas Fortune, whose socialist views were deeply alien to Washington's, was one of his closer Northern friends. Fortune, who was less stable than Washington, needed a kind of support that Washington gave generously, while the two men were frank with each other in their differing views about strategy. It is not surprising, however, that Northern blacks should have been piqued and resentful at the leadership which white America, North and South, so readily accepted as representative of them. DuBois put the matter with respect for Washington's own attainments, not untinged with irony at the claims being made for him:

> If the best of the American Negroes receive by outer pressure a leader whom they had not recognised before, manifestly there is here a certain palpable gain. Yet there is also irrepa-

rable loss,—a loss of that peculiarly valuable education which a group receives when by search and criticism it finds and commissions its own leaders.[2]

DuBois paid due tribute to Washington for having built a bastion of strength surrounded by racial enemies. Professor Harlan records, moreover, that Washington refused repeated invitations to move to the North. He accepted the risks of the struggle because he knew by instinct and conviction that his work lay in the South—which, in some obscure way, he truly loved. A black Southerner could know, as Northerners found it difficult to appreciate, that the South was a creation of black labour and could never have developed without the black presence. In this as in other important strains, Washington was far more consistent than is perhaps generally realized. His protean role-playing supported rather than conflicted with certain basic and virtually unchanging attitudes.

The problem of the controversy raised initially by DuBois's challenge to his leadership therefore needs to be restated in slightly different terms. Whether DuBois had a programme that could have survived for more than six months in Alabama is a matter on which Washington remains entitled to his own opinion. But the claim that DuBois challenged was that of leadership for the Negroes throughout the United States. To judge all aspects of the Negro situation from the Southern angle of vision, and to advocate the policy of accommodation, which may have been the code of survival in the South, as the highest aim of the blacks as a whole, was to cripple Negro claims to advancement precisely where they could be most ambitious and effective. New York State actually passed an anti-discrimination law in 1890 at a time when Southern states were passing segregation laws. It is not to be wondered at that Northern blacks who had fought to establish their own position should have murmured against being 'led,' and authoritatively spoken for, by a Southern accommodationist imposed on them primarily by Southern whites.

2. DuBois, *op. cit.*, pp. 45–46.

In the light of this celebrated controversy it remains worth noting some similarities despite the contrasts between the two contestants. In temperament, in their styles of life and thought, they differed as much as they did in background. DuBois was of course far more attached to higher education than Washington, whose life did credit to the creed that all labour was honourable, who got up early to feed the farm animals, and had an endearing affection for pigs. But both men valued Negro culture, particularly in the genuine plantation songs, or 'sorrow songs' as DuBois called them, which they tried to preserve. Both read the signs of their times to the extent of recognizing the need for some accommodation, and would have accepted economic or educational restrictions on the suffrage. In fact neither of them was 'democratic' in the full modern sense—for they could both very clearly see that populist democracy was no respecter of the rights of minorities. Washington several times said that the Negro had been enfranchised too rapidly during Reconstruction; he would have accepted the 'impartial' but qualified suffrage for which some Republicans contended during the debates on the Fourteenth and Fifteenth amendments. Both men believed in leadership by an element of superior talent, though DuBois had a far firmer grasp of the role of higher education in selecting and training his 'talented tenth.'

Washington has often been accused of deviousness, of exploiting a variety of exchangeable postures in a manner now familiar through ideas of 'role-playing.' When Professor Harlan says that 'the complexity of Booker T. Washington's personality probably had its origins in being black in white America. He was forced from childhood to deceive, to simulate, to wear the mask' (p. viii) one may be tempted to ask why, in that case, the same was not true of all Negroes in America? According to Professor Harlan, Washington was devious and competitive towards Negro rivals and colleagues. Were they equally devious and competitive towards him? As a study in character, this kind of problem becomes more interesting when the mask becomes part of the wearer's face; but Washington's role-playing, though devious, was not essentially mysterious. Like many people of his basic disposition, he was instinctively supple towards his masters while revealing his authoritarian personality towards subordinates. It seems highly likely that he would have been much the same in a black or a non-racially conscious society, if the power structure had required it of him; but Professor Harlan's explanation would not then have been available. Many individuals carry contradictory strands in their personalities just as most of us do in our desires—that in itself is not extraordinary. What made Washington remarkable in this respect was that his variety of roles does not seem to have been a source of internal strain or conflict. Each had its proper place and each had an important part to play. His power thus seems to have emerged from the harmony of these inner diversities, which gave him public efficiency and private balance. He should have derived some amusement from the mystery he created.

Professor Harlan leaves the reader free to observe all of Washington's characteristics without bias and without impediment. The sheer power of his personality must have stamped itself wherever he moved. In his early years at Tuskegee there were streaks of an unexpected, almost reckless daring when he sometimes committed the school to contracts for which the funds did not yet exist; events justified his faith, and no doubt established his confidence. These struggles also proved his terrific tenacity; his practical quickness and natural command of situations were those of a great general or business executive; they stand in contrast to his flat and platitudinous use of language. (Though, as Professor Harlan observes, he knew how to manipulate his platitudes.) His sense of humour was an instrument of control; but he irritated black contemporaries by introducing racially deprecatory remarks before white audiences. The technique relieved the tension and set them at ease; but other blacks caught the implication that Washington and his white audiences might enjoy some common understanding from which the black masses were excluded. In many ways he emerges as a type remarkable for its familiarity among the operators of American interest groups—that familiarity being disguised by skin pigmentation. He worked assiduously within the system, to whose economic and political conventions he faithfully subscribed; he took conservative views of larger social causes while showing great tactical skill in maintaining his own personal power base. Similar things could be said of—for example—Samuel Gompers!

DuBois understood well enough that Washington was obliged to bend before superior forces (they would have deterred, or broken, weaker men) and he hinted at knowledge of Washington's secret activities in defence of Negro civil rights.[3] Professor Harlan reveals these secret activities, which obviously redeem Washington from charges of mere subservience to white domination. The *Papers* disclose him as having been deeply hurt by aspersions on his race—as who would not have been—and demonstrate that he too thought about the psychological obstacles to Negro self-esteem, noted the need for 'black history' in order to give his race a sense of its own past—and its own heroes—and understood some of those inner complexities which remained so largely concealed not only from the white world but even from the blacks (*Papers, I*, 405; 422).

> . . . One cannot always tell what is going on deep down in their hearts merely from looking in their faces. Sometimes the Negro laughs when he is angry and cries when he is happy. Very often, it has seemed to me, the Negro himself does not know or fully understand what is going on in the depth of his own mind and heart.

Undoubtedly, as Professor Harlan says, Washington loved power; the maintenance of his own influence through the 'Tuskegee machine' came to be an end in itself. In this, once again, he really resembled many American sectional leaders more closely than his black skin allowed compatriots to see.

3. 'It would be unjust to Mr. Washington not to acknowledge that in several instances he has opposed movements in the South that were unjust to the Negro; he sent memorials to the Louisiana and Alabama constitutional conventions, he has spoken against lynching, and in other ways he has openly or silently set his influence against sinister schemes or unfortunate happenings.' DuBois, *op. cit.*, p. 57.

The publication of these *Papers* will serve to inform students of Southern history of ordinary incidents which were seldom reported and little known. In a bitter letter to the (Hampton) *Southern Workman* in 1885, Washington quoted this press cutting: 'The feet of a coloured boy rotted off a few days ago. This was caused by his being worked in the county chain-gang all the winter without shoes' (*Papers, II,* 296). Yet Washington always managed to curb his anger by pointing to alleviating developments, whether or not they were actually taking place. There are certainly moments when one wonders at his power to reconcile the horrors of the Southern penal system and judicial practices, the increase of Jim Crow practices and the menace of lynching, with his curiously persistent optimism. An address before a society at Lincoln University in Pennsylvania in 1888 (*Papers, II,* 439–50) represents one of his most reflective attempts to explain, at the same time, both the abominations and the grounds for hope. Washington based his hopes on the great increases in Negro population. Avoiding—perhaps unaware of—Malthusian anxieties, he proclamied that numbers alone would give the Negro strength to resist oppression.

Yet it is distressingly clear from the *Papers* (vol. II) that something close to a siege mentality was building up among Southern blacks during the late 1880s. Dr. Dorsette, one of only six black physicians in Alabama, who comes through these pages as a man of great courage and integrity, is an important witness to several phases of the struggle. He told Washington that a threatened Negro should put up a sign of his intention to hold his ground and refuse to be run out of town, by opening a store or operating a business, which Dorsette himself meant to do; yet he was surrounded by murderous enemies and knew his danger. It was against this background that Washington could claim that prejudice was diminishing in Alabama and that within twenty-five years civil rights would be as strong there as in Philadelphia (*Papers, II,* 443). His famous powers of deception do sometimes seem to have extended to himself.

Perhaps the central weakness in his position appears in his attempt to counterattack against the growth of railroad segregation. Writing to the press in April 1885, he conceded nine-tenths of the case for equality: 'I wish to say a few words from a purely business standpoint. It is not a subject on which to mix social equality or anything bordering on it. To the negro it is a matter of dollars and cents.' (The newspaper no doubt lowered the case of 'Negro,' which Washington habitually capitalized.) It was most certainly not merely a 'matter of dollars and cents' any more in the South than in the North; in putting the issue to his white neighbours in language he supposed they could understand, he risked corroding the self-respect of his own race. At the outcome of the *Civil Rights Cases* (1883) when the Supreme Court held the Civil Rights Act of 1875 unconstitutional, he expressed no dismay. Even his denunciations of lynching were qualified by the implication that the victims were often guilty of rape, in which case they deserved their fate—a guilt from which he exonerated the graduates of Negro institutions of higher education. He seemed not to realize that the economic base he wanted blacks to build for themselves in order to earn the respect of American whites would need the protection of all the civil rights that the law could afford. Charitably—or was it merely an excuse for his racial inertia?—he often reminded Negroes that the whites needed time to overcome their schooling in 200 years of racial prejudice. But the truth was that it was getting worse, not being overcome; by the end of the period it was hardening into law.

Professor Harlan develops all these themes with an authority acquired from many years of exhaustive work in the Washington records. Many forgotten people come to life in his pages, which give us the first large-scale modern edition of the works of a great American of the Negro race. The most attractive of these individuals is Olivia Davidson, who became Washington's second wife. She and Washington spent many weary summer months in the North trudging separately from house to house in search of funds for the School for which they both lived. After their marriage her dulcifying influence is perceptible in his style as well as in his

8

Slavery, Race, and the Debate on Personality (1976)

Slaves have always had a very bad name. With a few occasional and local variations, the unflattering characteristics attributed to them have been remarkable for their consistency. 'Throughout history,' as David Brion Davis has observed, 'it has been said that slaves, although occasionally as loyal and faithful as good dogs, were for the most part lazy, irresponsible, cunning, rebellious, untrustworthy, and sexually promiscuous.'[1] To these defects might be added the slaves' deplorable failure to appreciate the sanctity of private property. They were notoriously given to petty theft, which sometimes extended to the extreme form of absconding with their own persons from their lawful owners. Frederick Douglass, who as a young slave was chronically underfed, explains in his au-

---

1. David Brion Davis, *The Problem of Slavery in the Age of Revolution 1770–1823,* (Ithaca, N.Y., 1975), p. 41.

In 1976 the faculties of Classics and History at Cambridge jointly arranged a series of lectures on Slavery, which was repeated in 1977 by the Faculty of History. This essay is a revised version of my own contribution. The other lecturers were M. I. Finley, Robert W. Fogel, J. M. Lonsdale, Betty Wood, and Eugene D. Genovese. I have retained in the text occasional references to other lectures in the series.

tobiography[2] how he resolved in his conscience the problem of satisfying his hunger without committing theft, by transferring his master's food from the bran tub to his stomach, where it remained just as much his master's property as before.

There were so many ways of being a bad slave, and the opportunity was so frequently seized, that one may reasonably ask what were the ideal qualities of slave personality, the true characteristics of a good slave? Following Aristotle's justification of slavery,[3] a good slave would possess in the right proportions those attributes required by the state of slavery: only enough of the faculty of reason to understand orders, but not enough to think for himself; physical strength, an obedient disposition, and skill enough to do whatever his duties required of him—not enough to arouse interests of his own.

Enquiry into the meaning of these desiderata could not go far without raising contradictions. Suppose, for example, that the master's instructions for a particular task called for an effort of interpretation if the slave found that conditions were not exactly as had been expected? Must not the slave in that case enter into his master's intentions in order to understand what he wished him to do? But if he did that, would he not begin to share the forbidden territory of his master's capacity for reason? It is hardly surprising that Aristotle felt obliged to admit that one quite often found people in the condition of slaves who were not intended by nature for slavery. In another section of the *Politics*,[4] Aristotle discusses the question of whether the characteristics of the good citizen are the same as those of the good man. In discussing slave personality, it seems reasonable to reverse this question by asking whether a good slave need be a good man?

For Aristotle this question would presumably have been absurd, since a slave could not possibly possess the qualities of justice and

2. Frederick Douglass, *The Life and Times of Frederick Douglass* (New York, 1962), pp. 104–5.
3. Aristotle, *Politics*, I, v.
4. *Ibid.*, III, iv.

wisdom—though I suppose he might get by with a touch of the other cardinal Greek virtues of fortitude and temperance. A good slave would presumably have to possess those attributes which his master, or his work, required of him. No doubt, therefore, the best possible slave could exist only under the best possible master; in this way the slave's maximum potentiality would be fulfilled, being a potentiality only for service.

One cannot even begin to embark on an analysis of the demands made by slavery on the individual personality without encountering the issue of responsibility—of the paradox that slaves were held to be responsible for their moral conduct while being denied the attributes of reason and a sense of justice. The significance of this issue emerges again and again in different periods in the discovery that although slavery lies at one extreme of what Professor Finley has described[5] as the spectrum of social status from slavery to freedom, it still does require a relationship of some sort between master and slave. This may perhaps not have been true of galley slaves, or of those whose labours built the pyramids, and hardly true either of slaves on Caribbean sugar plantations. It is an important qualification in any discussion of this sort that the nature of the relationship will be determined by the expendability of the slaves in relation to the labour force. And that tells us something of the special character of slavery in North America, where slaves became an increasingly valuable capital asset as a result of a specific conjunction of forces unknown elsewhere. The primary forces were the rise in the price of cotton on world markets after the passage of an act of Congress which at least formally brought to an end the importation of fresh slaves from overseas. I suspect that an additional, though incalculable, influence may have been exerted by the consideration that the Southern states were themselves only part of a Union, in the rest of which slavery was regarded, at best as an anomaly in a notionally free Republic, and at worst as an abomination that contrasted violently with every value for which

5. M. I. Finley, 'Between Slavery and Freedom,' *Comparative Studies in Society & History*, VI, 1963–64, 233–49.

the Republic claimed to stand. But this aspect—the influence of Northern opinion on the character of Southern slavery—would be very hard to investigate, and it is not surprising that the attempt (so far as I know) has not been made.

Even from this cursory introduction it is clear that in talking about slavery and personality, we are talking about the effects of slavery on slave-owners as well as on slaves—and indeed of the effects of slavery on entire political systems.

The psychological consequences of the master-slave relation are the subject of Professor Genovese's final lecture. The brief comments I shall make are derived in part from his own published work, but are preparatory to some comments I want to make about the implications of slavery for the system of government, especially a system such as that of the nineteenth-century United States, which made unusually strenuous claims of respect for individual rights, equality, and freedom.

For the master class, the problems may be considered under three headings, the first being Natural Justice.

Aristotle held systematically that the proper order of relationship between animate beings was that of the ruling element to the inferior element, whose nature was to be ruled. This was the principle which legitimized slavery in cases where slavery was the proper relationship, as he explained in these words: 'We may thus conclude that all men who differ from others as much as the body differs from the soul, or an animal from a man (and this is the case with all whose function is bodily service)—all such are by their nature slaves, and it is better for them, on the very same principle as in the other cases just mentioned, to be ruled by a master.'[6]

But the Greeks, like other peoples, disapproved of enslaving their own kith and kin, and about 330 B.C. Lycurgus prohibited Athenians from purchasing as slaves any free men taken in war. After the abolition of debt bondage by Solon, no Athenian could be a slave in Athens.[7] So that Aristotle's comments in any case refer

6. Aristotle, *Politics*, I, v.
7. Finley, 'Between Slavery and Freedom,' 239.

to foreigners, not to natives, and even among foreigners he recognizes that a person who ought not to have been enslaved—for example because he had a noble rank or nature—is not really correctly defined as a slave. This is an important distinction, because it lays down lines which if followed out in policy would actually enable such persons to acquire their freedom.

The argument that foreigners—or barbarians—who were not one's kith and kin, and who by nature were fitted for slavery, especially if their condition derived from capture in war, were natural slaves, and were, therefore, better off as slaves, was to give considerable comfort to defenders of Negro slavery when the system came under attack in the United States in the 1830s.

Meanwhile, I am not sure whether Western civilization, and particularly Christianity, were making progress, or merely marking time, while the fathers of the Church disposed of the problem of slavery by explaining that all mankind are slaves to *sin*. [8] That was the real enslavement of the human race, and what we all ought to be worrying about. By contrast, the transient relationship between rulers and ruled, masters and slaves, on this earth was of trivial and ephemeral importance; and those who were enslaved could not claim not to have deserved it. St. Thomas was able to satisfy himself on these lines that a master was entitled to all the fruits of his slave's labour, including that of his wife and children, thus founding what proved to be a long-lived school of Uncle Thomists. The one theme that was maintained with a reasonable degree of consistency was that Christians ought not to enslave Christians, and this led to some moments of anxiety when Negro slaves began to undergo conversions to Christianity. But once that question had been settled in favour of slavery, which was effected in Virginia as early as the 1660s, religion, as before, raised no obstacles to the recruitment and maintenance of a slave labour force.

A more serious question came to a head—or at least to a point where it seemed to some persons to present a crisis of principle—

8. D. B. Davis, *Slavery in W. Culture,* pp. 88–89.

when Britain's American colonies declared their independence. When the Americans renounced the monarchy they also rejected all claims of hereditary rights in government. This course of events, and the success of the War of Independence, presented the Americans with a Republic, for which they had been prepared in theory and practice by a long experience of virtual self-government in their assemblies, and by the reception for more than one generation of a quasi-republican or 'Commonwealth' strand of English political thought. The idea of republican government meant different things to different people, varying widely through different states; but it certainly meant that no class or individual could claim to rule another by inherited status. In which case, what became of slavery?

According to prevailing views, codified by Montesquieu in *De l'esprit des lois,* perhaps the most widely read of recent works of political philosophy, each form of government was maintained by a spirit essential to its survival. The spirit essential to a republic was virtue—very much what we would call public spirit.[9] Most slave-owning Americans probably lost very little sleep over the question of whether owning slaves was in any way damaging to their qualifications as citizens of the Republic. But Thomas Jefferson was deeply imbued with a belief that a republic required a homogeneous political mind; and such a public political mind would be endangered by any form of anti-republican principle. For this reason Jefferson feared that American republicanism might be weakened by immigration from countries whose peoples had no experience of republican government; and he also feared the corrupting influence of slavery on the manners of citizens—a corruption that began in childhood.[10] Children would imitate the temper tantrums of their elders in the exercise of despotic power over slaves. Slavery, a fit training ground for tyranny, was the antithesis of the education needed by a free republic. Jefferson then went on to show

9. Montesquieu, *De l'esprit des lois* (Paris, 1961 ed.), III, 3.
10. Thomas Jefferson, *Notes on the State of Virginia*, ed. William Peden (New York, 1954) Onery xviii, pp. 162–63.

concern for the slaves, and the moral seriousness of this concern
has perhaps been a little underrated in recent years; but the main
thrust of the passage, which is one of the more powerful in Jefferson's eloquent but often rather cool style of rhetoric, is directed
towards the consequences of slavery for the manners and principles of the whites. Jefferson, after all, did not envisage a situation
in which the blacks would ever share political responsibility or
social equality with whites, and it was the whites who bore the
whole responsibility for the Republic.

These were private fears which Jefferson did not originally
intend to publish and which he tried to suppress. That does not perhaps detract from their seriousness but it strongly suggests that
he had little practical hope that the political processes open to the
free citizens of Virginia could ever be expected to turn against slavery. Yet he sensed that if the free remained silent, retribution would
follow, and he hinted strongly that it would take the form of divine
intervention. In this thought if in few others there seems to be a
link between Jefferson and the Lincoln of the Second Inaugural.
Silence itself could offer no solutions and no hope; yet Jefferson
shrank from the consequences of putting the abolition of slavery
on Virginia's political agenda, and failed to take advantage of his
Presidency to make it an issue of national politics; while in 1854
Lincoln told an audience at Peoria that if all earthly power were
given to him he would not know what to do about the existing institution. If Lincoln had been able to reach back to the Jefferson of
the revolutionary era he might have been tempted to do so in the
language of his favourite author:

> If thou art privy to thy country's fate
> Which happily foreknowing may avoid,
> O speak!

There was a reply, however, to the anti-slavery argument, which
Southerners did little to develop until their system came under
open external attack in the 1830s. Then, dipping freely into ancient history, Aristotle's philosophy, the Old Testament's frequent

references to bondsmen and to servitude as a punishment, and into the New Testament's manifest moral silence on the widespread existence of various forms of slavery, Southern spokesmen began to extol the American South as a new Athens—more extensive in territory, and destined to rise even higher in science and philosophy. In the hands of John C. Calhoun, Thornton Stringfellow, Edmund Ruffin, and others, slavery became a positive benefit to all concerned; it brought the savage African up to the highest level of civilization he could attain, and enabled his masters to found a new and higher civilization still. With the works of George Fitzhugh, these arguments were reinforced by a new and well-informed application of the very modern concepts of sociology. Josiah Knott in the 1850s added a dash of irreverence in the form of an open attack on the sanctity of the Biblical account of the creation—which opened the way for the doctrine that the Negro was a separate, and inferior, being from the white.[11] A curious, ironic convergence now took place between the modernistic argument for slavery and the contemporaneous attack, being developed by Marx and Engels, on industrial capitalism. The difference was that Fitzhugh and Calhoun saw no wrong in the system and would have been strangers to the concept of alienation—for which reason the analogy between these two lines of criticism should never be pressed too far. They did maintain, however, that history showed that all civilization rested on some degree of exploitation, that labour was never given voluntarily, and that absolute judgements based on philosophical abstractions about human rights were worthless as instruments of social policy.

Nothing in this view was inconsistent with a sense of responsibility to the slaves in one's own care. It was the anti-slavery argument which consistently represented the system as one of absolute domination reflected by total submission, and posited this domination on the unrestrained use of brute force. Among historians of

11. Usefully collected by Eric McKitrick in *Slavery Defended* (Englewood Cliffs, N.J., 1963). George Fitzhugh, *Sociology for the South* (Richmond, 1854). Josiah Knott, *Types of Mankind* (1830).

the American South, an alternative approach, which preferred to think of the relationship as paternalistic, was founded by Ulrich B. Phillips, whose fundamental work, *American Negro Slavery,* appeared in 1918. Phillips had the field largely to himself for nearly forty years. In other respects Phillips was a product of the current type of 'Progressive' history, arguing the force of economic conditions as determinants of social policy; on the whole these views fitted very nicely with a latent Northern preference for leaving the Negro to the care and protection of the South, and constitute perhaps a minor but not trivial example of the ways in which historical interpretations, without shaping social policy, can establish moulds of thought which assist in the process.

When Kenneth M. Stampp attacked Phillips in *The Peculiar Institution,*[12] he returned in effect to the view that slavery was a system of arbitrary domination; the shift of emphasis that he provided was obtained by concentrating on the varieties of slave resistance. But with the work of Professor Genovese,[13] the paternalistic concept has re-emerged in a far more sophisticated form than anything envisaged by Phillips. Genovese defines Southern paternalism as a reciprocal system of patronage and dependence, controlled from above, but capable of subtle modifications by the slaves into a defence against dehumanization.

The Abolitionists cited abundant evidence of brutality—a power of domination virtually unrestrained by any force of law. This gave rise to what really became the mainstream and certainly the liberal tradition as to what Southern slavery was like as a way of life. On the other hand, plantation records, diaries, and letters are replete with evidence from masters and families who felt a keen sense of personal responsibility for the well-being of their slaves. Both these views are true, in the sense that both can be illustrated from factual records; both, in any case, reflect a system of arbitrary power sanctioned by force and based on a concept of fundamental

12. Kenneth M. Stampp, *The Peculiar Institution: Slavery in the Ante Bellum South* (New York, 1956).
13. Eugene D. Genovese, *Roll, Jordon, Roll* (London, 1975), pp. 6–7.

inequality—an inequality in which a supposed difference of natural endowment is translated into a moral inequality of rights. There could be no way of equating this situation with the idea of republican government and the rule of law, for which reason the idea of the fundamental nature of racial difference became increasingly and critically important to the defence of the entire Southern structure.

The case for the idea of responsibility is beautifully illustrated in the letters of the Jones family, of Liberty County, Georgia, in an immense volume, *The Children of Pride*,[14] edited by Robert Manson Myers. Over and over again we find that Mary Jones's anxieties over slaves' illnesses and deaths are those of a member of the family; letters to other branches constantly contain greetings to the servants; whites, moreover, are intimately aware of the individual qualities of their slaves. But the Jones family fatally reveal themselves over the fate of the slave Jane, who ran away to Savannah, where she was eventually found and arrested, and of her entire family. The trouble with this family was that they never really seemed to understand slavery; however well they were treated, they didn't settle down and never appreciated or returned the good will of their masters. Reciprocally, the Joneses, who worried about the problem a great deal, never understood the family's persistent, stubborn rebelliousness. The clearest comparison was with that of the behaviour of unreformably bad children. But in this case they were bad children who had eventually to be got rid of.

The meaning of paternalism on both sides began to grow clearer during the Civil War when federal forces drew near and slaves began to desert. Both when slaves absconded in ordinary times, and when they deserted their masters during the War, or even as free servants after Emancipation, there issued from their masters and mistresses a persistent, plaintive note of having been ill-used. At last Mary Jones herself—a woman, I must say, of great fortitude and integrity, who had spent her life doing right according to her

14. *The Children of Pride: A True Story of Georgia and the Civil War*, ed. Robert Manson Myers (New Haven, 1972).

own lights—comments after a theft of some cotton, 'My heart is pained and sickened by their vileness and falsehood in every way. I long to be delivered from the race.'[15] This sense of grievance can best be explained by the heavy moral investment that the master class had made in their own idea of paternalism: a real protection, which the slaves really needed. Through these lamentations the masters expressed a pervasive white belief that Negroes could not look after themselves, and that without white protection they would degenerate and even die out. This belief persisted after the Civil War, when Carl Schurz, investigating conditions in the South, found that whites in general still believed that blacks would work only under compulsion.[16]

Both linguistically and practically, the corollary to paternalism was childishness. And this proves to be the one most general, unifying keynote in white conceptions of black slaves. The irresponsibility which whites thought they discerned in the Negro temperament, the laziness, the lack of forethought, the lack of persistent application, together with the much more spontaneous emotionalism with its rapid alternations of laughter and sorrow, and the love of display—all these seemed to the whites to be quite typical manifestations of savage or childish temperaments—and were not white children in part savages, treading the path to civilization under the refining influences of education and religion? The difference, of course, was that the *adult* Negro was thought to resemble a white child, in whom no further development was to be expected.

In her lecture on slavery in the colonial period, Dr. Wood[17] has suggested a rather different picture of master and slave relations. There seems no reason to believe that resistance or manifestations of discontent diminished in the latter part of the eighteenth cen-

15. *Ibid.*, p. 1313.
16. Carl Schurz "Report on the Condition of the South." Rep. ed. (New York, 1970).
17. Dr. B. C. Wood's lecture in this series was devoted to slave rebellion and resistance in colonial America and to consequent white expectations of resistance: the anti-Sambo image.

tury. On the contrary, one would expect them to have increased as a direct result of the Revolution. The blacks who served in the Continental armies were presumably free—but their presence there was not likely to have remained unknown among slaves. Southern officers were very uneasy about the use of Negroes as soldiers and did their best to weed them out. The language of colonial resistance stressed the contrast between slavery and freedom—and such thoughts were infectious.

It has been argued recently by Ira Berlin [18] that the Revolution, by leading to a substantial number of manumissions, created for the first time in American history a correspondingly substantial population of free blacks. The free black communities, living as they did between the free world and the slave world, became a common feature of American life in the nineteenth century, took their origin from these events, and constituted for the slaves a possible model for alternatives to rebellion. Certainly their very existence was an incentive to escape. We know that the white South viewed the free blacks with suspicion and distrust; but we do not yet know very much about the relationship between free blacks and slaves, and the tensions created by free black communities would be a worthy subject for further research.

The advance of the nineteenth century brought important changes. The legal closure of the African slave trade in 1808 introduced a defensive note into the Southern position. Whatever claims Southern spokesmen might make for the virtues and benefits of slavery, it was now established as national policy that the forced removal of Africans from their own homes was wrong, and if wrong now, then presumably wrong in the past. Even though the enforcement of the suppression of the slave trade may have been very much less efficient than historians generally suppose, we may I think regard the arrival of newly captured Africans as an exception rather than a rule, and to that extent the American slave force

18. Ira Berlin, 'The Revolution in Black Life' in Alfred F. Young, ed., *The American Revolution: Explorations in the History of American Radicalism* (Dekalb, Ill., 1976).

was not much reinforced by the arrivals with African memories.

It seems significant that both Stampp and Genovese assume a more fixed and definitive character to American slavery after about 1830. After the Nat Turner rising of 1831, Southern states everywhere tightened their precautions against all forms of collective action; the patrols set up to police the roads and pathways were a constant terror to Negroes. Genovese points out[19] that from about this time, the opportunities for escape from the system by *any* means sharply diminished—but also that, as a corollary, actual conditions became more tolerable, at least in the material sense (though this hardly comports with the increasing restrictions on slave education). It is hardly likely to be a mere matter of chance that most of the evidence for the kind of slave so often reported by travellers as well as believed in by masters—the childish, irresponsible, spontaneous figure characterized by the name Sambo— comes from this later period. So, incidentally, does most of Professor Genovese's evidence of paternalism among masters.

This characterization convinced Stanley Elkins that the only way to break out of a dialogue about slavery which had become sterile, was to accept the truth of the reports, and to proceed to ask by what means this infantilization of the American Negro slave had been brought about.[20] Elkins drew a powerful analogy with the deterioration of personality among the inmates of Nazi concentration camps, a process that led to a childlike dependence on the guards. He suggested that a similar demoralizing trauma must have taken place when Africans were captured, marched to the African coast, carried across the middle passage, and dispersed to forced labour in America. Elkins's basic suggestion was that these things must have caused a breakdown and disorganization which completely demoralized the newly enslaved Africans; and this, with some elaboration, was held to be the basic explanation for the observed 'Sambo' condition.

19. Genovese, *Roll, Jordan, Roll*, pp. 50–51.
20. Stanley M. Elkins, *Slavery: A Problem in American Institutional and Intellectual Life* (Chicago, 1959).

This interpretation was well received, and made rapid progress before it began to encounter obstacles, both in the reawakening of an offended black consciousness, and in logical and evidential objections raised by scholars.[21]

I do not intend to retrace the ground of this well-known controversy. Three points, however, do seem to me to deserve rather more notice than they have received despite the welter of literature.

The first is that if Professor Elkins's thesis were correct, then African arrivals would have been the most demoralized and the least inclined to rebel or to escape. But the evidence adduced by Dr. Betty Wood and by another recent scholar[22] strongly suggests that African-born slaves were *more* rebellious than those who had been born into slavery.

The second point concerns the comparison between the slave prisoners of the Nazis and the slaves of American plantations and households, and in my view goes a long way to falsify the analogy. The vital difference between the two was that the concentration camp victims were not part of any important productive process— they were entirely expendable. American slaves, by contrast, constituted the productive labour force of the Southern economy, and had every opportunity to know that their labour was of crucial importance to their masters. Whatever other differences existed— and there were many of different kinds—this difference constitutes a fatal flaw in the analogy from the point of view of the relationship of slave to master: he knew that his master needed him.

Elkins adopted Sullivan's theory of 'significant others' in order to give his own observations their orientation. My third point turns on his use of this theory. Its application seems in general terms to be an acceptable and even an ingenious method of approaching the problem of master and slave as a relationship rather than as a mat-

21. For which see Ann J. Lane, ed., *The Debate Over Slavery: Stanley Elkins and His Critics* (Urbana, Ill., 1971).
22. Peter H. Wood, *Black Majority. Negroes in South Carolina from 1670 through the Stono Rebellion* (New York, 1975), pp. 249–50.

ter of mere domination, though it was domination rather than relationship with which Elkins seemed to be preoccupied. The shortcoming here was the absence of any clear theory of the personality of the slaves themselves. They stand as mere recipients of whatever is done to them, not reacting in differing ways according to differences of nationality or tribe, training or religion, or even, as far as he is concerned, sex. And there is no follow-through to their subsequent behaviour. This seems to be a development which the theory would entitle us to expect. It would surely be of the utmost importance to ask whether an 'infantilized' character continued to behave in infantilized ways after emancipation—and if not, why not?

To this question Professor Elkins returns, if obliquely, in a later review of the controversy.[23] In reconsidering the relationship between emphasis on damage to personality, which emerges as the aspect to which he has made the most significant contribution, and emphasis on resistance, he observes that 'as resistance looms larger . . . the damage shrinks. . . .' That is a reference to the literary emphasis on these alternatives; but it had historical connotations which concern us. To what extent did specific *forms* of resistance reflect the damage done by slavery to slave personalities? How did their *subsequent* management of their lives reflect it? If Elkins's theory of damage is to continue to serve the purposes of enquiry it seems to require a follow-through into Reconstruction.

The more it appears that slaves were able to devise ways of coping with their situation, and especially the more it appears that they were capable of appraising their own needs—emotional as well as material—and of acting upon reasonable inferences from the appraisal, the more likely it will seem that the observations so often reported of slave behaviour will have been observations of role rather than of personality.

The reports we have of slave behaviour, and particularly of conversation, often seem to be more descriptive of roles than of total

23. Stanley M. Elkins, 'The Slavery Debate,' *Commentary* (December 1975), 40.

personalities. The experience of Robert Smalls is instructive.[24] As a personal servant he felt superior to the field slaves until his master left him behind on the plantation for a few days, and it was only then that he learnt about Frederick Douglass from the field slaves whom he had despised. This experience determined him to gain his freedom. Early in Reconstruction he established himself as the political representative of the Sea Island area, from which base he became a political influence in South Carolina and retained his seat long after nearly all other blacks had been driven out of the Assembly.

The stupidity of Negro slaves, which gave their masters so much exasperation, and so repeatedly confirmed the impression of their unreformable childishness, on closer examination displays a remarkable consistency in serving the slaves' own interests. It so often seems to have served the dual purpose of lightening their labours while permitting them the pleasure of frustrating their masters. A broken tool could not be used; an order misunderstood could not be properly carried out. And this stupidity was frequently allied to the frequently reported vice of deceitful cunning. As we look at these conversations it appears to be the white reporter or interlocutor who fails to take advantage of his superior intelligence to interpret correctly what was being said. Here, for example, is an episode recounted by Genovese:[25]

> A minister was telling Uncle Junk, to work him to repentance, how the devil tormented those who went to hell. Junk hoped that 'good Mas'r Debble' wouldn't be so cruel. The minister reproved him for speaking of the devil in such polite terms. 'Well, you see, Mas'r,' replied the old Negro, 'no telling but the enemy might cotch me, and den I trust he remember as how I spoke of him perlitely, an jest de same as if he was a white man.'

24. Willie Lee Rose, *Rehearsal for Reconstruction: The Port Royal Experiment* (Indianapolis, 1965), pp. 131–32.
25. Genovese, *Roll, Jordon, Roll,* p. 219.

Another telling episode comes from Higginson's *Army Life in a Black Regiment*.[26] Colonel Higginson—the commander of the first regiment of black troops to serve in the Civil War, whose diaries give an extraordinarily closely observed record of incidents, speech, songs, and actions—reports how he overheard a black soldier tell how he got a Confederate soldier to tell him the location of the federal troops:

> 'Den I go up to de white man, berry humble, and say would he please get ole man a mouthful for eat?'
> 'He say he must have the valeration of half a dollar.'
> 'Den I look berry sorry, and turn for go away.'
> 'Den he say I might give him dat hatchet I had.'
> 'Den I say,' (this in tragic vein) 'dat I must hab dat hatchet for defend myself *from de dogs!*'
> (Immense applause and one appreciating auditor says, chuckling, 'Dat was your arms, ole man,' which brings the house down again.)
> 'Den he say de Yankee pickets was nearby, and I must be very keerful.'
> 'Den I say, "Good Lord, Mas'r, am dey?" '
> Words cannot express the complete dissimulation with which these accents of terror were uttered—this being precisely the piece of information he wished to obtain.

Role-playing is a common phenomenon, and using it to explain all the varieties of slave behaviour is perhaps to risk assimilating the pressures which produced these slave responses too closely to those of everyday life in the world we know. In any case it always seems to me that theories about role-playing tend to assume rather too easily that roles are assumed and discarded voluntarily. But what are we to say when the mask melts into and transforms the face—as in some cases it surely does? This is another reason why the question of personality needs to be pursued beyond slavery, and indeed beyond the South.

26. Thomas Wentworth Higginson, *Army Life in a Black Regiment* (n.p. 1969 ed.), p. 37.

Slaves stood up under the strains and terrors that pressed upon them throughout their lives by means of a wide variety of beliefs, traditions, and relationships of their own, which owed little or nothing to the proximity of the civilization which kept them in slavery.

The most fearful risk facing slaves was that of the loss of their own immediate kin. Their very family life was insecure. Even though the statistics may now suggest that slave marriages were disrupted less often than used to be supposed, their fate and that of their families was not in their own hands. And in any case, my own reading of the statistics that have been produced by Professor Blassingame and by Fogel and Engerman[27] makes the disruption of marriage by sale and separation quite frequent enough to have been a subject of intermittent, in some cases perhaps of constant, fear and insecurity.

American slaves attempted to compensate for this insecurity by their own convention of stewardship—a form of collective responsibility. Herbert Gutman[28] has developed this theme in great depth from the records of several large plantations, one set of which was kept—remarkably—over four generations. These records reveal a continuity of family groupings, some of whose earliest members were African-born. Another inference is a configuration of sexual patterns which differed from those of the whites but was subject to the group's own rules. The giving and taking of names was also of matter of group custom. Surnames seem to have been normally taken from former masters, not from the present one. The slave communities studied by Professor Gutman had built up a collective network of relationships which he calls 'fictive kin,' capable of absorbing some of the shocks of sale and separation. I take this to be very close to what Genovese calls 'steward-

---

27. John L. Blassingame, *The Slave Community* (New York, 1972), pp. 77–103. Robert W. Fogel and Stanley L. Engerman, *Time on the Cross* (London, 1976 ed.), p. 49.

28. Herbert G. Gutman, *The Black Family in Slavery and Freedom, 1750–1925* (Oxford, 1976).

ship.' Although the two authors might not particularly welcome the assurance, their studies, built on massive foundations of research, tend to support each other. It would in my view be much more alarming if they did not.

The feature that seems to emerge from the more recent studies is the remarkable degree of moral autonomy that slaves managed to create and maintain for themselves, at least on the larger plantations. I doubt if it was possible on the smaller ones, and one must remember that although the larger plantations have left the more durable records, there is no more reason to regard them as typical of the life and circumstances of American slaves than to say the same of the medium or smaller ones.

Where the slave force was large in numbers and the quarters at night hummed with an independent life into which the planters could not enter (though they might occasionally have imagined that they were doing so), the slave culture was sustained by a very distinctive religious faith and religious observance.

Afro-Americans seem to have retained a capacity for faith in nature as a manifestation of divinity; they were not inhibited by the corrosive sense of sin bestowed on Catholics and Protestants alike by the legacy of Paul and Augustine. They also made use of Christian and Jewish iconography in ways that responded intimately to their own needs.[29] One of the most significant examples of this tendency was the practice, which white ministers must have found incredible, of conflating the figures of Christ and Moses. We, however, can afford to remind ourselves that while Christ promised deliverance in another life, Moses led his people towards a promised land in this world. That was the meaning, too, of the River Jordan, and why the crossing of the river played such a part in Negro song and lore. They also possessed and developed a rich body of folk-tales, of which the Brer' Rabbit stories are no doubt the best known, if not the most lovable. Brer' Rabbit is often represented as the black getting his revenge against the white

29. These remarks owe much to Genovese, *Roll, Jordon, Roll*; and to lectures and conversation of Professor G. S. Shepperson.

world; but if we consider his criminal record, which includes boil-
ing Brer' Wolf's grandmother, tricking Brer' Wolf into eating her,
and then sacrificing his own wife and children in order to escape
Brer' Wolf's revenge, we may begin to doubt whether the comparison to slave personality is particularly flattering. If the Brer' Rabbit stories were to be taken at any of the first two or three levels of
ambiguity, he might be considered about the most satisfactory evidence for the theory of damaged personality.

I have suggested that the record of how slaves behaved on their
emancipation—which in many cases they anticipated by escaping
into federal lines—should be regarded as important evidence of
personality. And the record is extremely interesting. From many
parts of the South and from many different sources the records tell
us that slaves deserted their masters and mistresses in large numbers. Their manner of doing so often struck their former owners as
proof of base ingratitude; but what seems to me the more remarkable is the general lack of malice. Ex-slaves distinguished clearly
among their former masters. Some, they knew, were cruel and
spiteful, others within the limits of the system were kind and
decent. But there seems to have been a remarkable understanding
that the masters, too, were locked into the system, beside which
overwhelming fact their personal characters were of little account.
There was astonishingly little violence or revenge; but on the other
hand there was no sense of obligation. The slaves had never owed
their owners anything and they knew it.[30] It was this coolness, this
total sense of non-obligation, that the former masters regarded as
ingratitude; they had so often believed they were succeeding in
making the relationship personal, gaining the joint advantages of
high productivity and a reputation for humanity among the slaves
themselves. There can moreover be no doubt at all that they often
felt warm affection for individual slaves. But there is much evidence that the slaves were not taken in.

Yet it must be recognized that most slaves, most of their lives,

---

30. See Rose, *Rehearsal for Reconstruction,* p. 102.

had no expectation of liberty—indeed, as I remarked, that any such expectation was diminishing for thirty years before the Civil War. Slaves with no African memories could get their idea of liberty only by observing the white world or glimpsing the free Negro world, of each of which they enjoyed only a constricted view. While I cannot now pursue this theme, which seems to me to need further research, it seems likely that in many cases this constriction of experience of the ordinary modes of procedure, of the language and assumptions of the free world, may have constituted a form of damage, or deprivation, whose effects would have been felt when the slaves were precipitated into freedom.

But slaves did not live their lives in the expectation of freedom, and in order to bear their condition they had to find ways to accommodate themselves to it. This problem of accommodation has become deeply contentious, although I think unnecessarily so. The problem of accommodating ourselves to the slave solutions to the problem is that accommodation can easily pass into ways that have the smell of collaboration about them. The more slave life is made to appear normal, as the acceptance of one form of extractive labour among others, the less it seems unbearable; the inference that comes from the study of the historical evidence thus assimilates American slaves to their condition of slavery, and never loses sight of the fact that American slaves were Negroes. In the eyes of most Southern whites, this assimilation took place, not as a result of slavery, but because it reflected the proper and natural relationship between the races. The Aristotelian formula had been confirmed: the Negro was a slave by nature! The whole problem of slave personality was therefore complicated, not only under slavery but ever since, by the cardinal fact that American slavery was *racial* slavery. The result of this was that in the United States, and one should add to a certain extent in the British Empire and in other European cultural perceptions, the slave personality became conflated with the Negro personality. As early as 1765, for example, the French *Encyclopédie* used 'slave' and 'Negro' almost interchangeably.

It is now quite clear that American Negroes under slavery preserved, constructed, and handed down a collective life that was rich in the resources of mutual support, religion, and music; but the historian of these things would commit a fundamental error of historical imagination if he were to suppose that this type of collective accommodation to fate represented any sort of free choice. Insecurity, fear, and the knowledge that your fate is in other, not necessarily friendly, hands, tend to breed fatalism and helplessness. As Professor Elkins has shrewdly observed,[31] powerlessness corrupts just as surely as power does.

In such circumstances, self-help was closely allied to self-preservation, and one of the most obviously sensitive points in question was the protection of one's person against physical abuse. This is one of the issues on which recent controversy has been understandably severe. Professors Fogel and Engerman reported that on the estate of Bennett Barrow, for which a written record survived, each hand could expect to be whipped only 0.7 times in any one year, a percentage which they clearly regarded as representing a very small threat to the average individual. Since then we have learnt that an alternative rendering of the same figures shows that one slave was whipped every four days.[32] It seems probable that some slaves were whipped often, others hardly ever. More recently Professor Fogel has stated that a much more thorough search of the slave narratives has tended to substantiate the conclusion that whipping was comparatively rare; only 20 per cent of slaves were ever whipped at all.[33]

These statistics, as usual, could be accounted for by more than one hypothesis. It might be the case that 80 per cent of slaves had masters who did not like to see slaves whipped, but who resorted to other methods of persuasion, such as confinement or short rations; but on the other hand, the 80 per cent who were not whipped might have witnessed the whipping of the other 20 per

31. Elkins, 'The Slavery Debate,' 40.
32. Fogel and Engerman, *Time on the Cross*, pp. 145–46. Herbert G. Gutman, *Slavery and the Numbers Game* (Urbana, Ill., 1975), p. 19.
33. At a seminar in Cambridge University, 1975–76.

cent, and might not have liked what they saw. One whipping in a lifetime would be enough to terrify many ordinarily fearful men and women. The use of statistics without imagination is far more misleading and dangerous than the use of no statistics at all.

The Negro in white society, and particularly it seems in Anglo-Saxon society, has not been victimized by slavery alone. He has been the victim of certain very distinct and selective attitudes, the consequences of which have contributed to the social identity, and therefore to some extent to the self-image, of Negroes ever since.[34] The issue here is very important and very sensitive. Those who observe the history of blacks in relation to whites, and of whites in relation to blacks, have been obliged to do so in a context in which their own sense of identity arose in part from that history. It is impossible to be sure, but important not to forget to ask, to what extent we may be defined by the preconceptions of others. Frederick Douglass, the greatest symbol of slave defiance since Nat Turner, once remarked that he had found Negroes who were convinced that either they or their ancestors must have done something wicked to have deserved their fates; Booker Washington, who does not usually convey the impression of a subtle sensibility, observed inner conflicts so deep that the Negro did not know how to speak for himself. The pain which these attitudes caused was produced because men like Douglass and Washington—they were not the only ones—knew that this was not the language of liberty and was hardly that of self-respect; it was the language of people cowed by generations of misery and by the prospect of perpetual misery at the hands of their white masters. But Douglass as a young man broke the nerve of Covey the slave-breaker, who had been given the job of breaking him; and he later remarked that the slave who got whipped was the slave who was whippable.[35]

White attitudes to Africans and to their descendants changed

34. I have discussed this question in *The Pursuit of Equality in American History* (Berkeley, 1978), pp. 344–45.
35. *Life and Times of Frederick Douglas*, pp. 134–44, Louis R. Harlan, ed. *The Booker T. Washington Papers* (Urbana, Ill., 1972), I, p. 405.

significantly over time, and with these changes came different explanations of African character. There is abundant evidence that sixteenth- and seventeenth-century Europeans regarded Africans as extraordinarily different from themselves—and if we had records from the other side I am sure we should find corresponding African expressions of amazement, possibly of disgust, at the appearance and morals of Europeans. It is also clear that Europeans often felt animosity—sometimes covert envy—of Africans. For reasons partly connected with this animosity, partly with the particular circumstances of the European encounter with Africa, when the demands of economic growth called for a labour force capable of heavy work in sub-tropical conditions, the African became a prime candidate for enslavement: as much because of his vulnerability, and the ease of identification, as for any other reason.

This identification was of course primarily a matter of pigmentation. From Herodotus onwards, Europeans had speculated on how the African had acquired his colour—though it seems never to have occurred to theorists on this question that it might have been put the wrong way round, and ought to have taken the form of asking how the dweller in northern climates had lost his natural colour. The observation of colour in any case did not give rise to any fixed concept of *race*. Dr. Johnson's *Dictionary* gives no clue to the idea of race that was to arise in the nineteenth century and has come to define the subject. The word does not appear at all in the first edition of the *Encyclopaedia Britannica,* published in 1771. The theory that biological origins determined the natural propensities and abilities, the psychological and intellectual endowments of different clusters of persons, may have had some of its beginnings in Linnaeus's methods of classification, but did not begin to take root until the emergence of the anthropology of the early nineteenth century. I rather suspect you would find its presence at the level of popular lore earlier than in the treatises of such investigators of cranial and skeletal structure as Dr. Samuel Morton of Philadelphia, who himself was restrained from drawing some of the more racialist inferences because of their conflict with the record according to Genesis. There was no difficulty, however, in handling ideas of hierarchy, which had always ruled human society. When the idea of race as biologically distinctive and permanent got linked with older and well-established ideas of hierarchy, the status of the Negro actually suffered from the advance of the still elementary forms of the science of anthropology.

White Americans who were concerned about racial typology and who were most sympathetic to the Negro, made no attempt to conceal from themselves that white and black personalities were considerably different: that, for them, was the problem. But it is important to notice that recognition of difference did not commit observers to the concept of *inferiority*. The New York emancipationist—and feminist—Theodore Tilton argued in 1862 that the Negro was the nearest equivalent among the races to the feminine qualities. The passage is expressive; Tilton regarded it as a mistake,

> to rank men only by a superiority of intellectual faculties. God has given to man a higher dignity than the reason. It is the moral nature . . . In all those intellectual activities which take their strange quickening from the moral faculties— processes which we call instincts, or intuitions—the negro is superior to the white man, equal to the white woman. The negro is the feminine race of the world . . .
>
> We have need of the negro for his aesthetic faculties . . . We have need of the negro for his music . . . But let us stop questioning whether the negro is a man. In many respects he is a superior man. In a few respects he is the greatest of men.[36]

Again Moncure Daniel Conway, a former Virginian slave-owner turned abolitionist, declared that, 'In our practical, anxious, unimaginative country, we need an infusion of this fervid African element, so child-like, exuberant and hopeful; we ought to prize it, as

36. Theodore Tilton, *The Negro,* quoted by James M. McPherson, 'A Brief for Equality: The Abolitionist Reply to the Racist Myth, 1860–1865,' in Martin Duberman, ed., *The Antislavery Vanguard* (Princeton, N.J., 1965), p. 166.

we do rare woods and glowing gems imported from the gorgeous tropics.'[37]

From a more scientific standpoint the weakness of these perceptions lay in their failure to offer, or to see any need for, an explanation of how these observed characteristics were acquired or transmitted. They were the perceptions of people who clearly discerned the deficiencies of North American civilization's fierce and often destructive competitiveness, its intensely economic vision, and its aims which seemed to concentrate all ideas of self-advancement into a narrow individualism. But it is significant that these views did not threaten that civilization with any risks from the consequences of Negro emancipation or Negro citizenship; for these Abolitionists, also sometimes called 'romantic racists,' sincerely believed that native Negro intelligence lacked the hard, analytical characteristics that had made European and American civilization, and the inference was that in an exposure to untrammelled competition in that society, the Negro would suffer and fail. Unless he were specially protected, or educated into its hard, competitive ways, he would go under.

These were in any case the views of a small minority. When theories of biological race, linked to notions of genetic and therefore ineradicable inferiority, had singled out the Negro—a process which, as I have suggested, popular attitudes and folklore had begun long before the beginnings of physical anthropology—the Negro's *visibility* placed him in a position of permanent exposure which by its nature was one of permanent vulnerability. To be regarded as inferior, to be the subject of expectations of inferior performance, particularly in children, leads to a loss of self-confidence and to a corresponding failure of performance. But emancipated slaves were also victims of the social system which the slave South had created. There had been a prolonged and chronic under-investment in the South's own human resources, most notably in education. Blacks and poor whites alike were abject victims

37. Quoted, *ibid.*, pp. 165–66.

of illiteracy and semi-literacy. One of the more interesting though admittedly difficult challenges that research into past social structures could now undertake would be an investigation of the vocabulary and linguistic resources available to the poor, and of the implications of vocabulary and language for the power to form concepts beyond those required for day-to-day life.

Psychological and social damage was inevitable when Negroes, who had been sealed off from the competitive world by slavery itself, were precipitated into conflict and competition with forces which were already quite capable of grinding each other to death. Slavery had prepared the large majority of Negroes only for exploitation, with some mutual support in their troubles; it did not undertake to prepare them for the world they were going to encounter. The consequences did not escape the comments of either W. E. B. DuBois or of Booker Washington. At the risk of a rather long quotation I would like to draw attention to DuBois's comments—those of a highly educated Massachusetts Negro, who was to emerge as one of America's most profound social thinkers and also, perhaps, its finest literary stylist—on the central question of slavery and personality; of the problem we have been discussing, that is, of 'damage':

> It is no idle regret with which the white South mourns the loss of the old-time Negro,—the frank, honest, simple old servant who stood for the earlier religious age of submission and humility. With all his laziness and lack of many elements of true manhood, he was at least open-hearted, faithful, and sincere. To-day he is gone, but who is to blame for his going? Is it not those very persons who mourn for him? Is it not the tendency, born of Reconstruction and Reaction, to found a society on lawlessness and deception, to tamper with the moral fibre of a naturally honest and straightforward people until the whites threaten to become ungovernable tyrants and the blacks criminals and hypocrites? Deception is the natural defence of the weak against the strong, and the South used it for many years against its conquerors; to-day it must be prepared to see its black proletariat turn the same two-edged weapon against itself. And how natural this is! The death of Denmark

Vesey and Nat Turner proved long since to the Negro the present hopelessness of physical defence. Political defence is becoming less and less available, and economic defence is only partially effective. But there is a patent defence at hand,—the defence of deception and flattery, of cajoling and lying. It is the same defence which the Jews of the Middle Age used and which left its stamp on their character for centuries. To-day the young Negro of the South who would succeed cannot be frank and open, honest and self-assertive, but rather he is daily tempted to be silent and wary, politic and sly; he must flatter and be pleasant, endure petty insults with a smile, shut his eyes to wrong; in too many cases he sees positive personal advantage in deception and lying. His real thoughts, his real aspirations, must be guarded in whispers; he must not criticize, he must not complain. Patience, humility, and adroitness must, in these growing black youth, replace impulse, manliness and courage. With this sacrifice there is an economic opening, and perhaps peace and some prosperity. Without this there is riot, migration, or crime. Nor is this situation peculiar to the Southern United States,— is it not rather the only method by which undeveloped races have gained the right to share modern culture? The price of culture is a Lie.[38]

The generation of black leaders and spokesmen who succeeded the end, and failure, of Reconstruction, were sometimes severely critical of what they regarded as the over-ambitious and exploitative aims of the Radical Republicans who engineered the principal acts of Reconstruction. Booker Washington made no secret of his belief that Negro enfranchisement had been brought into effect before the freedmen were ready for it, and had been exercised with a degree of indiscretion which had been directly responsible for bitterness and bloodshed.[39] This, together with the consequences of launching them into a world for which they had received no preparation and in which they were pawns of competing white political parties none of which had the Negro interest at

38. W. E. B. DuBois, *The Souls of Black Folk* (Chicago, 1903), pp. 203–4.
39. Louis R. Harlan, ed., *The Booker T. Washington Papers*, II, 258; *Up from Slavery*, p. 284.

heart, he held to be responsible, not only for the plight of the Southern Negroes, but for the state of moral deterioration which in turn crippled their ability to fight back. Washington, himself a past master of role-playing, did not believe that the Southern Negro could take his place in American society without first achieving a large measure of self-regeneration, and his deprecatory remarks on his own race often caused offence among his black contemporaries. Whatever the merits of his diagnosis, he applied it with a view to a cure. But the condition was desperate. In a competitive society, the Negro American was dogged by a peculiarly tenacious and damaging set of disadvantages. He was legally and nominally free, but he was not free in the full sense in which republican theory envisaged freedom.

In 1861, four years before the final abolition of slavery in the United States, Sir Henry Maine published his *Ancient Law*, in which he promulgated the famous dictum that the tendency of 'progressive societies' was to move 'from status to contract.'[40] American Negro slavery furnished an ironically complex commentary on this perspective. Slavery had defined the Negro's status in terms to which contract was irrelevant; but after emancipation, status continued to limit and often to determine the terms of contract. The development even suggests a modification of the original thesis. The tendency was clear enough; but previous status tends to determine and to be reflected in the kind of contract that the emancipated class can make.

Thomas Jefferson, whom I quoted early in this lecture, feared that slavery would corrupt the manners requisite for a republican government. He was thinking of the effect on the whites, but his observation was more accurate and more profound than even he would have realized. For Jefferson himself shared in the white belief that denied to Negroes the credit for being capable, through their own development, of taking their part in a republican government. The long shadow of this prevalent white belief was natu-

40. Sir Henry Maine, *Ancient Law* (London, 1888 ed.), pp. 169–70.

rally cast among Negroes, who had to struggle to convince not only the white world but themselves of their ability to hold their own and match the whites in attaining the standards that seemed to be called for by white civilization. The generation of post-Reconstruction Negro leaders generally accepted these standards and admitted the comparative shortcomings of many of their own race. They disagreed with white racialists about the reasons for this shortfall in performance. In a later generation, James Baldwin attempted to redress this imbalance by attacking the moral standards of white civilization and asking, 'Who wants to be integrated into a burning house?' And he also redressed the aesthetic imbalance by telling his contemporaries, black and white, that 'Black is beautiful.'[41]

That was something that DuBois had known long before. And the last word in all this still, I think, belongs to DuBois, who drew a moving picture of the dualism of the black standpoint for viewing the world of which he was a part but which remained outside himself:[42]

> After the Egyptian and the Indian, the Greek and the Roman, the Teuton and the Mongolian, the Negro is a sort of seventh son, born with a veil, and gifted with second sight in this American world,—a world which yields him no true self-consciousness, but only lets him see himself through the revelation of the other world. It is a peculiar sensation, this double-consciousness, this sense of always looking at oneself through the eyes of others, of measuring one's soul by the tape of a world that looks on in amused contempt and pity. One ever feels his two-ness,—an American, a Negro—two souls, two thoughts, two unreconciled strivings; two warring ideals in one dark body, whose dogged strength alone keeps it from being torn asunder.

DuBois, who had never been a slave, was talking entirely about the black experience of the world after slavery. But that only gives his reflections deeper significance. For his experience was of a white world whose conception of the Negro, if not originally

41. James Baldwin, *The Fire Next Time* (New York, 1963), p. 101.
42. DuBois, *The Souls of Black Folk,* p. 3.

formed by slavery, had certainly been reinforced and informed by two hundred and fifty years of America's peculiar institution.

It is for this reason that I conclude by returning to the forebodings of Thomas Jefferson. For despite his own unfriendliness towards Negroes—as a race if not always as individuals—and his skepticism about their potentiality for equal achievement, he appreciated rather more clearly than most of his contemporaries that Negroes were not the only victims, but that the white personality, and therefore the entire Republic, were among the casualties of black slavery.

Section Three

9

Historians and the Problem of Early American Democracy (1962)

The earliest national period of United States history combines two themes. It is a period of revolution and also of constitution making. Charter governments, whether royal or proprietary, give way to new governments which claim to derive the whole of their authority from the American electorate. The Americans, though working from experience, build for the future. This fact is of cardinal importance for any attempt to understand their work or the state of mind in which it was undertaken.

The claim of the new government raises a problem that was not solved by the mere exercise of effective, but revolutionary powers. Was their authority strictly compatible with the doctrine that governments derive their just powers from the consent of the governed? What was meant by 'consent'? How was such consent obtained or certified?

The attempt to answer these questions leads the historian into a reconstruction of the character of these early institutions and an inquiry into the ideas by which they were governed. In the light of

This essay was first published in *American Historical Review*, April 1962.

224 Paths to the American Past

subsequent American development, it has led historians to address themselves to the problem of deciding whether or not these institutions were democratic. Whether or not we choose to adopt this particular definition, whether or not we regard it as a useful tool of analysis, the underlying problem is one that the historian cannot easily avoid. No history of the American Revolution and of constitution making could be written without discussion of the doctrines on which the Americans based their resistance, the question of what meaning these doctrines bore for the different American participants, and of the degree of participation, the attitude and purposes of different elements in American society.

There is a problem of the relationship of ideas to institutions; there is a previous problem of the ideas themselves. I do not think that the broad and undifferentiated use of the term 'democracy' helps either to describe the institutions or to explain the ideas. I do not even think that our analysis of these matters will be much affected by the use of this concept. But the thesis has been advanced[1] that the American colonies were already full-fledged democracies before the American Revolution began, from which it follows that the cardinal principle of the Revolution was a defence of democratic institutions against royal or parliamentary tyranny. It is a thesis that has the advantage of an attractive simplicity, and it is one that can be supported by a good deal of evidence, especially if that evidence is read without much relation to the context of eighteenth-century political ideas. It also has the merit of providing the occasion, and in order that the argument should not go by default, the necessity of a more searching inquiry into the realities.

To use the word 'democracy' is to raise, but not I think to solve, a problem of definition. And it is not an easy one. There is so little agreement about what is meant by 'democracy,' and the discussion has such a strong tendency to slide noiselessly from what we *do* mean to what we *ought* to mean, that for purposes of definition it seems to be applicable only in the broadest sense. And this sense

1. Robert E. Brown, *Middle-Class Democracy and the Revolution in Massachusetts, 1691–1780* (Ithaca, N.Y., 1955), esp. pp. 401–8.

has the effect of limiting, rather than of advancing, our under-standing of the past.

But I must certainly admit that if I did think the word 'democ-racy' in fact did justice to the problem, then I would have to accept it despite the risks involved. More than this: we ought to have some agreement as to what meaning it can be made to bear. It makes good sense in a purely comparative view to call the Ameri-can colonies and early states democratic when contrasting them with the Prussia of Frederick II or the Hapsburg Empire; they were in the same sense democratic compared with France or with England, with which they had so much in common. There might be less unintended irony in calling them part of the 'free world' than in doing the same today with Spain, Formosa, or the Union of South Africa. In the broad strokes we use to differentiate between tyrannies and free states the term will serve as a starting point, but not as a conclusion. It is interesting, when one begins to look more closely at the structure of the complex societies of the eighteenth century, how rapidly these broad distinctions lose their value and cease to serve any analytical purpose. As R. R. Palmer has recently remarked, surveying the Western world before the French Revo-lution, 'No one except a few disgruntled literary men supposed that he lived under a despotism.'[2] When one considers how com-plex the machinery of administration, of justice, for the redress of grievances and, if any, of political representation must become in any ancient and intricately diversified society, it is easy to feel that the more democratic virtues of the American societies were re-lated, more than anything else, to their relative simplicity and lack of economic and functional diversity. But a closer inspection, not only of the structure, but of the development, of colonial institu-tions reveals a tendency that puts the matter in another light; for these institutions were unmistakably moulded in the shape of En-glish institutions and were conforming themselves, both socially and politically, to the conventions of the period.

2. R. R. Palmer, *The Age of the Democratic Revolution* (Princeton, N.J., 1959), p. 51.

The alternative view, which I want to suggest, does not confine itself merely to rejecting the 'democratic' interpretation by putting in its place a flat, anti-democratic account of the same set of institutions. What it does, I think, is to see the democratic elements in their proper perspective by adding a further dimension without which the rest is flat, incomplete, and, for all its turbulence, essentially lifeless. This is the dimension of what Cecelia Kenyon has called 'institutional thought.'[3]

To take this view, one has to free oneself from a tendency that has become very difficult to resist. I mean the strong, though wholly anachronistic tendency to suppose that when people who were accustomed to ways and ideas which have largely disappeared into the past felt grievances against their government, they must necessarily have wanted to express their dissatisfaction by applying the remedies of modern democracy; and, again, that when their demands were satisfied, the aspirations thus fulfilled must have been modern, democratic aspirations.

The idea that the great mass of the common people might actually have given their consent to concepts of government that limited their own participation in ways completely at variance with the principles of modern democracy is one that lies completely outside the compass or comprehension of the 'democratic' interpretation. That interpretation insists on the all-importance of certain democratic features of political life, backed by certain egalitarian features of social life having a strong influence on political institutions. What it misses is that these features belonged within a framework which—to polarize the issue at the risk of using another broad term—was known to the world as Whiggism. The institutions of representative government derived from the time when the Whig concept of representative government was being worked out in England and, both by extension and by original experience, in the American colonies (and when the foundations were

3. Cecelia M. Kenyon, 'Men of Little Faith: The Anti-Federalists on the Nature of Representative Government,' *William and Mary Quarterly*, XII (January 1955), 4.

laid for the Whig interpretation of history). Even where democratic elements were strong and dominant, the animating ideas belonged to a whole Whig world of both politics and society. More than this, the colonial and early national period in which they played so important a part was pervaded by the belief in and a sense of the propriety of social order guided and strengthened by principles of dignity on the one hand and deference on the other. It was, to use the term coined by Walter Bagehot in his account of Victorian England, a deferential society.[4]

There is, of course, nothing very new about the theory that early American society was relatively egalitarian and that this situation was reflected in political institutions and conduct. It was a view that became fashionable in the days of George Bancroft. But it has been reformulated, with formidable documentation, in Robert E. Brown's work on Massachusetts and in his attack on Charles Beard.[5] To regain our perspective it seems necessary for a moment to go back to Beard.

Beard, as we know, distinguished in his study of the Constitution between two leading types of propertied interest, basically those of land and commerce. Commercial property was supposed to have been strongly represented in the Constitutional Convention, landed property outside. The opposition in some of the state ratifying conventions was supposed to have arisen from the outraged interests of the landed classes.

Despite intense opposition in certain states, the Constitution was eventually ratified. But here Beard went further. He asserted that ratification was not a true expression of the will of the people. He based this argument on the prevalence of property qualifications for the suffrage, which meant that only a minority of freeholders and other owners of property could participate in the elec-

4. See also E. S. Griffith, *History of American City Government: Colonial Period* (New York, 1938), p. 191; Clifford K. Shipton, review of Brown, *Middle-Class Democracy*, *Political Science Quarterly*, LXXI (No. 2, 1956), 306–8.

5. Robert E. Brown, *Charles Beard and the Constitution: A Critical Analysis of 'An Economic Interpretation of the Constitution'* (Princeton, N.J., 1956).

tions to the ratifying conventions, which in consequence were not truly representative. There are two elements in Beard's hypothesis, as Brown has pointed out.[6] On the one hand, Beard advances the alleged clash between the mercantile and landed interests, with the mercantile coming out on top because of the power conferred by its economic advantages; on the other, he implies the existence of a connection between the landed opposition to ratification and the supposedly disfranchised masses, whose silence so damagingly detracts from the authority of the Constitution. It is not my purpose to discuss the questions as to whether Beard's argument has stood the test of recent scrutiny. Another aspect, which may be called that of the moral consequences of Beard's work, deserves more consideration than it has received.

The Philadelphia Convention was described by Thomas Jefferson as 'an assembly of demi-gods,' a judgement to which posterity murmured 'Amen.' There are, however, marked disadvantages about being descended from demi-gods; they not only lack a sense of humour, but they set an appallingly high standard. What a relief it must have been, after the first shock of Beard's iconoclasm had died down, to find that they were only human after all! Beard had questioned the Constitution at two points. In the first place, by implying that it was the work of men motivated by private economic interests he made it possible to reconsider its wisdom and justice; but in the second place, when he denied that it had received the sanction of a genuine, popular ratification he made it possible—perhaps obligatory—to question the authority of the Constitution precisely because it did not owe its origin to the only recognized source of such authority in the whole science of government as understood in America: the consent of the governed.

To this problem, Brown's critique of Beard is directly relevant. He not only pursues Beard with a determination that recalls John Horace Round's pursuit of Edward Freeman, but in his work on Massachusetts, he makes a thorough and painstaking investigation

6. *Ibid.*, pp. 50–51, 53–55, 180–81, 194.

of the institutions of that province, in which he reaches the conclusion that colonial Massachusetts was already so fully democratic that no case can be made for an interpretation of the American Revolution there in terms of an internal 'class war.' It is in this connection that Brown broadens his front to develop an attack on Carl Becker.[7] The Revolution was a war of secession, fought for the preservation of American democracy against the anti-democratic policy of the crown. Nothing more, and nothing less. The joint foundations of all this are the wide extent of the suffrage franchise and the wide distribution of middling quantities of property.

The consequences are obvious. If the states, and not only the states but the colonies, were ruled by the consent of the governed, then Beard's unenfranchised masses disappear, and the Constitution is restored to its high place not only in the affection of the American people, but in their scale of approbation.

American history has been written not merely as the story of the people who went to, and lived in, America. It has been developed as the history of liberty. Innumerable books carry in their titles the message that colonial development was a progress toward liberty; since the Revolution, it has sometimes been possible to discern in accounts of American history a certain messianic quality, which some have felt to have been reflected periodically in American diplomacy. History written in this way frequently finds itself obliged to ask how a man, or a movement, stands in relation to the particular values for which American history is responsible. A recent study of Alexander Hamilton's place in the origins of political parties, for example, speaks of the need to determine Hamilton's 'rightful place in our history.'[8] It becomes important, not just to write a man's biography or to assess his contribution, but to place

7. Brown, *Middle-Class Democracy*, chap. IV.
8. Joseph E. Charles, 'Hamilton and Washington,' *William and Mary Quarterly*, XII (April 1955), 226. A further example in connection with Hamilton, whose career provokes this kind of judgement, is found in the title of Louis M. Hacker's *Alexander Hamilton in the American Tradition* (New York, 1957).

him correctly on the eternal curve upon which American political performances seem to be graded.

The writing of history thus becomes a matter, not only of finding out what actually happened, but of judging the past. It is a process that cuts both ways. For earlier generations of Americans were keenly—almost disconcertingly—aware of the example they were setting for their descendants. (There is a town meeting entry in Massachusetts, in 1766, which calls the attention of future generations to the sacrifices the townsmen were making for their liberties.[9]) They knew that they would be judged. They were not only building institutions, they were setting standards, for the future. This can become a nerve-racking business. As has been remarked in a different connection (by a writer in the *Times Literary Supplement*) the past and the present seem to watch each other warily as from opposite boxes at the opera, each suspecting the other of being about to commit a *faux pas*.[10]

The two great instruments of American nationhood were the Revolution with its banner, the Declaration of Independence, and the Constitution. Baptism and confirmation. It would be hard to imagine a more important commitment, not only for the interpretation of the American experience, but one might almost say for the emotional stability of the interpreter, than to place his own values in their proper relation to these events, or if that cannot be done, then to place these events in their proper relation to his values.

Accordingly, historians have brought the problem of values firmly into their assessment of history. They ask, 'How democratic was early American society?' And they do not hesitate to reply, if their findings tell them so, that it was not democratic enough. Or, which is still more confusing, that it was struggling forward toward a fuller ideal of democracy. Accounts of this period repeatedly

---

9. Lucius R. Paige, *A History of Cambridge, Massachusetts, 1630–1877* (New York, 1883), p. 137.

10. 'Imaginative Historians: Telling the News about the Past,' *Times Literary Supplement, Special Supplement on the American Imagination*, November 6, 1959.

explain that such features of government as property qualifications for the suffrage and political office were still regarded as necessary at that time. 'Still.' These people had the right instincts; they were coming on nicely; but, unlike ourselves, they had not yet arrived.

There thus develops a tendency to adopt a completely anachronistic note of apology for the insufficiency of democratic principles in early American institutions.[11]

I would like here to anticipate the objection that I am advocating that moral judgements should be taken out of historical writing. Neither do I deny that major developments can and ought to be traced to their minor origins. Moral judgements about the past are not necessarily anachronistic. It is not, I think, unhistorical to believe that some of the acts of treachery and cruelty or of violent aggression which comprise so great a proportion of recorded human activity were morally wrong, or even to maintain that they influenced the course of events for the worse. But when judgements of moral value are applied to complex social systems, they expose the judge to a peculiar danger of self-deception, perhaps even of self-incrimination. The historian must not only be careful, he must also be highly self-critical, when he embarks on assessments of the moral shortcomings of the past.

The reading of values into historical analysis is particularly liable to deception when the values of the present are themselves made the basis for the selection of materials, which are then judged in the light of the values in question. This may happen when the importance of different institutions or opinions is estimated on the basis of our own opinion of the role they ought to have played in their own time.

Without doubt there is a place for such judgements. There is a place for criticism of the Hanoverian House of Commons—rather a

---

11. Even Brown does so. In pointing out how few men were disfranchised in Massachusetts, he significantly remarks, 'We cannot condone the practice of excluding those few,' though he rightly adds that it makes a tremendous difference whether they were 95 per cent or 5 per cent. Brown, *Middle-Class Democracy*, p. 402.

large place. But when we discuss that body our task is not that of apologizing for the fact that the bright light of nineteenth-century democracy had not yet broken on such persons as Pitt or Burke or Shelburne or Fox. Our problem, as I understand it, is that of reconstructing the inner nature of political society in their age and of asking how far Parliament answered the needs of that society, and how far it did not. And that is a matter of what history was actually about, not what it ought to have been about. The historian has a responsibility to the past, but it is not that of deciding within what limits he can recommend it to the approbation of his readers.

The American Revolution was certainly a war for self-determination. But self-determination and democracy are not interchangeable terms, though they can be confused with a facility that has not been without its significance in American diplomacy. A society need not be democratic in order to achieve a high degree of internal unity when fighting for self-determination. Again, a measure of democracy, or a wider diffusion of political power, may well be brought about as an outcome of such a struggle. Such a development was in fact one of the most important consequences of the American Revolution.

It must be acknowledged that the sources of colonial history supply an impressive quantity of material that can be marshalled against my own views of this subject, though not enough as yet to weaken my conviction of the validity of historical evidence.

Much evidence of this sort comes from New England, and Massachusetts is rich in examples. In 1768 General Thomas Gage wrote to Viscount Hillsborough, 'from what has been said, your lordship will conclude, that there is no government in Boston, there is in truth, very little at present, and the constitution of the province leans so much to democracy, that the governor has not the power to remedy the disorders which happen in it.'[12] The next year Sir Francis Bernard wrote to Viscount Barrington,

12. *Correspondence of General Thomas Gage* . . . , ed. Clarence E. Carter (2 vols., New Haven, 1931, 1933), I, p. 205.

> . . . for these 4 years past so uniform a system for bringing all power into the hands of the people has been prosecuted without interruption and with such success that all fear, reverence, respect and awe which before formed a tolerable balance against the power of the people, are annihilated, and the artificial weights being removed, the royal scale mounts up and kicks the beam. . . . It would be better that Mass. Bay should be a complete republic like Connecticut than to remain with so few ingredients of royalty as shall be insufficient to maintain the real royal character.[13]

In 1766 Thomas Hutchinson reported: 'In the town of Boston a plebeian party always has and I fear always will command and for some months past they have governed the province.'[14] Describing elections in 1772, Hutchinson told Hillsborough, 'By the constitution forty pounds sterl.—which they say may be in clothes household furniture or any sort of property is a qualification and even into that there is scarce ever any inquiry and anything with the appearance of a man is admitted without scrutiny.'[15]

The franchise was certainly broad. Brown has shown that in many towns as many as 80 per cent of the adult male population, in some more than 90 per cent, were qualified by their property to vote in provincial elections.[16] Three towns appear in the nineties, three in the fifties, the rest in between. These findings tend to confirm and strengthen the impression that prevailed among contemporaries, that Massachusetts was a hotbed of 'democratical' or 'levelling' principles: the more so after the Boston junta got control of the General Court.

These expressions raise two issues, one of definition, the other of interpretation.

The point of definition first: when the indignant officers of government described these provinces as 'democratical,' they were of

13. Quoted by R. V. Harlow, *History of Legislative Methods before 1825* (New Haven, 1917), pp. 39–40.
14. Brown, *Middle-Class Democracy*, p. 57.
15. *Ibid.*, p. 291.
16. *Ibid.*, p. 50.

course not talking about representative government with universal suffrage. They shared not only with their correspondents, but in the last analysis even with their political opponents, the assumption that the constitutions of the colonies, like that of Britain, were made up of mixed elements; they were mixed constitutions, in which the commons were represented in the assembly or commons house. In each constitution there were different orders, and the justification, the *raison d'être*, of such a constitution was that it gave security to each. When they said that the government was becoming 'too democratical' or 'leaned towards democracy' they meant that the popular element was too weighty for the proper balance of a mixed constitution. They used these expressions as terms of abuse. Not that that matters: we may be impressed by their indignation, but we are not obliged to share it. What is more important to the historian is that the leaders of these movements which took control of the assemblies were in general prepared to accept the same set of definitions.

This they demonstrated when they came to establish new constitutions. The theory of mixed government was maintained with as little adulteration as possible. The difference they had to face was that all the 'orders' now drew their position in the government from some form of popular representation. Most of the new constitutions represented the adaptation of institutions which undeniably received their authority from the people, an authority conceived, if not in liberty, then certainly in a revolutionary situation, to the traditional and equally important theory of balanced government.

This does not dispose of the second point, that of interpretation. Suppose that, in this form of mixed government, the 'democratical' arm actually gathers up a preponderance of political power. This, after all, was what happened in the Revolution and had been happening long before. Does this give us a democracy? It is a question of crucial importance and one to which one school of thought returns an uncritically affirmative answer. Much of the power and internal influence within each colony was indeed concentrated in its assembly. This concentration reflected, or rather represented, the distribution of power and influence in the colony in general. If the domestic distribution of power tends toward oligarchy rather than democracy—to use the language of the time—then the power of that oligarchy will be exercised in, and through, the assembly itself: just as in the House of Commons. A difference of degree, not of kind. And in fact this most significant aspect of the domestic situation in the colonies applied with hardly less force in levelling Boston than in high-toned Virginia.

In Virginia one feels that an immigrant from England would at once have been at home.[17] There were many instances of hotly contested elections, of treating and corruption, of sharp practice by sheriffs. It would not be difficult, however, to adduce evidence of democratic tendencies in Virginia elections. Especially in the spring elections of 1776 there were many signs that the freeholders were taking their choice seriously, and several distinguished gentlemen were either turned out of their seats or given a nasty fright. But it is an unmistakable feature of Virginia elections that although the freeholders participated often quite fully, the contests were almost invariably between members of the gentry. To seek election to the House of Burgesses was to stake a distinct claim to social rank. Virginia elections were of course conducted viva voce under the friendly supervision of the local magnates. The comparatively broad base of politics in Virginia makes it all the more instructive to look into the real concentration of political power. There were two main areas: the House of Burgesses and the county courts (not taking account of the council and governor).

Effective power in the House of Burgesses was concentrated in a few hands. The house began to use the committee system in the late seventeenth century and had brought it to a high efficiency well before the middle of the eighteenth.[18] The famous Virginia

17. Charles S. Sydnor, *Gentlemen Freeholders* (Chapel Hill, 1952); David J. Mays, *Edmund Pendleton, 1721–1803* (2 vols., Cambridge, Mass., 1952); J. R. Pole, 'Representation and Authority in Virginia from the Revolution to Reform,' *Journal of Southern History*, XXIV (February 1958), 16–50.

18. Harlow, *Legislative Methods*, pp. 10–11.

ruling families of this era always occupied a large share of the key positions, enough to ensure their own domination. Before the Revolution, of some hundred members who regularly attended the house, only about twenty took an active part in proceedings. Three families, the Robinsons, the Randolphs, and the Lees, provided most of the leaders. A very recent study shows that of 630 members between 1720 and 1776, only 110 belonged throughout the period to the 'select few who dominated the proceedings of the house.'[19]

These men, many of whom were linked by ties of family, had the characteristics of a strong social and political elite. They were large landowners and generally were substantial slave-owners. Some were merchants. A few, such as Edmund Pendleton, had arrived by intellectual ability and hard work combined with legal training. But Pendleton had the patronage of a great family. All those with ambition were land speculators. This gave them an interest in western development, an interest which no doubt extended to the policy of making western areas attractive to the prospective settler. Probably for this reason they wanted to extend the suffrage, which they twice tried to do in the 1760s by reducing the amount of uncleared land required as a qualification. The crown disallowed these acts, though on other grounds. This reform was completed in the first election law after the Revolution. Despite the famous reforms pressed through by Jefferson, no concessions were made on matters of fundamental importance. It is a striking tribute to the tremendous security of their hold on the country that in the new state constitution there was no provision for special qualifications for membership in the legislature. The qualifications of voters and of representatives for the time being remained as before. It is a silent piece of evidence, possibly, but one that speaks loudly of their eminent self-confidence.

Life in the counties was dominated by the county courts, which

19. Jack P. Greene, 'Foundations of Political Power in the Virginia House of Burgesses, 1720–1766,' *William and Mary Quarterly*, XVI (October 1959), 485–506; quotation from p. 485.

touched the interests of the common people far more closely than did the remote and occasional meetings of the legislature. The courts, which knew little of any doctrine of separation of powers, exercised all the main functions of both legislative and judicial administration. These included tax assessment, granting licenses, supervising highways, and authorizing constructions. They had nothing elective in their nature. Membership was by co-option. The courts made the important county nominations for confirmation by the governor. And the county courts were made up of the leading men of the county, representing at the local level the material of which the House of Burgesses was composed at the central. They seem on the whole to have worked well enough. And it is likely that if they had in fact been elected by the freeholders, their membership would have been about the same. Assuredly they were not tyrannical; equally certainly they were not democratic. They were a good example of what is usually meant by oligarchy.

What happened in the American Revolution in Virginia was that the policies of the British government clashed with the interests of this ambitious, proud, self-assured, and highly competent provincial government. In arguing its case, both to the British authorities and to its own people, this government appealed to the principles on which it claimed to be founded, which were philosophically the same and historically comparable to those of Parliament itself. For historical reasons, the Virginia Whigs were somewhat closer to the radical, or popular side, of the Whig spectrum. But in Virginia as in other provinces, it was the principles generally understood as Whig principles that were at stake, and it was these principles which were affirmed and re-established in the new set of domestic state constitutions.

From time to time, as the war went on, the upper classes felt tremors of alarm in which they revealed something of their relationship to the common people.

Thus John Augustine Washington, writing to Richard Henry Lee of the difficulties of getting the militia to obey a marching order, and the secret proceedings by which they bound themselves to stand by each other in refusing to leave the state, remarked: 'I fear we have among us some designing dangerous characters who misrepresent to ignorant, uninformed people, the situation of our affairs and the nature of the contest, making them believe it is a war produced by the wantonness of the gentlemen, and that the poor are very little, if any interested.'[20] Another of Lee's correspondents, on the need to arouse popular support, wrote: 'The spark of liberty is not yet extinct among our people, and if properly fanned by the Gentlemen of Influence will, I make no doubt, burst out again into a flame.'[21]

These hints, these references which illuminate the assumptions of political life, often reveal more than formal expositions of doctrine, or even the official records.

These 'Gentlemen of Influence,' the ruling class, were prepared to extend the suffrage when it suited their interest to do so in the 1760s, but refused to take the same step when it would have opened the question of political power, a generation later. The first demands for reform, in both suffrage and distribution of representation, began to appear about the turn of the century. And these demands were met with a prolonged and bitter resistance, leading only to reluctant and unsatisfactory concessions even in the famous constitutional convention of 1829–30. The struggle was carried on until a more substantial extension of political rights was at last achieved in 1850. The forces that Virginia's political leadership so long and so determinedly held at bay can, I think, without exaggeration, be called the forces of democracy.

It is a very familiar fact about the early state constitutions that they were generally conservative in character, in that they retained much of the principles and structure of the governments of the colonies. The colonies were already self-governing in the main, and this self-government was administered by representative institutions. When one's attention is confined to these institutions, it can soon become rather difficult to see in what respect they were

20. Quoted in Pole, 'Representation and Authority in Virginia,' 28.
21. *Ibid.*, pp. 28–29.

not, in a common-sense use of the word, democratic. After all, they were accessible to the people, they received petitions and redressed grievances, they possessed the inestimable right of free speech, and in the battles they fought, they were often engaged, in the interest of the colonies, against royal governors.

All these features were not merely consistent with, they were the formative elements of, the great Whig tradition of Parliament since the Glorious Revolution and before. They were, like so many other things, derivable from Locke. With certain exceptions, such as the difficulty of the Regulator rising in North Carolina, it would be true that colonial assemblies lay closer to the people than did the British House of Commons. For one thing, there were far more representatives per head of population in the colonies than in Britain. Parliament had one member to every 14,300 persons, the colonies approximately one to every 1,200.[22] And this meant that legislative methods and principles were more likely to be familiar to the ordinary colonist. To put it in contemporary terms, the colonies, on the whole, had a great many more constituencies like Middlesex or Westminster, except that they were mostly country and not town constituencies. It might be very close to the mark to press the analogy further and say that they had a great many constituencies that very much resembled Yorkshire—the Yorkshire of Sir George Savile, the Yorkshire of Christopher Wyvill.

What does seem striking about these in many ways highly representative colonial assemblies is, as I suggested earlier, the determination and sureness of touch with which they assumed the characteristics of Parliament. These were characteristics originally designed to secure the liberty of the people's representatives: free speech in debate, freedom of members from arrest or molestation, and freedom of the assembly from abuse by breach of privilege. But there were all too many occasions on which it must have seemed that these safeguards were designed to secure the as-

22. Mary P. Clarke, *Parliamentary Privilege in the American Colonies* (New Haven, 1943), p. 268.

semblies against abuse, in the form of free speech and fair comment, by their own constituents.[23]

The colonial assemblies became extraordinarily sensitive to the question of privilege. Strictly from an institutional viewpoint, they were deliberately building on the tradition of Parliament. But institutional studies always seem to tempt the historian to arrive at his answer the short way, by examining structure, without asking questions about development.

Much research has recently been done on what Palmer calls the 'constituted bodies'[24] which held a strong and growing position in the Western world in the eighteenth century. They were numerous and differed greatly, one from another, and from one century to another—first of all the variety of political or judicial bodies: diets, estates, assemblies, parlements; then the professional associations or guilds; as well as religious orders, and those of the nobilities of Europe.

There seems strong reason for holding that the colonial assemblies were behaving in close conformity with the other bodies of this general type. At their best they were closer to local interests, but no less characteristically, they displayed a remarkable diligence in the adoption of parliamentary abuses. They would send their messengers far into the outlying country to bring to the bar of the house some individual who was to be humbled for having committed a breach of privilege, which very often meant some private action affecting the dignity or even the property of the sitting member. Criticism of the assemblies, either verbal or written, was a risky business. The freedom of the colonial press was very largely at the mercy of the assembly's sense of its own dignity, so much so that a recent investigator doubts whether the famous Zenger case,[25] which is supposed to have done so much toward the es-

23. *Ibid.*, p. 127.
24. Palmer, *Democratic Revolution*, pp. 27–44.
25. Leonard W. Levy, 'Did the Zenger Case Really Matter? Freedom of the Press in Colonial New York,' *William and Mary Quarterly*, XVII (January 1960), 35–50.

tablishment of freedom of the press in the colonies, really had any general significance or immediate consequences. The fact is that restrictions on free press comment on assembly actions were not the policy of the crown but the policy of the assemblies.

Expulsions from colonial assemblies were frequent. And in case a parallel with the action of the Commons in the Wilkes case were needed to round off the picture, we may remark that colonial assemblies repeatedly excluded members who had been lawfully elected by their constituents.[26]

There was another feature in which these assemblies showed their affinity with the outlook of their times. In spite of the amount of choice open to the electors, there was a growing tendency for public office, both the elective and the appointive kinds, to become hereditary. It was of course very pronounced in Europe; it is surely no less significant when we see it at work in America. The same family names occur, from generation to generation, in similar positions. And this was no less true in New England than in Virginia or South Carolina or Maryland.

If this was democracy, it was a democracy that wore its cockade firmly pinned into its periwig.

One of the most interesting consequences of the revolution situation was that it demanded of political leaders a declaration of their principles. Thus we get the famous Virginia Bill of Rights, the work of George Mason; the Declaration of Rights attached to the 1780 constitution of Massachusetts; and the constitutions themselves, with all that they reveal or imply of political ideas; and in the case of Massachusetts we can go even further, for there survive also, in the archives of that state in Boston, the returns of the town meetings which debated that constitution and in many cases recorded their vote, clause by clause.

This constitution, in fact, was submitted to the ratification of what counted then as the whole people—all the adult males in the state. The constitutional convention had been elected on the same

26. Clarke, *Parliamentary Privilege*, pp. 194–96.

basis. The constitution which was framed on this impressive foundation of popular sovereignty was certainly not a democratic instrument. It was an articulate, indeed a refined expression, of the Whig view of government—of government-in-society—as applied to the existing conditions in Massachusetts, and as interpreted by John Adams.

The property qualifications for the suffrage were, in round figures, about what they had been under the charter. In practice they proved to have very little effect by way of restricting participation in elections. The introduction of decidedly steeper qualifications for membership in the assembly meant that the body would be composed of the owners of the common, upward of one-hundred-acre family farm, and their mercantile equivalent. The pyramid narrowed again to the senate, and came to a point in the position of governor. These restrictions were new, but gave little offense to the general sense of political propriety; the suffrage qualifications were objected to in about one-fifth of the recorded town meeting debates.[27]

The house and senate represented different types of constituency, and the difference is one of the clues to institutional thought. The house represented the persons of the electorate living in corporate towns, which were entitled to representation according to a numerical scale of population; very small communities were excluded. The town remained the basic unit of representation. The senate, on the other hand, represented the property of the state arranged in districts corresponding to the counties; the number of members to which each county was entitled depended, not on population, but on the taxes it had paid into the state treasury. The

27. The constitution of 1780 is discussed in: S. E. Morison, 'The Struggle over the Adoption of the Constitution of Massachusetts, 1780,' Massachusetts Historical Society *Proceedings*, L (Boston, 1916–17), 353–412; Robert J. Taylor, *Western Massachusetts in the Revolution* (Providence, R.I., 1954); J. R. Pole, 'Suffrage and Representation in Massachusetts: A Statistical Note,' *William and Mary Quarterly*, XIV (October 1957), 560–92. The town meeting records are in Volumes CCLXXVI and CCLXXVII in the Massachusetts Department of Archives, the State House, Boston.

result in distribution of representatives in the senate was not actually much different from the apportionment that would have been obtained by population,[28] but the intention was there, and the plan conformed to the principles of political order by which the delegates were guided.[29]

New York, which established popular election of its governor, and North Carolina took the matter further by differentiating between the qualifications of voters for the senate and the house of representatives.

How then are we to explain the paradox of popular consent to a scheme of government which systematically excluded the common people from the more responsible positions of political power? The historian who wishes to adopt the word 'democracy' as a definition must first satisfy himself that it can be applied to a carefully ordered hierarchy, under the aegis of which power and authority are related to a conscientiously designed scale of social and economic rank, both actual and prospective; if this test fails him, then he must ask himself whether he can call the system a democracy, on the ground that it was a form of government established with the consent of the governed. Those who wish to argue this line have the advantage of finding much serviceable material that can be adopted without the rigors, or the risks, of a historically minded analysis. It is possible to concentrate all attention on those aspects of the system which we would now call democratic, to assert that these elements exerted a controlling influence and that all the rest was a sort of obsolescent window dressing. Such a view may not be particularly subtle, but on the other hand it is not absolute nonsense. It is, perhaps, the easiest view to arrive at through an extensive reading of local economic records in the light of a clear, but vastly simplified interpretation of the political process; but it leaves

28. As noted by Palmer, *Democratic Revolution*, p. 226.

29. It may be permissible to mention that Brown, in his study of this constitution, omits to note this provision for tax payment as the basis of county representation. In itself, this may seem a small clue, but the thread leads into another world of political ideas than that of modern democracy. Brown, *Middle-Class Democracy*, p. 393.

unfulfilled the rather more complex task of perceiving the democratic elements in their proper place within a system conceived in another age, under a different inspiration.

In the Whig philosophy of government the basic principle, preceding representative institutions, is the compact. The people already owned their property by natural right, and they are supposed to have come into the compact quite voluntarily to secure protection both to their property and to their persons. For these purposes government was formed. What was done in Massachusetts seems to have been a solemn attempt to re-enact the original compact in the new making of the state. It was even possible to deploy the theory of compact as an excuse for seizing other people's property: in 1782 the legislature of Virginia resolved that the estates of British subjects might be confiscated because they had not been parties to the original contract of the people of that state.[30] And the Virginia constitution had not even been submitted for popular ratification!

Massachusetts and New Hampshire, in fact, were the only states in which popular ratification was sought for the revolutionary constitution. In a society whose moral cohesion was supplied by the sense of deference and dignity, it was possible for the broad mass of the people to consent to a scheme of government in which their own share would be limited. Some of them of course expected to graduate to the higher levels; government was not controlled by inherited rank.

This factor—the expectation of advancement—is an important feature of the American experience; it is one which is often used to excuse the injustice of exclusion from government by economic status. The *Address* that the Massachusetts convention delegates drew up in 1780 to expound the principles on which they had acted makes the point that most of those excluded by the suffrage qualification could expect to rise sufficiently in their own property to reach the level of voters. The exclusion of the artisan and la-

30. Edmund Randolph to James Madison, Richmond, December 27, 1782, Madison Papers, Manuscript Division, Library of Congress.

bourer from the assembly was, however, more likely to prove permanent.

It would be a mistake to suppose that the body of citizens included in the electoral system at one level or another, or expecting to gain their inclusion, was really the whole body. There are always farm labourers, journeymen, migrant workers, and one may suspect that the numbers excluded by law were larger than the terms of the *Address* suggest. But even if we are disposed to accept the high level of popular participation in elections as being weighty enough to determine our definitions, it is surely wise to pause even over the legal disfranchisement of one man in every four or five, and in some towns one man in three.

This constitutional scheme was derived from a mixture of experience, theory, and intention. It is the intention for the future which seems to call for scrutiny when we attempt a satisfactory definition of these institutions.

In the first place there is the deliberate disfranchisement of the small, perhaps the unfortunate, minority; the fact that the number is small is not more significant than that the exclusion is deliberate. In the second place, there is the installation of orders of government corresponding to orders of society; the fact that the lines are imprecise and that the results are uncertain is again not more significant than that the scale is deliberate.

It was a rule of Whig ideology that participation in matters of government was the legitimate concern only of those who possessed what was commonly called 'a stake in society.' In concrete terms this stake in society was one's property, for the protection of which, government had been originally formed. As a means to that protection, he was entitled, under a government so formed, to a voice: to some form of representation.

But there is a further problem. To put it briefly, what is to happen if the expected general economic advancement does not take place? Accumulations of wealth were far from being unknown; what if the further accumulation of wealth and the advance of the economy were to leave an ever-increasing residue of the popula-

tion outside the political limits set by these constitutions? It is unlikely that their framers were ignorant of such possibilities. The
growth of Sheffield, Manchester, and Leeds was not unknown;
London was not easy to overlook; the Americans had close ties
with Liverpool and Bristol. The fact is that a future town proletariat would be specifically excluded by the arrangements that were
being made.

The historian who insists that this system was a model of democracy may find that the advance of the economy, a tendency already
affecting America in many ways, leaves him holding a very un-
democratic-looking baby. In the Philadelphia Convention, James
Madison bluntly predicted that in future times 'the great majority'
would be 'not only without landed, but any other sort of,
property'—a state in which they would either combine, to the
peril of property and liberty, or become the tools of opulence and
ambition, leading to 'equal danger on the other side.'[31] The objection became common when state constitutions were under reform.
Opponents of suffrage extension in the constitutions of the 1820s,
who included many of the recognized leaders of political life, had a
better right than their opponents to claim to be the legitimate
heirs of the Whig constitution makers of the revolutionary era.

The constitution of the two legislative houses was based on the
view that society was formed for the protection of persons and
their property and that these two elements required separate protection and separate representation. This was one of the leading
political commonplaces of the day. It is implied by Montesquieu;
Jefferson accepts it in his *Notes on Virginia;* Madison held the view
throughout his career; Hamilton treated it as a point of common
agreement.[32] It is worth adding that it lay behind the original con-

31. *Records of the Federal Convention,* ed. Max Farrand (4 vols., New Haven,
  1927), II, 203–4.
32. Charles de Secondat, Baron de Montesquieu, *Œuvres complètes* (Paris, 1838),
  De l'esprit des lois, p. 267; James Madison, *Writings,* ed. Gaillard Hunt (9
  vols., New York, 1910), V, p. 287; Hamilton's speech in *Debates and Proceedings of Convention of New York, at Poughkeepsie 1788* (Poughkeepsie, N.Y.,
  1905), p. 26.

ception of the United States Senate in the form envisaged by the
Virginia plan, a form which subverted when the Senate became
the representative chamber of the states. The whole subject was,
of course, familiar to John Adams, who went on thinking about it
long after he had drawn up a draft for the constitution of his state
in 1780.

John Adams, as he himself anticipated, has been a much-misun-
derstood man. But it is important that we should get him right. No
American was more loyal to Whig principles, and none was more
deeply read in political ideas.

Adams is often said to have been an admirer of aristocracy and of
monarchy. His admiration for the British constitution was easy to
treat as an admission of unrepublican principles. But he really
believed in the British constitution as it ought to have been, and
he prudently averted his gaze from what it was in his own day. If
Adams had lived in England in the 1780s, he would have been an
associator in Wyvill's parliamentary reform movement, rather than
a Foxite Whig.

Adams was profoundly impressed with the advantages enjoyed
by birth, wealth, superior education, and natural merit, and the
tendency for these advantages to become an inherited perquisite of
the families that enjoyed them. He was equally clear about the
corrupting influence of this sort of power. For this reason he
wanted to segregate the aristocracy in an upper chamber, a process
which he called 'a kind of ostracism.' The strong executive in
which he believed was intended as a check not on the commons so
much as on the aristocracy.

He developed this view of the function of the upper chamber in
his *Defence of the Constitutions of the United States* (1786–1787).
It is not wholly consistent with the view given in the *Address* [33] attached to the draft Massachusetts constitution of 1780, in which
the line taken was that persons and property require separate protection in different houses. This view is itself a reflection of more

33. This, however, was the work of Samuel Adams. (William V. Wells, *The Life
and Public Services of Samuel Adams* (3 vols., Boston, 1865), III, pp. 89–97.)

than one tradition. It reflects the traditional structure of the legislature—council and assembly, lords and commons; it reflects also the idea that the state is actually composed of different orders (a word of which John Adams was fond) and that these orders have in their own right specific interests which are entitled to specific recognition. They are entitled to it because it is the purpose of the state to secure and protect them: that in fact was why the state was supposed to have come into existence.

Adams once, in later years, wrote to Jefferson: 'Your *aristoi* are the most difficult animals to manage in the whole theory and practice of government. They will not suffer themselves to be governed.'[34] Yet in spite of his intense distrust of them, I think his attitude was two-sided. I find it difficult to read his account of the role played in society by the aristocracy without feeling that there was to him, as there is to many others, something peculiarly distinguished and attractive about these higher circles, elevated by nature and sustained by society above the ordinary run of men. And had he not, after all, sons for whom he had some hopes? Some hopes, perhaps, for the family of Adams?

Governor Bernard had lamented the disappearance from pre-Revolutionary Massachusetts of those balancing factors, 'Fear, reverence, respect and awe.' Disappearance at least toward the royal authority. They did not disappear so easily from domestic life. There is nothing which reveals these deferential attitudes more fully than in respect to birth and family, given on trust. Adams therefore tells us much, not only of himself but of his times, when he draws attention to inequality of birth:

> Let no man be surprised that this species of inequality is introduced here. Let the page in history be quoted, where any nation, ancient or modern, civilized or savage, is mentioned, among whom no difference was made, between the citizens, on account of their extraction. The truth is, that more influence is allowed to this advantage in free republics than in despotic governments, or would be allowed to it in simple mon-

34. Quoted in Palmer, *Democratic Revolution*, p. 273, n. 52.

archies, if severe laws had not been made from age to age to secure it. The children of illustrious families have generally greater advantages of education, and earlier opportunities to be acquainted with public characters, and informed of public affairs, than those of meaner ones, or even than those in middle life; and what is more than all, a habitual national veneration for their names, and the characters of their ancestors, described in history, or coming down by tradition, removes them farther from vulgar jealousy and popular envy, and secures them in some degree the favour, the affection, the respect of the public. Will any man pretend that the name of Andros, and that of Winthrop, are heard with the same sensations in any village of New England? Is not gratitude the sentiment that attends the latter? And disgust the feeling excited by the former? In the Massachusetts, then, there are persons descended from some of their ancient governors, counsellors, judges, whose fathers, grandfathers, and great-grandfathers, are mentioned in history with applause as benefactors to the country, while there are others who have no such advantage. May we go a step further,—Know thyself, is as useful a precept to nations as to men. Go into every village in New England, and you will find that the office of justice of the peace, and even the place of representative, which has ever depended only on the freest election of the people, have generally descended from generation to generation, in three or four families at most.[35]

Deference: it does not seem, in retrospect, a very secure cement to the union of social orders. Yet to those who live under its sway it can be almost irresistible.

It was beginning to weaken, no doubt, in Adams's own political lifetime. 'The distinction of classes,' Washington said to Brissot de Warville in 1788, 'begins to disappear.' But not easily, not all at once, not without a struggle.

It was this which collapsed in ruins in the upheaval of Jacksonian democracy. And that, perhaps, is why the election of so ambiguous a leader was accompanied by such an amazing uproar.

35. John Adams, *Defence of the Constitutions of the United States* . . . (3 vols., Philadelphia, 1797), I, pp. 110–11.

10

The American Past: Is It Still Usable?
(1967)

The past, in the course of its ever-recurring encounters with the demands inflicted on it by the present, enjoys one inestimable advantage: it cannot answer, it is not even listening. 'We ask and ask, thou smilest and art still,' we might almost say, giving to Arnold's ponderous lines a touch of unintended meaning. In spite of appearances to the contrary, even the American past is in the same position. Even after the lapse (the 'revolution,' as Gibbon would have said) of more than three and a half centuries of continuous settlement, the historian who has been educated entirely in the tradition and the environment of the United States needs rather more than his European contemporary's normal degree of subtlety if he is to free himself from the peculiarly American version of the space-time continuum.

Those Virginians who still talk about Mr. Jefferson as though he might, at any moment, train his telescope on them from Monticello, the distinguished historian of Reconstruction who, emerging from a Southern archive and blinking at the day's newspapers,

This essay was first published in *Journal of American Studies*, Vol. 1, No. 1 (1967).

felt a momentary uncertainty as to which century he was actually in or whether any time had passed, the politicians who invoke the ideals of the Founders as though these gentlemen, if alive, would not in fact be over 200 years old and possibly beyond giving a useful opinion, are all inhabitants of this remarkable continuum, this eternal triangle of space, time, and political ideology. It is as though any part of the continent, and any period, could be visited simply by virtue of the efficiency of the tourist trade. Although the people who lived in earlier centuries may, by some accident in the providential design, be technically dead, they remain to a peculiar degree the property of their heirs and successors; what one misses is that sense, inescapable in Europe, of the total, crumbled irrecoverability of the past, of its differentness, of the fact that it is dead.

This situation makes room for, and indeed it partly results from, the persistent force of what may well be called the American extension of the Whig interpretation of history.[1] In its cruder recent forms this attitude has been given by some of its critics the inelegant name of 'presentism'; by which is meant that the historian plants his own political values, or those which he thinks belong to his own time, in the minds of the people of the past, and approves of their achievements or judges their shortcomings according to these present-day standards. There are, of course, a number of variants, connected in part with varieties of temperament, and in large part with the prevailing political controversies amid which the historian has found himself; but the Whig interpretation, in American hands, has always taken the view that the United States as a nation was responsible for the preservation and advancement of certain ascertained values, and hence to discover, record, and celebrate these values was the peculiar duty that the historian owed to his country.

It would be impertinent to suggest that the Whigs have had it all their own way. But patriotic history has almost always been iden-

1. Herbert Butterfield, *The Whig Interpretation of History* (Cambridge, 1931).

tical with Whig history, and these two strands had an early meeting in the work of George Bancroft.[2] Bancroft, it is true, did not succeed in getting the story of America beyond the Federal Convention of 1787, but he was himself a Jacksonian politician and a dedicated Democrat, and it was he who gave the most effective impetus to the idea that American history should be celebrated as the triumph of democratic principles.

It follows that the works of American politicians and others must be evaluated according to their contributions to the advancement of those principles. Those who obstructed, or who saw their problems in some different light, or who sought a path that went over a precipice—these are mere historical curiosities: what defines them is that by the final test, that of democratic success, they are not truly American. It is the fate of the Loyalists, the Federalists, the Confederacy; if some historians of the New Deal have their way it may even prove the fate of the Republicans; even the Antifederalists have only narrowly escaped it.

Before the end of the nineteenth century, the issues of contemporary politics had begun to suggest the need for some redefinition of the actual objects of American democracy; and it was as a consequence of these conflicts that historians who were themselves dedicated to the Progressive movement began to forge American history into an instrument of political action. The immense, almost oppressive veneration for the Constitution, its use by the courts as itself an instrument of capital against labour, and the bitter strife that had grown up as a result of recent economic development—these things make it seem inevitable that social scientists and even historians should have begun to marshal their own resources on the side of reform. They knew what they were about and soon began to get the feeling of the resources at their disposal; certainly they were not driven blindly into this position by the circumstances of their times. The functional application of historical writing was deliberately proposed in 1912 by James Harvey Robin-

2. George Bancroft: *History of the United States*, 6 vols. (Boston, 1879); *Formation of the Constitution*, 2 vols. (Boston, 1882).

son in the cause of liberal reform,[3] and was carried forward by a giant stride with the appearance, the next year, of Beard's tract on the economic motives of the framers of the Constitution.[4]

This famous tract performed a service of intellectual liberation that was very badly needed, but it did more than that: by virtue of innuendoes whose implications Beard disclaimed, and by the selection of evidence to support a specific conclusion, it inflicted on more than a generation of historians an excessively narrow view of the issues and an almost unavoidable necessity to take sides in a controversy that even now is not fully worked out. Beard, of course, was striking a powerful blow, not at the Constitution of 1787 but at the Constitution in 1913; and this motive gives the clue to the instrumentalist direction that American historiography was to extract from its Whig foundations. Each stage in the argument was proposed, not by a question (in Collingwood's manner) but by an objective: the significance of the whole procedure being that the objective lay in the historian's own contemporary social and political interests rather than in those properly pertaining to the past.

Instrumental historians gained their sense of direction from social conflict. But in the intellectual development of their views of the nature of historical thought they owed a great deal to European as well as to American philosophy. The leading European influence was that of Benedetto Croce, who was a young man in the 1890s turned against the traditions of positivist realism and whose mature philosophy embraced history as a mode of the historian's own thought—a procedure that tied it down as an expression of 'present' experience. American instrumentalists saw in this thesis the justification for their own obvious relativism: if their historical thought were relative to their own values and interests, so had been

3. James Harvey Robison, *The New History* (New York, 1912), pp. 15, 24; Chester McArthur Destler, 'Some Observations on Contemporary Historical Theory,' *American Historical Review*, 55 (April 1950), 503, n. 3.
4. Charles A. Beard, *An Economic Interpretation of the Constitution of the United States* (New York, 1913).

those of all their rivals and predecessors! The reception of Freudian psychology, which began early in the century and had great influence in the 1920s, seemed to those who were inclined to read it in that light to go still further towards justifying a psychology and hence a philosophy of subjective and therefore relativist values. On the American side lay the active influence of the specifically 'instrumentalist' philosophy of John Dewey.[5]

Beard himself had absorbed much of the feeling of the American Populists and had adopted much of the method learnt from Marx. His instrumentalism, however, is characteristic of that of his more orthodox contemporaries in his method of selecting a simple dichotomy of opposed forces. The broad and rough outline of a division, discernible in the later eighteenth century, between mercantile and agrarian interests, became for Beard a precursor of the class war; the immense weight of landed interest that was thrown behind the Constitution could be by-passed as simply irrelevant to his view of what the struggle was all about. In lining up the two sides Beard assumed that the mercantile and moneyed interests, because 'capitalist,' were conservative, and by inference opposed to the democratic principles of American progress; which meant that the agricultural interest was also the popular and democratic side in the struggle. The fact that the leadership and probably the bulk of the agrarian interests were in important respects profoundly conservative, while the capitalists were, in an economic sense, dynamically progressive, was overlooked because it was irrelevant to the particular conflict on which his attention was riveted.

It was consistent with this method that when Beard came to the Civil War and to Reconstruction he applied a similar analysis, and that he and his disciples discovered in the capitalist North an aggressive business spirit whose interests explained the Radical Republican programme and their victory in the elections of 1866.[6]

5. Destler, 'Contemporary Historical Theory,' *loc. cit.*, pp. 503–6; R. G. Collingwood, *The Idea of History* (Oxford, 1946).
6. Howard K. Beale, *The Critical Year: A Study of Andrew Johnson and Reconstruction* (New York, 1930). Charles and Mary Beard, *The Rise of American Civilization*, revised edition (New York, 1949), chap. xviii.

The Civil War itself was interpreted as a collision between the capitalist North and the agrarian and basically feudal South—an extension of the dualism that Beard had found earlier in American history. It is perhaps odd that Beard, who wrote with great insight about the clash of interests in politics,[7] and who virtually discovered the 10th Federalist, should have yielded his powerful intellect so easily to the idea of a recurring dichotomy that he virtually overlooked the pluralistic nature of American politics.

These remarks are not made here for the sake of reviving controversies or reviewing the now familiar ground on which Beard and his disciples have grappled with their opponents, but to indicate one of the most persistent styles in American historiography. Running through all the grades of this style, a strand that is at once utilitarian and populistic seeks to explain to a skeptical audience that the justification for the study of history is practical; it helps us to understand the present, and can become, in dedicated hands, an instrument of action.

The most extreme statement of this instrumental view of history came, not from the Progressive Movement, but from Conyers Read, in his Presidential Address to the American Historical Association in 1949.[8] In a candid and unusual bid to qualify as the Zhdanov of the profession, Read disparaged both the work and the interests of those dedicated historians who take the past seriously for its own sake. 'It is the rare bird,' he said, 'who is interested in the past simply as the past—a world remote, apart, complete, such as Michael Oakeshott has envisaged.' Read took the view that the liberal age, 'characterized by a plurality of aims and values,' was a thing of the past, and that 'we must clearly assume a militant attitude if we are to survive.' This militant attitude involved the organization of resources and the disciplined interpretation of history towards the propagation of American doctrines. 'This sounds,' he added, 'like the advocacy of one form of social control as against

7. Charles A. Beard, *The Economic Basis of Politics and Related Writings,* comp. William Beard (New York, 1958).

8. Conyers Read, 'The Social Responsibilities of the Historian,' *American Historical Review,* 55, No. 2 (January 1950).

another. In short, it is. But I see no alternative in a divided world.' His reassurance that his concept of control meant 'no menace to essential freedoms' could hardly have satisfied those whose views and interests might have run the risk of proving inessential.

In a subtler form the instrumentalist version of the Whig tradition reappeared among certain historians whose early political memories were those of the New Deal. Arthur M. Schlesinger, Jr., whose *Age of Jackson* [9] remains after twenty years a work of extraordinary vitality and intelligence, quoted Franklin D. Roosevelt in his preface and argued explicitly that Roosevelt had carried forward a process which Jackson had inaugurated, but which had subsequently been submerged by other issues. It would not be altogether unfair to Professor Schlesinger (at any rate when he wrote *The Age of Jackson* at twenty-eight) to say that in his view the forces on the other side, the Bank of the United States, or the combinations of monopoly capitalism, represent reaction in much the same sense that the Roman Catholic Church represented reaction to earlier historians of Protestantism; and that the Democratic side, which happily emerges as the winning side, is the more American.

Historians of different temperament have always known that there was an alternative to all this. It begins with a fundamental respect for the integrity of the past in which the instrumental view has no place because its aims are irrelevant. It approaches the subject matter of history without intense presuppositions and with a mind in which convictions (however strongly held) about right and wrong have been subordinated to a profound curiosity as to what was thought about right and wrong in the period under scrutiny. It places a deep absorption in the substance and detail of history on a higher level of priority than the principles which it expects to discover; it starts, of course, with a hypothesis but this hypothesis is almost invariably modified if not abandoned in the course of the research.

9. Boston, 1946. In the same connection see Eric F. Goldman, *Rendezvous with Destiny* (New York, 1952).

The results often tend to be less spectacular and less susceptible of literary grandiosity than those of the progressive, or reactionary, instrumentalists. Yet they are worth noting, because, if they are properly understood, they not only come nearer the truth but they change the message received at this end of the line. Vernon L. Parrington, a literary historian whose work was an outstanding example of the Progressive school, thought that an early example of political progressiveness was to be discovered in Roger Williams, the founder of Rhode Island. Under this impression, Parrington chose to interpret Williams's work as being inspired by political interests and the ideals of democracy. But Professor Alan Simpson, in an article which should be carefully read for its general as well as its immediate reflections, went back to the texts of Roger Williams's work and showed that his preoccupations were overwhelmingly religious. If he was a 'democrat' it was by indirection and as a result of the circumstances he was in.[10]

It would be grossly unjust to suggest that the elders of the present generation have missed the complexities that are more clearly apparent to their successors. The difference has always been one rather of temperament and interest than of age. Professor Carl Bridenbaugh has built up for us a body of information about the early life of American cities in books that will last longer than many a fast-selling work of popularization or propaganda; and the works of those major New England historians, the late Perry Miller and Samuel Eliot Morison, do more to bring the past to life than those which have a point to prove about the present. But there is also, in recent years, an increasing appreciation of the variety of voices that speak from the past to those who are willing to listen, 'Each generation,' we are often told, 'reinterprets history in the light of its own interests.' But each generation happily contains many independent minds with a great variety of intelligent interests: so that the arguments for pure historical relativism lead either

10. Vernon Louis Parrington, *Main Currents in American Thought*, 3 vols. (New York, 1927–30); Alan Simpson, 'How Democratic was Roger Williams?' *William and Mary Quarterly* (January 1956).

towards solipsism or, more fortunately, to cancelling each other out.

In each of a variety of fields, the last fifteen or twenty years of American historical scholarship have produced indications of a kind of expertise that tends, not merely to a revision of the last opinion on the subject, but to the suggestion of new categories of question. The trend is perhaps nowhere clearer than in those reviews of twentieth-century foreign policy which have helped to advance our understanding by rejecting the old formalism which dominated American views of the outside world and which culminated, in the actual conduct of foreign relations, in the reign of John Foster Dulles as Secretary of State. George F. Kennan's trenchant critique of the dominance of moral attitudes in American foreign policy followed shortly after Professor John M. Blum's unfriendly but cogent analysis of Woodrow Wilson as an agent of moral preconceptions that limited his understanding of political reality.[11] Professor Blum writes from an extraordinary fund of knowledge of recent history and politics, and from a conviction, not perhaps expressed but clearly affecting his method, that the political system he knows so well has enough flexibility to contain and handle the problems that emerge from American society in political form. Meanwhile Professor Ernest R. May[12] has recently opened a searching inquiry into one of the most settled assumptions of American diplomatic historians, the prevailing belief that foreign policy reflects, and, in effect, enacts, public opinion on foreign affairs. It is not necessary for one moment to suppose that such writers have said the last word, or even to agree with their individual conclusions, in order to recognize that their style of approach is refreshing in its coolness, its liberation from the favoured American illusions, and its tone of skeptical pragmatism.

11. George F. Kennan, *American Diplomacy 1900–1950* (Chicago, 1951); John M. Blum, *Woodrow Wilson and the Politics of Morality* (Boston, 1956).
12. Ernest R. May, 'An American Tradition in Foreign Policy: The Role of Public Opinion,' in William H. Nelson (ed.), *Theory and Practice in American Politics* (Chicago, 1964).

The gains to scholarship resulting from this mood can be traced in such widely different fields as the American Revolution, the character of politics in the age of Jackson, and the motives and achievements of the several interests involved in Reconstruction. American historians of the Revolution are conducting the analysis of politics in a manner that owes, and acknowledges, a great debt to Namier; it is an appreciable irony of eighteenth-century studies that this stance of independence of the Whig tradition should in fact owe more to the example of Namier than to the argument of Butterfield. Students of British politics such as Professor C. R. Ritcheson (and Dr. Bernard Donoughue of the London School of Economics) and students of American politics such as Professor Jack P. Greene,[13] together with specialists in a valuable and increasing number of state or local histories, show a relish for facts, for building up the picture as it looked at the time, which gives us a deeper understanding of the kind of choices that were available at that time.

Revisionism does not invariably mean rethinking. It is often possible and sometimes easy to seem wiser than one's predecessors by virtue of some slight change in outlook which renders a new question more attractive. There is no period of American history under a more intense ferment of revision than that of Southern Reconstruction, and none, certainly, in which it is more important to try to distinguish what is the product of new thinking from what is the product of the altering social opinion. An immense amount of research has been put into Reconstruction during a period that corresponds, very roughly perhaps, with the time since the Supreme Court's decision in *Brown v. Board of Education*—the School Segregation Cases of 1954. Most of the results have appeared in articles, and no synthesis of the period in book form has yet ap-

13. C. R. Ritcheson, *British Politics and the American Revolution, 1763–1783* (Norman, 1954); Bernard Donoughue, *British Politics and the American Revolution . . . 1773–1775* (London, 1964); Jack P. Greene, *The Quest for Power: The Lower Houses of Assembly in the Southern Royal Colonies, 1689–1776* (Chapel Hill, 1963).

peared to do justice to the full depth of the work. Professor Kenneth M. Stampp's comparatively brief survey, *The Era of Reconstruction* (London, 1965), presents the principal findings of this revision (including of course Professor Stampp's own research) with the cogent persuasiveness of an authority. When Stampp hands down a verdict he does so in a manner from which there seems little room for appeal. Yet his standpoint is not the only one from which deeper levels of understanding might be attained.

The questions crowd so close upon each other, each entailing the answer to so many others, that any attempt to review the field would require at the least a full-length article to itself. In summary, we risk reducing the subject to a series of paradoxes. When, for example, LaWanda Cox[14] embarked on a study of the Northern movement to give to the freedmen that fundamentally American form of security, the tenure of freehold land, she clearly expected to find here one of the truly nobler and more redeeming features of the somewhat mixed story of Northern intentions. Her account is scholarly, sound, and full of interest: but the interest does not grow any less deep when she arrives, with obvious reluctance, at the discovery that at least some of the congressmen and senators behind this campaign were motivated principally by their anxiety to avert the danger of footloose freed Negroes flooding into the North. Free land would at least keep the Negroes in the South. To take up the problem of interpretation at another level, the historian who regrets the failure of Radical Reconstruction may put his finger on the antipathy between President Andrew Johnson and the Radical majority in the Congress, and may rightly blame the deadlock on the separation of powers, which emerges as a grave defect in the Constitution itself. But the historian who does not regret the failure of Reconstruction will have equal reason to applaud the wisdom of the Founders, who made it virtually impossible for a temporary majority in Congress to impose so sweeping a policy.

14. LaWanda Cox, 'The Promise of Land for the Freedmen', *Mississippi Valley Historical Review*, 45 (1958), 413–40.

The rewriting of Reconstruction history has produced notable advances in method which have suggested more complex and more interesting categories. The method which depended on imposing the concept of class conflict had the defect of introducing broad, inclusive but basically simple categories. Thus the real force behind the Radical Republicans was held to be that of the Northern business interests that were intent on exploiting the resources of the South, laid open for subjection by military defeat. But a significant article by Stanley Coben began the work of reconsideration by pointing out that no such unit as that of 'Northern business interests' had ever existed, and that in fact the business interests of the Northeast, which were supposed to be prominent in the movement, were not only various in content but divided over Southern policies.[15] Professor Unger's more recent and extensive examination of the social and economic history of the era demonstrates the complexity, the dividedness of the business interests, and renders the old categories obsolete.[16]

> If it is hard to see the consensus in post-bellum America, [Professor Unger observes] it is also difficult to detect a simple Beardian polarity. On the money question there were not two massive contending interests; there were many small ones. If the financial history of Reconstruction reveals nothing else of consequence, it does disclose a complex, pluralistic society in which issues were resolved—when they were not simply brushed aside—by the interaction of many forces.[17]

It can of course be argued that the great revision of Reconstruction history is itself a form of instrumentalism.[18] There would be

15. Stanley Coben, 'Northeastern Business and Radical Reconstruction: A Re-examination,' *Mississippi Valley Historical Review,* 46 (1959).
16. Irwin Unger, *The Greenback Era: A Social and Political History of American Finance, 1865–1878* (Princeton, 1964).
17. *Ibid.,* p. 405.
18. For a specific affirmation of these revisionist views (in this case of the Abolitionists) as serving an instrumentalist purpose, see Howard Zinn, 'Abolitionists, Freedom-Riders and the Tactics of Agitation' in Martin Duberman (ed.), *The Antislavery Vanguard: New Essays on the Abolitionists* (Princeton, N.J., 1965).

an element of truth in this criticism—an element not to be disregarded because of one's standpoint on civil rights. Yet much of it has been of such value in clearing away cartloads of erroneous information and pernicious mythology—errors about the content of legislation by Southern state assemblies under Radical rule, errors about the actual composition of Reconstruction conventions, myths about the scalawags, to name only a few—that the achievement has been an act of positive liberation.

Yet Southern history, as Vann Woodward has pointed out,[19] has on the whole been by-passed by the more exhilarating winds of the success story that Americans love to tell and to hear. The South, unlike the nation, had suffered a shattering military defeat, and the experience of its white population could never be wholly at one with that which was celebrated in the rest of the Union. The best that could be made of it was a great lost cause, to rank in history with those of the Stuarts or the victims of the French Revolution.

One sign of the critical sophistication about the past which seems to have developed since the Second World War has indeed been a moderate revival of interest in lost causes. The Federalists are now being taken more seriously than they used to be by any except political opponents of the Democrats (though it seems odd that a country that can put up a monument to Robert A. Taft cannot find the heart to commemorate Alexander Hamilton); and recent years have shown a new disposition to study and even to redeem the Loyalists of the Revolution. A most important attribute of this approach, not one confined to lost causes but to the rebuilding of historical knowledge in depth, is the attention which historians are giving to local and state history, and to the examination, in great detail, of the composition of communities. Perceptive monographs about New England towns and about state or provincial politics, amplified by articles based on very extensive use of local records, have appreciably added to our picture of the structure of society and the changes brought in it by the War of In-

19. 'The Irony of Southern History', *Journal of Southern History*, 19 (1953), reprinted in *The Burden of Southern History* (New York, 1960).

dependence; that picture seems to change before our eyes, exposing the frailty of surveys made from the continental centre of politics for the very simple reason that there was no centre.

The most influential single product of this detailed social realism has probably been Professor Lee Benson's book *The Concept of Jacksonian Democracy* (Princeton, 1961). Party divisions, and the ideological claims made by rival parties, have always seemed in the past to present an obvious and a legitimate scheme for organizing the political history of the period, and to lead straight from politics to social structure. But Professor Benson rejects these claims, reconstructing the parties from the social ingredients and finding in their rival policies a reflection of immediate electoral needs rather than serious differences of opinion or principle. Much the same attitude has influenced Professor Richard P. McCormick's important work, *The Second American Party System* (Chapel Hill, 1966). It stands out as an interesting conclusion of this study that by the time of the second American party system the capturing of the presidency had become the overriding aim of party organization, and that to this end the second American parties, unlike the first, were willing to subordinate almost all considerations of principle. 'Between 1824 and 1840, the "presidential question," rather than doctrinal disputes, was the axis around which politics revolved.'[20] These investigations will undoubtedly lead to further work on the same lines. They represent a brand of toughness, and a skepticism about the proclaimed ideals of party leaders and theorists, that not only appeals to the mood that has succeeded the Cold War, but is obviously producing tangible results.

Yet it would be a pity if this realism, with its useful appreciation of sociological techniques, were allowed to drive out all respect for the values or principles which Americans said they believed in. The history we have to record is that of the United States under Jackson and Van Buren, not under Clay; yet it is permissible to think that the history of that period would have been significantly

20. McCormick, *op. cit.*, p. 353.

different if Clay had been elected in 1832, and that such differences would have been due to genuine differences of purpose.
The United States without the Bank had a different economy from
the United States with the Bank—to name only one divisive
issue—and differences on the question certainly turned on matters
of substance.

The inevitable attraction of the great controversies has tended to
conceal what is in truth another very significant and at times a very
subtle division in American historiography. To put the matter with
that simplicity that always does injustice to the nuances, it is the
division between those who believe in the primacy of mind and
those who believe in the primacy of material fact. The obvious formative and ever-present ingredients of geographical circumstance
and economic interest—what may be called the urgency of the
economic problem—in American history have not prevented the
United States from becoming one of the leading centres of the profession of intellectual history. Even if we discount the influence,
which may indeed be very important, of the Puritan founders of
New England with their profound sense of mission and their habit
of interpreting human affairs as part of a theocentric order, we may
be justified at least in tracing the practice of giving a certain primacy to opinions and states of mind back to John Adams. 'The
Revolution,' he declared in a famous phrase, 'was effected before
the war commenced. The Revolution was in the minds and hearts
of the people.'[21]

Much of what has been styled the 'Whig' method in American
historiography has been involved in this process, because of its intense interest in motive. The search for the standard-bearers of
progress has meant the search for those who were conscious of
their mission; the concept of commitment to preconceived ideals
has always been a part of the Whig design for the understanding of
the past. It is perfectly legitimate in certain important instances,
such as that of the crusaders against slavery; but it becomes mis-

21. Quoted by Clinton Rossiter, *Seedtime of the Republic* (New York, 1953), p. 4.

leading to an equal extent when it generalizes and blurs the motives of campaigners who were attacking on some narrow front in
the cause of some special interest. And this kind of commitment is
more common, and in general more effective. Parrington, largely
because of the scale of his achievement, stands out as the leading
exponent of this mode of Whig intellectual history, exemplifying
both its clarity of design and its defects of interpretation. In contrast is the great example of Perry Miller, a historian who more
deeply understood the relation of the minds of earlier generations
to their own past and their own age.

Since their day Richard Hofstadter has emerged as the most influential of all the historians with a primary interest in states of
mind rather than conditions or series of events. In addition to his
own impressive and always slightly disturbing studies, he has
helped to inspire studies, such as that of Marvin Meyers on the
Jacksonians,[22] which may be said to counteract the progressivism
of the more conventional Whig thought. Hofstadter, whose extraordinarily trenchant insight—it is almost an instinct—for historical fallacy, has brought about a reorientation in the views of many
more conventional judgements over a variety of fields, has seldom
been the victim of any undue propensity for optimism—either
about the past or the future. In less incisive hands, the method he
has developed of re-creating past states of mind from the records of
published opinions, rather than from archival sources, could easily
become cloudy and inconclusive. Oddly enough (considering the
feeling he generates that something of value is under attack), it was
Hofstadter who proposed the view that American political history
should be reconsidered in the light of consensus rather than conflict.[23]

In view of the tremendous emphasis on the conflict of mighty
opposites which Parrington and Beard had imposed on their gener-

22. Marvin Meyers, *The Jacksonian Persuasion: Politics and Belief* (New York, 1957).
23. Richard Hofstadter, *The American Political Tradition and the Men Who Made It* (New York, 1951), Introduction.

ation, the suggestion that American history owed much to an underlying agreement was a very sensible direction to take. On this view, the successes of the American polity were more important and more enduring than its failures, and those successes were due to the absence of any fundamental divisions in ideology. It would be wrong to attribute the main development of the view to Hofstadter, however. Louis Hartz[24] expounded it in much greater detail on the basis of two principles which he discovered in American history. The first of these was Tocqueville's 'equality of conditions'—the absence of feudalism and of all the appurtenances and legacies which feudalism left in Europe. The second was an original 'liberal principle.' It was not the whole of English society, but what Hartz calls its liberal wing, that settled in America, and being settled it grew without the obstruction of any major contrary power or indeed of any contrary ideal.[25] Hofstadter might agree with Hartz that American development can be explained without recourse to fundamental clashes of ideology, though Hofstadter attaches much more importance to conflicts arising from deep social divisions; it seems that for Hartz the trouble with the Federalists or the Whigs was that they were victims of an intellectual error.

The idea of consensus was a useful direction-finder. It is not an explanation. In a sense it may be called a tautology, for the consensus extends only to the principles about which there is agreement, and deep disagreement may be concealed by different readings of the same sacred texts, when opposing sides affirm their allegiance to the source of these texts. Professor Hartz remarked in his Commonwealth Fund lectures that even the Civil War does not represent a real collapse of the American consensus because the Southern states claimed to have adhered to their own view of the Constitution, which they reproduced, with a few modifica-

24. Louis Hartz, *The Liberal Tradition in America* (New York, 1955).
25. A view developed in Professor Hartz's Commonwealth Fund lectures at University College, London, in 1962 and in *The Founding of New Societies*, ed. Hartz (New York, 1964).

tions, in that of the Confederacy. At this point consensus may be thought to have lost its usefulness. Might one not as well suggest that the French Wars of Religion do not represent a real religious cleavage because both Catholics and Huguenots avowed their faith in the Christian religion?

To reject the concept of basic ideological conflict is not the same thing as rejecting the influence of ideas, preconceptions, states of mind. In contrast to the entire school of intellectual historians there stands a different tradition, whose exponents emphasize the primacy of material forces. The great progenitor of this line was Turner, who seemed to feel that democracy, and all that was genuinely American about American institutions, rose up like a sort of ground mist from the soil of the continent and entered into the bones of the settlers. It was Turner who really implanted this deep strand of geophysical determinism whose influence has affected so much subsequent historical writing but has aroused such deep resentment—partly, perhaps, because its implicit rejection of the formative influence of ideas seems to be a veiled attack on the commitment of the intellectual life of the historian himself.

The great modern exponent of this style of historical thought, though he has arrived there by his own route and his debt to Turner is indirect, is Daniel J. Boorstin. Professor Boorstin has devoted one book to the thesis that the success of American government, the great ability that Americans have shown in overcoming their practical and political problems, is in fact due to their rejection of preconceived ideological schemes of government. In his major works that have followed, he has extended the same concept to social history in its broadest sense, deliberately extruding ideas or ideals from his terms of reference. As Boorstin shows, in the process of settlement, community came first, government afterwards. Boorstin is not unlike Namier in his hostility to the importation of ideals, ideology, or indeed any form of systematic beliefs—and also, incidentally, in his keen eye for the revealing incident. No contemporary surpasses him in the ability to re-create scenes and situations that bring the past to life; this, we feel, is what it really felt like to be there.[26]

Yet Professor Boorstin's remarkable persuasive powers and the obvious cogency of much of his argument should not conceal two points: First, that it *is* an argument, and as such that it explains the sort of phenomena that primarily interest Professor Boorstin far better than other phenomena that, however, remain significant. The deep and principled convictions that brought about the early political parties, the passions of the anti-slavery movement, the ratiocinations of Calhoun and other speculative writers, are slighted. And, secondly, that the things that interest the author are presented not merely as one aspect of what he calls 'the national experience': they *are* the national experience. The rest is worthy only of rejection because, presumably, it is contrary to the true American genius. The rejects of history that fall into this state of gracelessness, because of that failure, can be rather large, and include the second Bank of the United States, which plays no part in the book which covers its lifetime.

Boorstin is far more subtle and complex in his appreciation of American development than Turner was, and his originality and persuasiveness are sure to exert great influence; much indeed of what he says is more important than what he chooses to leave out. Like Turner before him he sings the virtue of the land, and might for a text have reversed a line of Robert Frost's to read 'We were the land's before the land was ours.' It is not the less important on this account to appreciate the extent to which his own ideas form a system.

The deep division of interpretation that has been suggested here is concealed by the fact that Boorstin, Hofstadter, and Hartz join in some measure of belief, shared by such a solid political historian as McCormick, that ideological conflict has not dominated American life; that agreement to work the machinery has been much

26. Daniel J. Boorstin: *The Genius of American Politics* (Chicago, 1953); *The Americans: The Colonial Experience* (New York, 1958); *The National Experience* (New York, 1965).

more important than conflict over principles. But the fact that rival parties agree to work the same machinery does not mean that they intend to work it for the same objects; and the machinery itself sometimes changes shape under the pressure of strong personalities or principles. The machinery of politics is not neutral; it is not 'matter,' even though it sometimes seems to be treated as though it were of the order of natural or environmental phenomena rather than of those made by man in America.

This division between mind and matter is less dramatic than those in which the participants are to some extent ideological partisans. It results perhaps from a contrast of temperaments rather than ideals. Yet these alternative views cut deep enough to affect any interpretation of specific events or decisions. It may seem strange that American historians should be moved to take sides over the very question of whether there are any sides to take. But an explanation may lie, to some extent, in the actual nature of the theories that have played so dominant a part in the rewriting of American history during the present century. The Populists, the Progressive instrumentalists, and the Marxists asserted the historical primacy of an ideological conflict; and it appears that some historians, anxious to escape this dilemma and convinced of its irrelevance to American development, have in fact been trapped by it. The word 'ideology' has itself been given too much work. Ideologies have been thought of as all-embracing, as embodying fundamental views of the state and society, to be wholly accepted or resisted; so that if one rejected 'ideological' interpretations one was easily led to deny the relevance, and minimize the intellectual seriousness, of any profound differences of opinion on matters of principle or policy.

But this approach makes too much of the general problem and so, in the end, makes too little of the particular issues. Ideological conflicts may be relatively short-lived, like that between the Federalists and Jeffersonians, and yet intense while they last. Such conflicts, especially when they lead to the adoption of divisive policies, require to be incorporated, not by-passed, in the writing of history. Another of our needs in these matters is to distinguish between the parties who do hold a total view of society and those who are committed to a narrower cause; but it will always be a mistake to trivialize past differences merely because they disappeared with the passage of time.

Time, to come back to the beginning, is the element with which many American historians have had the greatest difficulty in coming to terms; yet they will see into the past, so far as it is given to us to do so, only when they recognise it, in its integrity, as the past. Time is not the enemy of the historian but it is not his friend; it is the prism, the only one, through which we may hope to perceive the dead.

11

The New History and the Sense of Social Purpose in American Historical Writing (1972)

Historians have often been inspired by the power of spiritually high ideals or socially good intentions, sometimes by both. Orosius, a disciple of Augustine, composed his *Seven Books of History Against the Pagans* to prove that nations which had submitted themselves to non-Christian rulers had thereby incurred a series of disasters. The legend that Brutus of Troy had founded Britain was thought useful by King James I. Both in the earlier and later stages of the development of concepts of verification with regard to historical records, the idea of a past whose example points the way to present and future conduct or which gives validity to the regime of the present has been an extraordinarily potent instrument of social policy. The social instrumentalists who emerged, among the political scientists, economists, sociologists, philosophers, and historians of the Western world about the end of the last century were hardly less ambitious than their predecessors. Among them, the Ameri-

This essay, which was read as a paper before the Royal Historical Society on October 20, 1972, was published in *Transactions* of the Royal Historical Society in 1973. It represents a further reflection on the ideas in "The American Past: Is It Still Usable?" Readers will notice that at one or two points I have worked from the same material, but I hope the argument as a whole represents an advance.

can school was particularly confident of what could be achieved by wresting the study, teaching and writing of history from the hands of its orthodox exponents and redirecting the entire subject in the interests of social advance. There is an obvious temptation to describe this school as historical utilitarians, a word that suggests itself particularly because of their long emphasis on the use and usability of the past. But the term is inappropriate. Utilitarianism is a system which envisages the greatest good of the greatest number; whereas an instrumental view could be directed to special problems or be intended to promote the interests of a particular group.

The driving force of the school were those who proclaimed the New History. The phrase had been used several times before 1912, when James Harvey Robinson unfurled the banner bearing that device;[1] by 1938, after Robinson's death, Harry Elmer Barnes, the most pugnacious of the school's propagandists, who by this time had been obliged to recognize that the New History's intellectual pedigree could be traced back to Voltaire, was able to proclaim the outcome of the struggle in buoyant terms:

> Down to the present time the exponents of the new history have found it necessary to engage in a campaign of persistent propaganda and education. . . . They have now definitely won the victory and can henceforth concentrate their energy upon perfecting the basis of the new history and on providing the training of those who will be competent to practice the new history.[2]

In view of this declaration, it seems important to recognize from the outset that several of the major figures of the period, including Osgood, Andrews, Morison, Wertenbaker, Miller, and Nevins, were writing history that would probably have been exactly the same if the New History school had never existed; and later commentators, so far from accepting the triumph of the New History, came to the conclusion that, by at latest the end of World War II,

1. James Harvey Robinson, *The New History* (New York, 1912).
2. Henry Elmer Barnes, *History of Historical Writing* (Norman, Okla., 1932).

its frontier of settlement had closed.[3] But if, as seems to be generally agreed, that impulse was spent, it would still be superficial to suppose that the influence was exhausted. The New Historians were one manifestation of the broader cultural phenomenon of the Progressive Movement, and in 1959 Henry May remarked that 'We still tend to see American history through the eyes of the Progressive Era.'[4] The Progressives, moreover, had powerful survivors and successors who carried the historical torch for the New Deal, and for a succession of reformers who seemed always to be struggling against those ever-renewed forces of reaction and oppression.

Thus although the phenomenon with which this paper is concerned lies in the past, it seems equally significant that by the time the nucleus of the New, or more broadly of Progressive, History, had spent its specific impulse, it had succeeded in infiltrating a much wider segment of the corporate body of historians in which it continued to live. The New History's aims could be summarized with a simplicity which does no injustice to its practitioners by saying that they proposed to convert history into a positive instrument of social progress through the clarification of the historical origins of current problems; and further, that the New History intended to enlist the full range of the more recent social sciences in an attempt to comprehend and interpret every aspect of the life of the past.

It is the first of these aims that I have called 'instrumentalism.' The second aim seems to serve the first, but if it became an end in itself then it would seem to endanger the priority of the first. The details or logic of these priorities were not quite clearly established, even when set out by Barnes in his *History of Historical Writing* in 1938.

I doubt whether I should have come to write this paper if I were

3. Richard Hofstadter, *The Progressive Historians: Turner, Beard, Parrington* (New York, 1968), p. 438; John Higham, *History: The Development of Historical Studies in the United States* (Englewood Cliffs, N.J., 1965), p. 131.
4. Henry F. May, *The End of American Innocence* (New York, 1960), p. 164.

entirely satisfied that I agreed with the view that the New History, in all its manifestations, had passed away with its own generation of historians. There is, therefore, a sense in which I am exposed to the accusation of being engaged in a similarly instrumental activity myself. As an episode in the history of American thought, the New History calls for both identification and explanation; but the views that we develop are bound to be informed by the necessity for a critical consideration of the New History's longer-term intellectual consequences. Not that all the thinking that bears an instrumentalist stamp has necessarily been dedicated to social reform—a danger shrewdly seen, in 1935, by Theodore Clarke Smith,[5] who expressed his fears for the future if historians allowed themselves to be swayed by Charles Beard's presidential address to the American Historical Association, 'Written History as an Act of Faith.'[6] Smith observed that there was already Soviet History and Fascist History, and there would be national socialist history as soon as it could be manufactured, 'in each case based on a definite philosophy as an act of faith.' He foresaw that history would come to be permitted only as an entertainment or as a form of social control. Neither these words nor the events of the next few years, appear to have supported the democratic faith of Conyers Read, who, as President of the Association in 1949,[7] disparaged those historians who interested themselves in the past for its own sake; in his view the liberal world, with its plurality of aims and values, was a thing of the past, and for the future, 'we must clearly assume a militant attitude if we are to survive.' The theme of this militant attitude, involving the organization of resources and the disciplined interpretation of history, was to be the propagation of American doctrines. 'This sounds,' he added, 'like the advocacy of one form of social control against another. In short, it is. But I see

5. Theodore Clarke Smith, 'The Writing of American History in America from 1884 to 1934,' *American Historical Review*, 40 (April 1935).
6. Charles A. Beard, 'Written History as an Act of Faith,' *American Historical Review*, 39 (January 1934).
7. Conyers Read, 'The Social Responsibilities of the Historian,' *American Historical Review*, 55 (January 1950).

no alternative in a divided world.' He reassured his hearers that his concept of control meant 'no menace to essential freedoms,' but left it to be inferred that the controllers of policy would decide which freedoms were essential.

Social control in this organized sense has certainly never been an aim of historians writing in the general tradition of the New or Progressive History, but equally certainly it was within their compass to aim at the kind of intellectual influence that could help to shape social policy. The achievements of American historians were proclaimed by a Social Science Research Council Report of 1946, to have been 'frankly functional.'[8] As recently as 1966, Professor Eric Goldman is reported to have said on the 'Open Mind' television programme that 'most historians' were 'in agreement' that history was, to use his own word, a 'weapon'; and it was 'employed in determining peoples' ideas and attitudes'; he went further, for there was 'a certain measure of responsibility on the part of the historian for making sure that he writes history in such a way that it will bring about the kind of action that he wants.'[9] Mr. Goldman's distinguished predecessors had chosen some sort of historical relativism, but it might be unfair to them to describe his assertion as lying logically at the end of that road. I don't think it does; it is better thought of as a wrong turning, but unfortunately it carries a great deal of traffic, some heavy, much light, and most of it noisy. Mr. Goldman's statement is not better for being the counterpart of Conyers Read's presidential address, or of comparable declarations more recently from the New Left,[10] all of which stand before us as bleak warnings of what lies in store when the basic concept of historical truth has been discarded as irrelevant

8. J. H. Randall, Jr. and George Haines IV, 'Controlling Assumptions,' in *Theory and Practice in Historical Study: A Report of the Committee on Historiography*, ed. Merle Curti, SSRC Bulletin 54 (New York, 1946), p. 51.

9. James J. Martin, 'History and Social Intelligence,' in *Harry Elmer Barnes, Learned Crusader*, ed. Arthur Goddard (Colorado Springs, 1968), p. 241.

10. For example, Howard Zinn, 'Abolitionists, Freedom-Riders and the Tactics of Agitation,' in *The Anti-Slavery Vanguard: New Essays on the Abolitionists*, ed. Martin Duberman (Princeton, 1965).

for the excellent reason that it has ceased to serve any useful purpose. They tend to justify Voltaire's cynical remark that history is nothing but a pack of tricks we play on the dead.

With these reverberations in mind, it will be timely to turn back to the beginnings of the school which claimed the rubric of the 'New History.' These historians were in fact not all of one mind, and were on occasion capable of differing from each other quite sharply. But on one common piece of ground they felt very firm: they had cleared away the dense undergrowth of pietistic rhetoric to uncover the nature of reality. The matter was stated by Arthur F. Bentley, with Charles Beard's warm approval: 'Reality is in group interests acting on political institutions, not in the hearts or minds or thoughts or feelings of the people.'[11] Similarly, Turner's preoccupation with the significance of the frontier amounted to a primitive form of geo-economic determinism. He was almost blindly unwilling to admit of the influence of ideas, of institutions, or of the cultural inheritances of language or religion; and, as Hofstadter observed, he never seriously applied himself to the problems of cultural transmission.[12] A little below the surface of agreement, his views were bound to separate from those of such social critics as the political scientists Bentley and Goodnow or the socialists Gustavus Myers and Algie Simons.

In its substance and style, the new movement was distinctly American, but it would be wrong to suppose that it grew out of a condition of intellectual isolation, or that its exponents were in any way confined to America. Charles Beard as an undergraduate at DePauw University had already read Arnold Toynbee's *Lectures on the Industrial Revolution* (1884), whose message was of formative importance for him:

> You must pursue facts for their own sake, but penetrated with a vivid sense of the problems of your own time. This is not a principle of perversion, but a principle of selection, and you

11. In Beard's review of Arthur F. Bentley, *The Process of Government* (1908), *Political Science Quarterly,* 23 (1908).
12. Hofstadter, *The Progressive Historians,* p. 141.

> could not have a better one than to pay special attention to
> the history of the social problems that are agitating the world
> now.[13]

The bibliography of Beard's first book, a little essay on the same
subject—*The Industrial Revolution* (1901)—written during his
years at Oxford and addressed to the British working classes, bore
all the traces of his own intellectual debts to the new social consciousness in Britain; he listed *Fabian Essays,* and the works of the
Webbs, of Hobson, and of Ruskin, who had moved him so deeply
that he is said to have carried a copy of *Unto This Last* in his
pocket for several years. The college which Beard helped to found
was to be called Ruskin Hall. Behind all these, with their strong
sense of social purpose, stood J. R. Green's famous *Short History
of the English People* (1876), perhaps the first actual work of history to manifest the new historical spirit. Green, who disagreed
with Freeman's dictum that 'History is past politics, politics is
present history' and made it his aim to tell the story of the people
as a whole, enjoyed enormous sales in the United States long
before his approach had become acceptable to the more professional of American historians.

Beard dropped an oblique, perhaps unintended hint as to his
own future direction when in 1906 he reviewed Jean Jaurès's new
venture, the *Histoire socialiste,*[14] and remarked that the socialists
had not yet made any great contributions to history because
lengthy treatises did not serve the purposes of party propaganda.
'Nevertheless,' he significantly continued, 'the avowed purpose of
the Socialists to force a disintegration of the intellectual synthesis
on which the defence of the present order rests will compel them,
in time, to open the whole question of historical interpretation and
construction.' In the light of Beard's current beliefs about the na-

13. Burleigh Taylor Wilkins, 'Frederick York Powell and Charles A. Beard. A
    Study in Anglo-American Historiography and Social Thought,' *American Quar-
    terly,* 11 (1959); Arnold Toynbee, *Lectures on the Industrial Revolution* (Lon-
    don, 1884).
14. *Political Science Quarterly,* 21 (1906).

ture of reality, one may wonder how fully he was aware of this implied commitment to the view that the defence of an economic and political order did in fact rest on an intellectual synthesis. But the prophetic quality of this observation seems to reveal as much about Beard's own prospective development as about that of the socialists. He might not have agreed that he ever intended 'to force a disintegration' of the American synthesis of his time, but as soon as he discovered the appropriate historical records he proved himself ready to deploy the resources of scholarship to expose the revered institutions of that order to the most skeptical and searching questions.

Yet Beard's iconoclasm was never unambiguously destructive. The tone of his short book, *The Supreme Court and the Constitution* (1912), which is constructed from sketchy evidence held together by faulty reasoning, is at least consistent with great respect for the Court, and it was meant to refute the allegation then current that judicial review was a usurped power. It thus seems reasonable to suppose that when Beard discovered the Treasury records showing the financial holdings of the Founders of the Constitution, which appreciated after its inauguration, the evidence may have influenced his views about their motives. But the influence, if so, was exerted on a mind that was already in a high state of susceptibility, and although his scrutiny was remarkably hasty and inconclusive, it was enough to satisfy him and, more surprisingly, for some forty years it satisfied an increasing proportion of his readers. His iconoclasm, in any case, was in keeping with the tone of the period, whose most devastating blast, perhaps surprisingly, had been sounded a few years earlier in England. In 1904 the English legal scholar Edward Jenks published in *The Independent Review* an astonishing article which denounced as a group of self-serving feudal reactionaries a body of strong-minded men who had for several centuries been honoured as the founders of the liberties of the English-speaking peoples. The article was called 'The Myth of Magna Carta.' By the time Beard, a close student of English history, reviewed Jaurès, he had read not only Jenks, but

McKechnie's *Magna Carta* (1905), and took advantage of the opportunity to mention that Jaurès had not. Without imputing a direct line of connection, one cannot but be struck by similarities of circumstance and tone. The peculiar role of the barons as the authors of a great and fundamental written charter of liberties was comparable, at least in a rhetorical sense, with that of the Founders of the Constitution in the history of the United States. When Beard came to write about the Founders he restrained his criticism to the level of innuendo; and he failed to resolve a certain ambivalence as to their achievement—for he never quite lost track of his own Midwestern Republican background. But in his attribution of motives and in his skepticism towards their exalted reputations for disinterested service, Beard was as clear about the Founding Fathers as Jenks about King John's barons.

It was James Harvey Robinson who in 1912 proclaimed the arrival and outlined the programme of the New History in a book of essays under that title. Robinson's interest in the theme was not new. As early as 1892, when a junior faculty member at the University of Pennsylvania, he had been named to the National Educational Association's Committee of Ten to make suggestions about the teaching of history in schools, and this was the beginning of a connection that lasted for twenty-five years. The Committee of 1892[15] (Woodrow Wilson was another member) stressed the importance of educating the majority of children who were not destined to go to college; the Committee felt strongly that all children should receive the same education, and that history and its allied subjects were 'better adapted than any other subject to promote the invaluable mental power we call the judgment.' They recommended the study of Greek, Roman, English, American, and French history. From that time onwards, Robinson took a leading part in leading the N.E.A.'s advisory committees to recommend the reduction of time spent on ancient and medieval history, and

15. U.S. Bureau of Education, *Report of the Committee on Secondary School Studies at the Meeting of the National Educational Association, July 9, 1892* (Washington, D.C., 1893).

280   *Paths to the American Past*

the advancement in the curriculum of modern and American history; and by 1899 that view had got so strong a hold that the American Historical Association's Committee of Seven for that year went so far as to advise that 'It is not desirable that much time should be devoted to the colonial history.'[16] By 1911, a committee reporting to the American Historical Association advised that medieval history be dropped, and Robinson later stated that in all the conferences on historical instruction on which he had served he had always urged that history for students and readers be directed to the understanding of present conditions and problems.[17] The last curriculum committee in which he took part, which met in 1916, recommended a heavy reorientation of school studies towards civics, vocational studies, and modern history. *The Social Studies in Secondary Education,* in which these proposals were made, quoted Robinson's *The New History* on the purpose of teaching history and showed much evidence of the influence of his views.

There can be no doubt of this Report's lasting influence on American school curricula; during the next ten years the United States Bureau of Education distributed 27,000 copies,[18] but the effects were by no means confined to the secondary schools. The university syllabus, or more accurately the courses offered for election, reflected a rising preoccupation with modern and recent history; and this tendency, as a result of which medieval and ancient history have had difficulty in holding any serious footing even in important universities, has never been effectively redressed. While it would be absurd to ascribe to Robinson's own influence the characteristic trend of the social as well as the intellectual life of the period, he was without doubt the most influential publicist and to that extent the most representative propagandist of these views. It becomes significant, therefore, that Robinson seems

16. *The Study of History in Schools. Report to the American Historical Association of the Committee of Seven* (New York, 1899), pp. 74–75.
17. Luther Vergil Hendricks, *James Harvey Robinson, Teacher of History* (New York, 1946), pp. 53–56. Robinson's influence on the work of educational committees is traced on pp. 35–61.
18. *Ibid.,* p. 63.

never to have differentiated seriously between the school, the university, and the general public. History had for all of them the same purposive social utility, and it was in that spirit that he wrote, both for the students of the rising state universities and for the mass readership that his books gained. The didactic emphasis on recent history appeared in the text-book *The Development of Modern Europe* (1907–8) written jointly with Beard, the preface to which declared that,

> In preparing the volume in hand, the writers have consciously subordinated the past to the present. It has been their ever conscious aim to enable the reader to catch up with his own times; to read intelligently the foreign news in the morning paper; to know what was the attitude of Leo III towards the social democrats even if he has forgotten that of Innocent III towards the Albigenses.

But in *The New History* Robinson's note was even more challenging:

> We must develop historical-mindedness upon a far more generous scale than hitherto, for this will add a still deficient element to our intellectual equipment and will promote rational progress as nothing else can do. The present has hitherto been the willing victim of the past; the time has now come when it should turn on the past and exploit it in the interests of advance.[19]

Historians, despite Robinson's belligerent tone, are generally rather fond of the past, whose inhabitants as they get to know them, appear at least as attractive as some of the historians' own contemporaries. Robinson's strangely resentful and hostile attitude, suggesting an adversary relationship with the main object of his own vocation, requires some explanation. The reasons are to be found, I think, in the combination of his enthusiasm for social advance with his intellectual inheritance of a Darwinian sociology.

Since approximately the 1880s, the Darwinian analysis of society

19. Robinson, *The New History*, p. 24.

had been breaking into splinters, duly appropriated as weapons by opposing sides in the social struggle. Although the logical flaw that lies at the root of social Darwinist thinking consists in the mechanical transposition of methods belonging to the explanation of a biological process to the analysis of social processes of an entirely different kind, it must be said in fairness to the early social Darwinists that they had a distinguished exemplar: Charles Darwin, in *The Descent of Man,* agreed with the view that the progress of the United States was the result of natural selection and that the Anglo-Saxon emigration to the west was the climactic event of all history.[20] The language of social science was permeated with Darwinian ideas, while ideas of progress, in vague and unsystematic forms, were pervasive. For Beard, in his book on the Industrial Revolution, it was natural to argue that the unity of tendency to be found in the apparent confusion of history was that of the progressive control of man over his environment. For both Beard and Robinson this control was itself one of the themes of history, though Beard placed a heavier and more assured emphasis on democracy and the common man as the objects for whose benefit the control was to be directed—that was what made it progressive.

Robinson was aware of the intellectual risks he was inviting. In *The New History* he found room for an explicit warning against the fallacy of believing that historical lessons give direct solutions to present problems;[21] he was well aware that every case differs and that past solutions hold good only for past problems. But as a historian Robinson did not go forward with his own programme; he seems to have been unable to commit himself to writing history in a way that would have exemplified his own thesis. In keeping with his own social convictions he involved himself in 1919 with the founding of the New School for Social Studies in New York; but his published work revealed no intellectual development. Ample in

20. Cushing Strout, *The Pragmatic Revolt in American History. Carl Becker and Charles Beard* (New Haven, 1958), p. 17; Charles Darwin, *The Descent of Man* (London, 1871), I, p. 179.
21. Robinson, *The New History*, pp. 17–18.

amount, and pitched as it was at the level of intelligent popularization, it became increasingly shallow and repetitive, sometimes drawing on materials that he had used twenty or thirty years earlier. His sales were enormous, and, a captive of the bestseller market, Robinson became a willing victim of the present.

When Robinson explained why historical studies were needed, he viewed the past as though the surviving evidence for its existence consisted largely of archaic relics forming stubborn, but reducible obstacles to social progress. 'If it be true,' he asked in *The New History*, '. . . that opinion tends, in the dynamic age in which we live, to lag far behind our changing environment, how can we better discover the anachronisms in our views than by studying their origin?'[22] This was left as a rhetorical question; better ways might well be thought of, and history may need rather more subtle justifications for the claims that it makes on time and resources in a rapidly changing environment. In a later book, *The Mind in the Making*, which achieved immense sales in the 1920s, Robinson observed that the physics of Aristotle had been completely discarded, yet his ethics and politics were still considered to be works of profound value; and their continuing influence he regarded as an anomaly. This argument suggests certain limitations to evolutionism as a useful system of thought; an heir to both Darwin and the Utilitarians, it did not occur to Robinson or to those who thought like him that ethics might not be susceptible to evolutionary analysis; physics, after all, was undeniably a natural science, but Aristotle, whom Robinson had invoked, specifically held that ethics was not a science.

It was a fundamental tenet of the New History, propounded by Robinson and repeated enthusiastically by Barnes, that the evolutionary attitude would give men the power to resolve the social problems that resulted from the past. Barnes declared that the 'genetic attitude'—a term for evolutionism—had been taught to historians by biologists; he described 'the principle of development

22. *Ibid.*, p. 103.

and the genetic attitude' as 'the cornerstone of the more vital phases of the new history.'[23] Barnes, even more explicitly than Robinson, insisted that historical mindedness would enable people to diagnose those obstacles left behind by the past, apparently somewhat resembling geological deposits that had somehow been carried along, as perhaps at the foot of a glacier; but the deepest consequences of these doctrines were, not the inculcation of what they called historical mindedness, but a weakening of historical perspective. Robinson produced an analogy,[24] which Barnes fondly adopted, by which the age of the earth was depicted as on a clock with the beginning at midnight and the present at mid-day. By this way of measuring, Babylonian and Egyptian civilization had appeared on earth at about twenty minutes to twelve, while Greek literature, philosophy, and science were about seven minutes old; Bacon's *Advancement of Learning* appeared at one minute to twelve, and not half a minute had elapsed since the first steam engine. To Robinson the inference from his imaginary time-scale led to firm and practical conclusions: 'This makes it obvious that those whom we call the ancients are really our contemporaries . . . They now belong to our own age.' It was Francis Bacon who first observed that there was something amiss about the traditional conception of the 'ancients'; they had really lived in the youth of the world. But Robinson was not interested in such subtleties. What he wanted to do was to annihilate all differences between antiquity and modernity. Yet an unusual burden seems to rest on his use of the word 'really.' Why, we may ask, are people who lived and died some thousands, or hundreds, of years ago, under different ecological systems, believing in different cosmologies, obeying different laws, and worshipping different gods, 'really our contemporaries'? The human perspective, though enlarged by knowledge of geology, natural history, and human development, is still contained in the human life-span, and the merging of past and present into one glutinous, undifferentiated mass is a form of *Ge-*

23. Barnes, *History of Historical Writing*, p. 376.
24. Robinson, *The New History*, p. 239.

mütlichkeit that is antipathetic to any genuinely historical vision. That fundamental respect for the distance and differentness of the past, which is an indispensable element of the historical understanding, was absent from the historically innocent mind of Vernon Louis Parrington, whose influence was for a period greater even than that of Beard or Robinson. A poll taken in 1950 disclosed that, of books published between 1920 and 1950, Parrington's *Main Currents of American Thought* (1927–30) was the work most highly esteemed by the majority of historians working on American history.[25] Perhaps still more important is the lasting debt to Parrington that is warmly avowed by Henry Steele Commager.[26] Parrington, a professor of literature, had apparently received no historical training when he embarked on his amibitous history of American thought. He was not the first to accept the notion of an essential contemporaneity between past and present, or between different past periods, for Beard had argued that the late-nineteenth-century struggles of the Populist farmers of the West and South amounted to a virtual re-enactment of the great struggles a century earlier over the adoption of the Constitution, and Turner took a similar view. A kind of textually thinned and intellectually simplified Whig view of history enabled Parrington to see the American past as a series of encounters between progress and privilege, enlightened democracy and obscurantist reaction, with an immediacy that transcended any necessity for the historical context of the problems. He was thus able to describe Roger Williams as 'contemporary with successive generations of prophets from his day to ours.' As for the colonists, with their up-to-date ideas of liberty and democracy, they were 'old-fashioned only in manners and dress.'[27] The point was that the issues they dealt with and the aims they strove for were modern.

25. Hofstadter, *The Progressive Historians*, p. 350.
26. H. S. Commager, *The American Mind* (New York, 1950), p. 303; see Hofstadter, *op. cit.*, p. 350, n.2.
27. Parrington, *Main Currents of American Thought*, I, iv, vi, 62–75; Hofstadter, *The Progressive Historians*, ch. 2, esp. at p. 398.

The New Historians had an urgent message for their contemporaries; but their purposeful emphasis on recent history and their denigration of the significance of events more distant in time formed in the minds of their readers a dangerously shallow attitude to the past itself. This attitude has involved not only for them but for those who have been formed under their influence, a depreciation of the intellectual difficulties involved in historical understanding; as Henry May has remarked, 'In Robinson's exuberant pages there is little hint of skepticism, except about long dead traditions, and no whisper of doubt about our ability to understand what was happening.'[28]

The New Historians supposed themselves to be breaking away from a tradition of erudite but arid fact-gathering. Robinson, in this as in other things to be repeated by Barnes, was fond of replying to the great architect of orthodox history, Leopold von Ranke, by asserting that he had placed too much emphasis on history *'wie es eigentlich gewesen'* to the neglect of the more important question of *'wie es eigentlich geworden'*—how it came about.[29] But neither Ranke's American disciples, who thought of themselves as pure historical scientists, nor his American opponents, who believed themselves to be in revolt against orthodox nineteenth-century historical science, seem to have understood Ranke's meaning. They thought of facts as hard little nuggets deposited in the past; but Ranke thought of them as the agents of moral forces, possibly of divine origin.[30] When Ranke used his famous phrase, *'wie es eigentlich gewesen,'* which he did in distinguishing true historical values from such aims as romantic nationalism, what he meant to convey was the sense of what it was like at the time. The translation into our current idiom might be, 'tell it like it was.'

Assuredly the achievements of the school deserve to be mea-

---

28. May, *End of American Innocence*, p. 161.
29. Robinson, *New History*, p. 47.
30. I depend here on Cushing Strout, *The Pragmatic Revolt in America: Carl Becker and Charles Beard*, p. 20; Morton G. White, *Social Thought in America: The Revolt against Formalism* (New York, 1947), pp. 221–22.

sured against the more complacent assumptions of the orthodoxies
to which they gave battle; and it is fair to say that they often wrote
with style, verve, and considerably wider learning than has been
thought necessary by many of their intellectual heirs. Robinson inaugurated the course on European intellectual history which for
many years attracted large attendances at Columbia, and the College catalogue for 1899–1900 indicates that a reading knowledge of
French, German, and Latin was required of undergraduates in his
courses.[31] Progressives could reasonably argue that orthodox histories served their own instrumental purposes by protecting the
reputations of established institutions;[32] and Progressives were
more than merely narrow instrumentalists when they showed that
history could be written with a sense of social commitment which
would compel the attention of people who had not formerly been
committed. But when these gains have been acknowledged, we
may continue to ask whether the cogency of their theoretical arguments or their achievements as working historians earned these
writers their remarkable and sustained influence over such an important sector of American intellectual life. For it cannot be said
that the New History's excessive preoccupation with the recent
past, and with the relevance of problems that seem to lie in a
direct line to current affairs, has served them well, or has done
much to deepen the respect felt by American students for the comparative aspects of the past or the different qualities of other cultures. Judgements about recently current affairs may in a sense be
just as important as those about the more remote past, but they
rest on a shorter time-scale and tend to be much more rapidly
superseded. Robinson's own example, put forward in the preface
to *The Development of Modern Europe*, rebounds upon him; for
some of the gravest problems of the authoritarian age into which
he survived, and which grew more forbidding after his death,
would probably gain more illumination from studying Innocent

31. Hendricks, *James Harvey Robinson*, p. 14.
32. See Barnes's attack on 'good taste' as a handicap to contemporary historical
writing; *History of Historical Writing*, p. 273.

III's crusade against the Albigenses than Leo III's attitude to the social democrats.

When the early proponents of new aims and methods demanded a major transformation of both, they strongly implied that their predecessors' intellectual foundations had been misconceived. Were orthodox historians working with correct methods but improper aims? Or were they the victims of a philosophical misconception about the nature of historical knowledge itself? Very few of the new school allowed themselves to be detained, still less deflected, by these questions; the impulses that bore them forward were social, not philosophical. Carl Becker, an ambiguous ally, was the only contemporary, apart from the philosopher Frederick J. Teggart—who wrote some of the most interesting discussions of the whole problem—to apply himself at all systematically to the investigation of the logical consequences of adopting a consistent position of philosophical relativism. Becker's teacher, Turner, had said in a sentence as early as 1891 all that most of the Progressive or New Historians thought it necessary to say by way of philosophical justification. In his eassy, 'The Significance of History,' Turner observed that 'Each age writes the history of the past anew with reference to the conditions upper-most in its own times.'[33] When reduced to its elements this statement was not a very careful expression of so important a principle; but it would do. People were already thinking in such terms, and Toynbee's lectures had made a similar point seven years earlier. Both were preceded by F. H. Bradley's *Presuppositions of Critical History,* published in 1874, the year of Beard's birth. Bradley argued that each period was capable of historical knowledge only to the extent made possible by the limits of its own assumptions. 'Inference,' he explained, 'depends on the character of our general consciousness—and so the past varies with the present, and can never do otherwise, since it is always the present on which it rests.'[34]

33. F. J. Turner, 'The Significance of History', can be found, *inter alia,* in *The Varieties of History,* ed. Fritz Stern (New York, 1956).
34. F. H. Bradley, *Presuppositions of Critical History* (Oxford, 1874), p. 15.

Turner does not seem to have read Bradley, although he may have done; but certainly he was offering a sharp hint that a new way of looking at both the aims and the subject matter of history might be at hand. The relativism implied by this turn of thought, however, contained hidden traps for the confident exponents of the newly fashionable geographical and economic determinism. It has already been observed that they were optimistically sure of their sense of reality—it was interests, economics, brute facts, that made history, not ideals or principles or thoughts. Beard and his contemporaries did not pause to ask themselves why a thought should be something less than a reality if it were in truth a real thought, or why, by prescribing modes of action, it should not contribute to the next set of material realities.

Turner had referred to 'each age' as though ages possessed general characters. Carl Becker, whose thinking in these matters appears to have owed much to Bradley, went on to develop a much fuller view of the characteristics of a historical age. J. B. Bury remarked that 'Ideas have their intellectual climates.'[35] Earlier, William James had argued for the recognition of a 'specious present' in which ideas encountered the tests of pragmatism. Becker believed A. N. Whitehead to have been the source of his own concept, but it was Becker himself who thought out the idea of 'climates of opinion' as virtual determinants of thought and knowledge. (We shall perhaps be fortunate if we escape without hearing them called paradigms.) Becker also took further than his American contemporaries the difficult enquiry into the status of the historical fact; he was the first of them to take seriously the problems arising from the observation that all knowledge of the past is necessarily present knowledge. However, Becker too was concerned to harness history to social improvement, and probably owed more to American pragmatism than to European idealism; his thinking at times suggested that he was heading for a form of epistemological relativism which would have kept very uneasy

35. J. B. Bury, *The Idea of Progress* (London, 1920).

company with Beard's or Robinson's hard-headed kind of interest in social advance; yet he withdrew sharply from the implication of solipsism that seemed to lie along that road. After his famous presidential address, 'Everyman His Own Historian,' Becker found himself obliged to reply to the criticism of William E. Dodd, who told him that he was afraid the address had undermined younger members of the profession in their confidence in the validity of historical research. Becker explained that he had tried to say that it was the duty of the historian 'to keep Mr. Everyman's history, so far as possible, in reasonable harmony with what actually happened.' In a critique of Maurice Mandelbaum he made clear that he did, after all, believe that historical knowledge was objectively ascertainable: the truth was to be searched for.[36]

This late recruit to the school of Ranke had at least taken the debate on to slightly higher ground. He had always been a little skeptical of the New Historians, and when he reviewed Robinson in 1912 he raised the question as to what was meant by 'progress,' suggesting that a scientific definition was needed before action followed.[37] Becker was also skeptical about the novelty of the New History, and it was he who obliged his contemporaries to notice that the *philosophes* had proclaimed their own 'New History' in order to disengage from the past the elements having universal validity which, conforming to the essential nature of man, would act as guiding principles for social regeneration. For Becker, historical thinking was an intrinsic part of any given society's intellectual process, and one of his more imaginative expressions suggested the needs to which he thought the process answered: 'The past,' he

36. Carl Becker, *Everyman His Own Historian* (New York, 1935); Charlotte Watkins Smith, *Carl Becker: On History and the Climate of Opinion* (Ithaca, N.Y., 1956), pp. 64, 69–76, 86. Burleigh Taylor Wilkins, *Carl Becker: A Biographical Study in American Intellectual History* (Cambridge, Mass., 1961), pp. 88–89, 194–95, 198, 205. On Becker's debt to pragmatism, David Noble in *Ethics*, 67 (1957). A distinction between evolution and progress in Becker's thought is suggested by David Noble, *The Paradox of Progressive Thought* (Minneapolis, 1958), pp. 18–33.

37. Smith, *op. cit.*, pp. 61–62.

said, 'is a kind of screen upon which each generation projects its vision of the future, and so long as hope springs in the human breast the "new history" will be a recurring phenomenon.'[38]

Becker was not alone in perceiving that ideas had, after all, their place in historical studies. That thought—for it was a thought, and no doubt a real one—began to trouble Charles Beard by 1926, when he hinted at his own waverings towards relativism in his presidential address to the American Political Science Association.[39] By 1932, in writing an introduction to the American edition of Bury's *Idea of Progress*, Beard could admit that 'the world is largely ruled by ideas, whether true or false.' This was a graver concession for Beard than it could have been for Robinson, who taught a course in intellectual history, or for Becker, to whom in any case it was obvious. Even in his celebrated interpretation of the Constitution, however, Beard had left unresolved problems of interpretation; he never clarified or appeared to recognize the distinction between economic determinism and economic interpretation; nor did he clear up the problems of moral responsibility involved in these views. But he had struck a resounding blow against time-honoured institutional certainties, and in his flashes of skepticism as in his profound conviction of the strength and future of democracy he always showed how deeply he shared the Progressive faith.

Faith became the theme of his pronouncement when he told the American Historical Association, in 1933, that he had lost his determinism but had gained a philosophy.[40] When he called written history 'an act of faith' he was as much concerned with the future as with the past. In a manner very like that of H. G. Wells, whom the New Historians tended to regard as one of their own,[41] Beard maintained that the correctness of the historian's judgement about

38. Becker, *op. cit.*, p. 170.
39. C. A. Beard, 'Time, Technology and the Creative Spirit in Political Science,' *The American Political Science Review*, 21 (February, 1927).
40. Charles Beard, 'Written History as an Act of Faith,' *American Historical Review*, 39.
41. See Barnes, *History of Historical Writing*, p. 142.

the past was to be measured by the extent to which his predictions about the future were verified by the course of events. Beard's own faith was pitched on the advance of democracy and the interests of the common man; his historical vision revealed to him that this was the course that history had progressively followed. This expansive statement failed to provide any guide to the explanation of specific historical problems. In later years Beard pursued these questions further, but he never seems to have been completely clear about the logical distinction between an analysis of a given historical situation based on a hypothesis, and a prior judgement of value which actually controls the historian's findings and opinions. The manifest courage with which Beard in his later years tackled these problems, attempting to enlist the names of Croce, Heussi, and Rietzler in his columns, does not help to establish that he understood them. His subsequent essays display his unfailing energy, his deep commitment to history as a hope for the solution of human problems, and his basic lack of comprehension of the differences between the types of problem involved. Croce was engaged with the problem of defining history as a mode of knowledge; Beard was never far removed from the question of how one was to interpret general or specific issues, how one was to come to terms with the admitted relativity of one's own judgement.[42]

The New History was not an exclusively American phenomenon, nor were its early standard-bearers fighting in pure intellectual isolation. Robinson's *Mind in the Making* had a preface by H. G. Wells, of whom a signed photograph appeared as the frontispiece; Barnes acknowledged a host of Europeans as pioneers and contemporaries of a common movement. Yet it is curious that while so much of the work of the Americans was frankly hortatory and propagandist, their British compeers were writing of the history of trade unions and local government, of the town and village la-

42. The debate was continued in C. A. Beard, 'That Noble Dream,' *American Historical Review*, 41 (1935); C. A. Beard and Alfred Vagts, 'Currents of Thought in Historiography,' *ibid.*, 42 (1937). For a bibliography, see Hofstadter, *The Progressive Historians*, p. 484.

bourer, and of the agrarian movement in the sixteenth century. There were significant national differences in emphasis, in the content of the work, perhaps even in aim; but there was also an international movement.

Karl Lamprecht of Leipzig was probably the first to bear the message in person. His book, *What Is History?*, was published in English in 1905, after he had lectured both at the 150th anniversary celebrations of Columbia University and at the World Fair in St. Louis. Lamprecht, whom Becker, it is comforting to note, found incomprehensible, announced that history was primarily a socio-psychological science. In the nineteenth century, he said, speaking of Germany, 'when the nation yearned with every fibre of its being for the long coveted political unity,' political history could be an instrument of national purposes—a statement which at least established the instrumental nature of history and the fact that its subject might change with different aims. The quality which Lamprecht wished history to recapture from the past was nothing less than a nation's soul-life,[43] a task for which the American profession was not perfectly equipped. But a sort of *Kulturgeschichte* was in fact attractive to the New Historians. Turner himself was excited by the spirit of American society, and in 1909 he wrote to Max Farrand that 'The new line for the future is the history of the development of American *society*, ideals, etc.'[44] The 'etc.' is not without pathos. Turner, proceeding with feverish enthusiasm into his labyrinths of research, could never quite specify the relationships between his ever exciting discoveries and his general ideas; his ideas were too general, his details too detailed. He seldom seems to have known precisely what question he was trying to answer.

Yet his one famous essay on the frontier influenced more than a generation of scholars; Beard's sketchy and inconclusive tract on the Constitution had almost captured the field by the mid-1930s; Robinson's books sold by the hundreds of thousands. These suc-

43. Karl Lamprecht, *What Is History?* (New York and London, 1905).
44. W. R. Jacobs, *The World of Frederick Jackson Turner* (New Haven, 1968), p. 99.

cesses deserve explanation, and an explanation should in turn depend on and help to reveal the more general character of American culture. When the proponents of the new approach began their work, the historical profession in America was still of recent growth. The various men of letters who had taken it upon themselves to write histories, usually in many volumes, during the nineteenth century, had often been men of independent means; few of them owed their opportunities for scholarship to university chairs. In fact posts of any sort were exceedingly sparse; in 1884 there were only about twenty full-time teachers of history in the 400 or so American institutions of higher education, and as late as 1907, when the Mississippi Valley Historical Association was founded, only 250 candidates had taken the degree of Ph.D. in history in all American universities.[45] The popular readership for history actually declined towards the end of the century, and in face of the rise of the social and political sciences, members of the historical profession had some reason to feel that their calling was in a defensive position.[46] The economic, social, and psychological problems which beset the country in the 1890s, which included such material events as the economic depression of 1893 and the closing of the frontier of settlement, did not dispose people to believe that the solution of their difficulties lay in the study of history. This state of affairs gives Turner's essay its special significance, not only for the theme it proposed to the American imagination, but for the historical perspective it cast on the present. Turner's message was that the crisis that would arise from the closing of the frontier could be understood only in the light of history, and this brilliant, if somewhat discoloured, flash of illumination gave new life to the hopes and self-respect of historians.

Turner, for the time being, had spent his force. It was far from clear that the detailed filling-in of the landscape he had lit up would be enough to serve the needs of the present, but profes-

45. Hofstadter, *The Progressive Historians*, p. 35; Higham, *History*, p. 19.
46. Higham, *op. cit.*, p. 71.

sional history still tended to be the home of political and economic orthodoxy. When Robinson in due course demanded that history be written to serve the cause of social advance, he not only failed, as Becker pointed out, to specify his meaning of progress in general, but he failed to explain precisely what kind of advance was needed and in what ways the study of history might serve it. Robinson, abetted in this by Beard, was satisfied to declare the aim of promoting history as the study of modern problems; they never seriously addressed their attention to the working out of the problems of method which their programme implied. But the concept of instrumentalism in history accommodates profound differences as to the aims which historical study may serve. It was one thing to believe, as Robinson, who actually declined to admit that he was a social reformer, could reasonably have maintained, that the general character of modern industrial problems called for knowledge of the history of the modern industry. It was another thing to identify some specific problems whose existence was due to the survival of mistaken beliefs or anachronistic institutions. Both Robinson and Barnes, in their optimism about the solvent powers of historical knowledge, seemed unwilling to face the fact that the obstacles to social advance possess a recrudescent character. They renew themselves and spring up afresh even in some cases as a result of the kind of progress that progressives desire. The critical problems for American society in their period were posed not by the legacy of the medieval church (of which Robinson was well aware) but by the new power of the trusts—in which he showed much less interest.

The New Historians only occasionally probed problems of this sort. Considered as historians, they were in fact substantially orthodox; nor did they contribute any refinements of technique. But their comprehensive embrace of the social sciences caused grave offence to those members of the profession who had spent their lives establishing the reputability of history in face of dangerous academic competition. George Burton Adams, one of the chief patrons of this school, gave vent to his feelings in a presidential address to the American Historical Association in 1908,[47] in which he defended history as an independent science of investigation against the encroachments of political scientists, geographers, economic interpreters, sociologists, and social psychologists. He asked whether the profession was moving from an age of investigation to one of speculation? Those interested in theories of aggression will note his use of the idea that what had happened was an 'invasion of territory.' Much the same point was made by William Sloane, the Low Professor at Columbia, in a memorandum to President Butler and the Trustees directed against the activities of Robinson and James T. Shotwell. They were accused of having departed from Columbia traditions in history by establishing courses in the history of thought and culture, 'in which courses they teach didactically from a modernist point of view . . . everything except history as understood by their colleagues.' According to him, the departments of economics and sociology had been disturbed by the 'trespass.'[48]

Yet the New History came increasingly into possession of the field, a process reflected in the increasing modernism of courses and a foreshortening of the perspectives of time. The explanation could not lie exclusively in the internal politics of the profession and its conflict of interest with other disciplines. In the broadest sense, the New History has to be understood in its relation to the emerging material of American culture. As early as 1892, the National Educational Association's Committee of Ten made a remark which reflected the peculiarity as well as the urgency of the social problem facing American education in general. 'An additional responsibility,' said the Report, 'is thrown on the American system of education by the great number of children of foreigners, children who must depend on the schools for their notions of American in-

47. G. B. Adams, 'History and the Philosophy of History,' *American Historical Review*, 14 (1909).
48. Richard Hofstadter, 'The Department of History,' in R. G. Hoxie, *History of the Faculty of Political Science, Columbia University* (New York, 1955), p. 227.

stitutions, or of anything outside their contracted circle.'[49] Mass immigration, on a scale out of all proportion to the experience of other countries, produced a complex of problems of which the most basic was that of language. It is not altogether surprising that educators should have begun to concern themselves with the problems not only of instruction and content but of communication in its broadest sense.

Robinson and Beard both felt that history could be useful to an industrial working class, of whose alienation they were clearly apprehensive, by explaining to them such mechanisms as the division of labour, by which the workers had come, through the growth of industry, to be contributors to a mighty system of which they were beneficiaries as well as servants.[50] These needs did not present themselves to such teachers as involving difficult philosophical questions about the status of historical knowledge; all that concerned them was their right to use history, recognizing the properly scientific methods for ascertaining facts, in their own way, to make it do what they wanted it to do.

All this was less new than it seemed to them. As Commager has argued, Americans had begun from an early date to shape their knowledge of American history into what he has called 'a usable past.'[51] The New History defined itself in relation to the conventions of subject matter and teaching that had established themselves in the small number of genuine institutions of higher learning, during a period of only some thirty years. Its practitioners might have established their claims with more conviction if they had spent more of their efforts in the writing of history as they conceived that it ought to be written, and correspondingly less in what Barnes frankly called 'propaganda.' As it was, the body of their work, when measured against the achievements of their less socially inspired contemporaries, does not seem to possess great

49. *The Study of History in Schools*, pp. 167–68.
50. Cf. Beard, *The Industrial Revolution;* and Robinson, 'History for the Common Man,' in *The New History*.
51. H. S. Commager, *The Search for a Usable Past* (New York, 1967).

powers of endurance. Yet their mood was in tune with the wider audience of the mass universities, their impatience with the remote past was more characteristic, their sense of relevance was constantly merging into their sense of what was American. The cast of mind was discerned, in another connection, by Momigliano,[52] who has remarked that 'The trust with which Americans welcome foreign historians who import new knowledge and ideas . . . must not conceal the fact that, in the end, the testing ground for the validity of historical theories of any kind is, in America, American history.' The phase of American culture to which these reflections applied as imperatives may, however, have begun to come to a close; there have been increasing and deep signs of a standpoint from which the historian, without feeling compelled to disengage himself from his own society, feels less driven by that society's immediate presence to take a functional and foreshortened view of the past. But that is only one view of the possible future, and I have no intention of committing myself to an act of faith.

52. A. D. Momigliano, *Studies in Historiography* (London, 1966), p. 231.

12

Daniel J. Boorstin
(1969)

The rediscovery of America, which takes place with each attempt
to comprehend the American experience as a whole, has always involved Europe. Even so nationally centered a historian as Turner
got his bearings by repudiating the theory that attributed American institutions to a long line of European descent. Professor Daniel J. Boorstin, whose work has grown to be one of the most ambitious and persuasive of all attempts to impose on American history
the vision of a unified interpretation, has never lost sight of the
necessity to plot his course by taking his bearings from Europe and
particularly from England.

The America that comes to life under Boorstin's hand is, in its
early periods, itself a country of contrasts and of varied cultures.
The main unifying effects of growing up on the American continent
came from the fact that the experience differed so completely from
that of Europe. But eventually a national quality was formed,
partly out of a direct experience of settlement and recent tradition,
partly out of shared hopes, partly out of myth. A powerful, per-

This essay was first published in *Past Masters: Politics and Politicians 1906–1939*
(New York: Harper and Row; London: Macmillan & Co., 1976).

suasive sense of homogeneity takes precedence over those divisions of time, of region, and of theory which are common to Europe. The contrast enables Boorstin to bring forward this theme of homogeneity, a theme that develops as he traces the shaping influences that rose from the problem presented by the creation and survival of society in an unsettled land.

Professor Boorstin draws on more than one tradition, the earliest being Frederick Jackson Turner's. The emphasis is on what was new, unexpected, and what Americans owed and still owe to the land. The older the settlement, the less part it plays in Boorstin's story; the Eastern seaboard, once left behind by the movement of civilization, lies at a lengthening distance from his centre of attention and his central themes. But these themes are far more varied and complex than Turner's. Where Turner's primary emphasis was on democracy and public institutions, Boorstin's is on the whole experience of a growing community, on the style and quality of the life it lived. Boorstin's method also makes him a partial exponent of comparative history; Turner merely revolted from an older tradition and then became absorbed in America, but Boorstin, without dwelling on Europe as a developing civilization, seldom loses sight of the alternatives it could propose. All this gives Boorstin a place of his own among the modern proponents of American consensus.

The view that America owed more—and particularly more of its successes—to a tradition of consensus about fundamental principles than to a tradition of internal conflict was advanced by Richard Hofstadter in 1948[1] and was reinforced from the point of view of comparative political science by Professor Louis Hartz.[2] Hartz, having created a large and receptive space by pointing out the fact that America lacked a feudal heritage, filled it by explaining the importance of the 'liberal' philosophy imported from Europe. Other scholars, both in early American history and in early and recent political science, have emphasized in recent years the im-

1. *The American Political Tradition and the Men Who Made It (New York, 1948),* Introduction.
2. *The Liberal Tradition in America* (New York, 1955).

mense amount of common ground shared by Americans in political practice and belief.[3] Boorstin's mature work on America has the density of a vast fund of carefully sifted facts, which contrasts with Hartz's and Hofstadter's interest in ideas, theories, and ideals; but Boorstin is concerned with the manner of the life based on those facts, and the definition of 'experience' includes imagination and sensibility. Each of his books is different, and his work continues to grow. The justification for reviewing his achievement at this stage is that it would continue to exert a profound influence over American historical thought even if he were now to make an entirely new departure. It may be said of Boorstin as perhaps of any major historian that his thought is both mature and incomplete.

Boorstin's strong sense of the comparative nature of his work has a biographical as well as a purely intellectual source; after graduating, *summa cum laude,* from Harvard in 1934, Boorstin went to Oxford as a Rhodes Scholar. His record there was remarkable; he took two degrees—those of B.A. and B.C.L.—getting first-class honours in both; contemplating a career in the law, he also ate the prescribed number of dinners at the Inner Temple, passed the examinations, and was called to the bar. At Balliol, the most distinct influence was perhaps that of A. D. Lindsay, who was Master, and under whom Boorstin read philosophy, and it was during his years at Balliol that he laid—or deepened—the foundation of a twofold interest that has had enduring significance. One of these is in this comparative method—the identification of America by comparison and contrast with Europe. The other is in law. Boorstin, having qualified as a barrister in England, took a J.D.S. degree at Yale Law School and also became a member of the Massachusetts bar; his double armament has been a source of strength, but he is not likely to need the qualifications of the lawyer, in the manner of

3. Robert E. Brown, *Middle-Class Democracy and the American Revolution in Massachusetts: 1691–1780* (Ithaca, N.Y., 1955); Benjamin F. Wright, *Consensus and Continuity* (Boston, 1958); Samuel Lubell, *The Future of American Politics* (New York, 1952); Richard P. McCormick, *The Second American Party System* (New York 1966).

many American politicians, to sustain him during intervals between tenures of office.

Boorstin began his work as a historian in a distinctively legal context. His first book, which he wrote as a law student at Yale and an instructor at Harvard, was a study of Blackstone (1941).[4] Even then Boorstin was not a historian of law; rather he used the view of social order and of political priorities implied in the legal system as an instrument for uncovering social history. In his Blackstone his method is explicit. In his later work, it is sometimes subdued, sometimes not required. But as an influence on his intellectual development it has never disappeared, and it is present in the shaping of his approach to some of the central questions that he has tackled. When he says of the American Revolution that it was 'a prudential decision taken by men of principle rather than the affirmation of a theory'—a remark to which it will be necessary to return—he seems to imply that the leaders had the attitude of lawyers acting in the true interests of their clients rather than in the heat, and risk, of anger or enthusiasm; it is perhaps the scholar of law, both as history and procedure, who inclines to see in this cool light the acts of the revolutionary leaders.

The study of law appears to have contributed to Boorstin's controlling sense of the distinction between theory and practice. In later works he develops the distinction with great care and an amplitude of illustration, reaching to a point at which theory seems not so much to support and explain practice as to stand over against it, as an alternative or even an obstruction to doing what needs to be done. It is as well to remind ourselves that in an amusing but by no means unserious remark made in a much later essay, he alluded to the American view of the law as being 'the ethical minimum.'[5]

Boorstin's first book was about England, his second, *The Lost World of Thomas Jefferson* (1948), was about America. Despite

4. *The Mysterious Science of the Law* (Cambridge, Mass., 1941).
5. 'A Dialogue of Two Histories,' in *America and the Image of Europe* (New York, 1960), p. 177.

these obvious differences, these two books belong to the same phase of his thought. Both are eighteenth-century studies; and they are concerned with historical problems of similar genre though dissimilar in subject matter. The problem is the reconstruction of a complete mode of thought—of the social and intellectual assumptions of an influential group of contemporaries who, in certain ways, gave laws or gave a style of their generation. Boorstin's analysis of Blackstone is little less than an analysis of the idea of law in eighteenth-century England. By contrast, though *The Lost World of Thomas Jefferson* is clearly consistent with the earlier study, the interests that dictated it were no longer so distinctly those of the student of law.

It is to the lawyer, as well as to 'the student of history and the student of method in the social sciences' that the study of Blackstone is addressed.[6] Blackstone's *Commentaries on the Laws of England*, which were delivered in his capacity as the first Vinerean Professor of English Law at Oxford and were published between 1765 and 1769, form for Boorstin a microcosm of the prevailing rules and values of English society. The explicit lesson is that 'the ostensibly impartial processes of reason are employed by the student of society to support whatever social values he accepts.'[7] What emerges, as the substance to support this conclusion, is an interpretation of the mind of Blackstone and his contemporaries accompanied by a subtle critique of Blackstone's reasoning. This critique is essential to Boorstin's purpose. Probably every system of law involves the acceptance of certain legal fictions, some tautology or circular reasoning; it is by the penetration of these points that we can see what the system means to its upholders, what they are most heavily committed, through its agency, to defending.

For Blackstone, as Boorstin shows, the discussion of every section of the law becomes the exposition of 'rational principles'[8] The laws of England might have been a disordered mass, their prac-

6. *Mysterious Science*, p. 1.
7. *Ibid.*
8. *Ibid.*, p. 20.

304 Paths to the American Past

tices piled on several centuries of precedents, statutes, and customs, but Blackstone found everywhere that the rule of reason prevailed, and he satisfied himself that the reasons to be discovered in English law were always the best reasons. The laws of England, in fact, were little other than the working application of the laws of God, and it was, perhaps, for this reason among others that although they were rational they were unfathomable. And in one of those observations with which Boorstin can epitomize a complex reflection he concludes, 'The conflict between Blackstone's science of Law and his Mystery of Law was never to be entirely resolved. For this was nothing less than the conflict between man's desire to understand and his fear that he might discover too much.'[9]

The laws of England protected three great values, Humanity, Liberty, and Property. Boorstin's analysis of them shows that, as all the principal requirements of natural law were already covered, no improvement was to be expected from tampering with institutions. As for Liberty, for which England was particularly admired, Blackstone showed that it represented first the free expression of the will of the individual and secondly the full assertion of his rights. Civil society itself sprang from the free exercise of the wills of individuals. But the rights that society protected marked the limits of those proclaimed in the name of Liberty; thus property restrictions on the suffrage were justified because they assured unfettered expression to the wills that were truly free; it was not to be desired that liberty should spread to those without property; liberty protected rights and the protection of rights was the primary end of government. In fact, Boorstin points out, the whole structure of the *Commentaries* is built on the concept of rights, the first and second books being on 'Rights' and the third and fourth on 'Wrongs.'[10] But the most important right and highest value was that of Property. Property was absolute. Blackstone's cry, as Boorstin says, would not have been 'Liberty and Property' but 'Liberty *of* Property.'[11]

9. *Ibid.*, p. 31.
10. *Ibid.*, p. 162.
11. *Ibid.*, p. 186.

Property was created by nature, and civil society recognized and protected it; yet the definition of property was to be found only in the laws of England: the protection of the law became the only test of the existence of a right of property. The circularity of this definition provides a clue to Blackstone's method; and Boorstin is at his best in explaining, without lack of sympathy, what values Blackstone meant to uphold, while exposing the flaws in his arguments. The circularity of much of Blackstone's reasoning, which treated law as an isolated and self-consistent system of logic and often assumed what it purported to prove, and in which 'tautology was often concealed by the copiousness of legal vocabulary'[12]—these are the intellectual methods by which he organized his immense mass of learning and reduced the laws of England to a system. The method is extensive. In principle, it governs Blackstone's use of the 'maxim' as the rule of common law. The authority of the maxim rests on general reception and usage, but Blackstone could give a maxim as the 'reason' for a specific rule. Blackstone, a recipient of Locke's psychology, attached importance to the doctrine that both ideas and knowledge were rooted in experience; he had no use for metaphysics but shared the prevailing belief in the utility of universal rules and principles. Experience, moreover, meant the experience of mankind; the principles that governed past civilizations would also be found in the present. Everywhere, he found a reason behind the received legal practice and related that reason to those values of eighteenth-century England which he regarded as sacred, as given by authority—in this case that of the Glorious Revolution—and therefore protected by law. If the method was circular the circle at least had a long circumference.

Boorstin, however, does not expose in order to destroy but rather to reconstruct. The rights of property at the heart of Blackstone's legal system were held in cohesion by the needs of a complex and largely customary society. Throughout, the reader appreciates that Blackstone was a part of a living world, and Boorstin criticizes those lawyers and social scientists who think institutions can be analyzed 'scientifically' without regard to the fact that the

12. *Ibid.*, pp. 122, 124.

agent is guided by what he believes to be good and is limited by the values of society. Blackstone, he observes, did insist that society had a moral purpose and that man should not let science lead him by the nose; he does not think that philosophical consistency is the only virtue to be praised, even in a work on law, and points out that Blackstone had a sort of *social* consistency; and he concludes by offering a defence of Blackstone's attempt to give a reason for defending a social and moral framework.[13]

The strength of this study does not rest on sympathy with Blackstone's ideas but rather on appreciation of his integrity of purpose. Boorstin already possessed the comparative insight essential to the historian. He knew that the first thing to grasp about the eighteenth century is that it was different from our own and did not hold itself responsible for twentieth-century values. Yet, as he shrewdly remarks, subsequent history has been written in the eighteenth century's own terms, so that trying to reconstruct its intellectual history is like trying to see the color red through red-coloured spectacles;[14] and this remark reveals an insight into the intellectual problems of relating past to present and a preoccupation with the need to do so that continue to pervade Boorstin's work.

He was still engaged primarily in intellectual history when he turned to the reconstruction of the philosophical and scientific world-picture of Thomas Jefferson.[15] But now both the scene and the sources were different. For the earlier work, the *Commentaries* of Blackstone, provided a solid, already organized foundation, but the picture of the world as seen through Jefferson's eyes had to be put together from the numerous and scattered writings of Jefferson and his philosophical contemporaries. The scene itself, of course, had shifted to North America—to be more exact, mostly to Philadelphia, where the American Philosophical Society held its sessions—and Boorstin constantly keeps before the reader the importance of the local experience.

13. *Ibid.*, pp. 187–90.
14. *Ibid.*, p. 5.
15. *The Lost World of Thomas Jefferson* (New York, 1948).

This theme opens the book; and here begins the published
record of Boorstin's lasting preoccupation with the influence of the
specifically American experience of life on the making of a specifically American mind.[16] Jefferson's intellectual circle formed a remarkably interesting group, and Boorstin is able to re-create the
frame of their shared ideas about nature and nature's God, about
the equality of the human species deriving from its descent from
an original creation, about the essential materialism of their psychological, moral, and religious beliefs, and about society and politics. The beliefs held in common by these men, without being
highly systematic, were closely related, and their inquiries into the
natural world were intended to supply information to prove what
they already believed.

Their interests were extremely wide, and in a sense it was the
seriousness of their commitment to certain preconceived ideas that
determined their incessant search for facts. They believed in original creation and human equality and hence, for example, sought to
explain the Negro's color as a medical abnormality; they believed
in the economy of nature and hence that no natural creation could
be either duplicated or extinct; and since they rejected the idea of
development, they believed in the sovereignty of the present generation and had little interest in history. Like Blackstone, they had
no use for metaphysics, and Jefferson maintained that the problems of moral perception could be reduced to those of a rarefield
but essentially practical form of anatomy. A keynote to their outlook is given by Benjamin Barton's claim that 'the strong democracy of facts should exert its wholesome sway,' and Boorstin adds
that 'by a "fact" the American philosopher meant anything recorda-

16. He is not describing Americans in general, though; the leading figures of this
work are David Rittenhouse, the astronomer; Benjamin Rush, the physician
and professor of medicine; Benjamin Smith Barton, the botanist; Joseph Priestley, the Unitarian theologian, radical, and chemist; Charles Willson Peale, the
artist; Thomas Paine, the radical publicist; and Thomas Jefferson, the Universal
Man. On the other hand James Madison, one of Jefferson's closest associates, is
conspicuous by his absence precisely because his attitude to history and the
works of man was so different.

ble by man's physical senses.'[17] It was wholly in keeping with their beliefs that even thought should have been reduced to a branch of physiology—'the mode of action called thinking.' But by rejecting the value of metaphysical speculation, the Jeffersonians isolated themselves within their own system and deprived themselves of the possibility of perceiving that it *was* a system, with gaps which they lacked the means to close. This comment contains an irony which later turns on its author. For Boorstin was soon to embark on a full-scale interpretation of American history that owes much to the Jeffersonian viewpoint; Boorstin sees American society as a product of American geography, denigrates the value of theoretical speculation, isolates himself within his own system, and exposes himself to the criticism he makes of the Jeffersonians.

When Professor Boorstin turns to the political science of the Jeffersonians we begin to perceive connections between the forgotten world of their vision and the continuing traditions that have been kept alive in American thought and institutions.

Rejecting the study of history, and any formal interest in institutions, Jeffersonians centered their political science on the relationship of man to nature. 'Jefferson's often quoted aphorism that the people were governed best who were governed least,' remarks Boorstin, 'was simply another way of insisting on [the] distinction between imperfect human institutions and the Creator's perfect rule.'[18] The dismissal of theoretical presuppositions, in a political philosophy based on natural rights, made successful action the final test of human institutions; and Boorstin insists that Jefferson took his cue from political science, not from any preconceived purpose 'but from the struggle already going on among men.'[19] But in what sense and how far may a philosophy of natural rights be said to involve metaphysical conceptions? It is here that Boorstin is more critical, perhaps, than anywhere else in his analysis of the Jeffersonian mind. 'All the Jeffersonians,' he says,

17. *Ibid.*, p. 129.
18. *Ibid.*, p. 173.
19. *Ibid.*, pp. 190, 201.

were great believers in 'Bills of Rights,' and the word 'rights'
is the most familiar and significant word in their political
idiom. Contrary to general belief, this emphasis did not
express a conscious reliance on metaphysical foundations, nor
a 'rationalistic' or abstract basis of the state. It revealed,
rather, the unsystematic and inarticulate character of Jeffersonian political theory. A list of 'rights' substituted for a systematic theory of government. 'Rights' are indefinitely enu-
merable, and (in the absence of a comprehensive theory of
'right') the addition or subtraction of any one does not necessarily require the subtraction or addition of others.[20]

We shall not often find Boorstin so strongly implying the advantages of a systematic theory of government. It was, he explains,
faith in the perfection of the Creator's design for mankind (within
which human conflicts seem to have cancelled each other out to
the attainment of an ultimate good), that 'saved the persistent
iteration of "rights" from seeming an anarchic individualism.'[21]
And he does not fail to point out that the insistence on rights is accompanied by a marked indifference to any complementary idea of
duties.

Despite these reservations, Boorstin's conclusions are affirmative. The American continent, awaiting settlement and the filling
out of the Jeffersonian expectations for society, provided a favour-
able setting for the confirmation of their dreams. 'The Jeffersonian
philosophy was futuristic without being utopian or apocalyptic,' he
observes; 'its vision of the future was foreshadowed not in any
sacred document nor in any private revelation, but in the American continent itself, and in the very shape of man.' The naturalistic
theme, which played so large a part in the Jeffersonian view of the
American future, was not to be fully played out until the end of the
nineteenth century.

One of the characteristic difficulties encountered by Americans,
when reviewing their history, is that of establishing, with what a
European might be forgiven for considering a normal degree of

20. *Ibid.*, p. 194.
21. *Ibid.*, p. 196.

clarity, the distinction between the past and the present. The problem is compounded by the innocence as to the possibility that such a problem might exist. But no one is more keenly aware of this difficulty than Professor Boorstin. His work shows a constant respect for the past, in its integrity, as the past. Yet he has also shown an equally constant and frequently anxious concern about the present; and an important feature—perhaps at times a motive—of his work has been the recognition of a need to establish that peculiarly subtle dialogue in which past can speak to present in a voice that it would recognize as its own. The need to do this by understanding history for its own sake is expressed in his penchant for quoting a remark of Charles H. McIlwain's that trying to teach the lessons of history is like trying to plant cut flowers.

It is clear that Boorstin had these problems very much in mind soon after he returned from Oxford. The appreciation of the fact that the past was not engaged in attempting to answer present questions, which marked his study of Blackstone, caused him to recoil from the profoundly unhistorical attitudes which prevailed in American law schools and dominated much of the writing of legal history in Britain. As early as 1941 he criticized in the *Harvard Law Review* the prevailing practice in the writing and teaching of the history of legal doctrines; the history of contract, for example, was treated as though medieval arrangements which had a touch of contract about them were to be considered as imperfectly realized attempts to achieve the modern law of contract.[22] Boorstin regretted 'the subservience of legal historian to practising lawyer' and attacked the use of 'present legal categories as the framework of legal history,' as a result of which 'the classifications found in legal textbooks and treatises have become the classifications for the material of legal history.' Seven years later he addressed to the Association of American Law Schools a powerful and eloquent plea for the recognition of historical values in the teaching of legal history.[23]

22. 'Tradition and Method in Legal History,' *Harvard Law Review*, 54 (1941), 960–75.
23. 'The Humane Study of Law,' *Yale Law School Journal*, 57 (1948), xiii.

Among the strong continuities marking the development of Boorstin's thought nothing is more consistent than his interest in the problem of the 'lessons' or moral of history, a moral that can be extracted only by absorbing oneself in the substance of history. 'Our past,' he wrote in the preface to *The Lost World of Thomas Jefferson*, 'must serve not as an anthology from which to cull apt phrases for current needs, but as a stage for observing in all their tantalizing complexity the actual ways in which men in America have faced the ancient problems of the human race.' In his introduction to *An American Primer*,[24] which is an anthology, not of 'apt phrases' but of carefully selected and edited documents, he juxtaposes the questions of the historian with those of the citizen: 'Historians reading the words of John Winthrop usually ask "What did they mean to him?" Citizens ask "What do they mean to us?" Historians are trained to seek the original meaning; all of us want to know the present meaning. These are two quite different quests which often get in each other's way.' He adds the hope that the book will 'remind us how to keep our traditions alive,' a hope that perhaps reveals more confidence than American traditions can be relied on to bear. It depends which tradition one chooses. Racial discrimination is an American tradition; so is civic corruption, so is violence; so also are equality, morality, and the rule of law. There is at least a hint of patriotic history in this expression of purpose and a satisfaction with the way things have turned out that not all Americans, past or present, appear to share. Americans have yielded to the general temptation, as Boorstin has elsewhere remarked, to homogenize experience, 'to empty each age of its vintage flavor in order to provide ever larger receptacles into which we can pour an insipid liquor of our own making. By homogenizing I mean the tendency to make ideas or things seem more alike in order to serve some current purpose.'[25] But he has, at this point, just issued a cogent reminder of what the true historian does: 'Our

24. Two vols. (Chicago, 1966).
25. 'The Myth of an American Enlightenment,' in *America and the Image of Europe* (New York, 1960), p. 67.

greatest historians—whatever else they may have done—have somehow added to our understanding of what it meant to be alive at a particular time and place in the past.'[26]

Boorstin clearly thinks that, as the American past differs from Europe's, so the American conception of the past differs from that which is commonly found in Europe. The great difficulty is to convince Americans that they have a past. They must discover that what they have in the space reserved for history is something other than a backward extension of the present.

The idea that the past and present exist in a sort of continuum which virtually permits them to talk to each other without raising their voices is supplemented, and the related intellectual difficulties are complicated, by the feeling Boorstin discerns that American ideals and institutions all derive from an experience that was 'given' rather than being historically accumulated. These views are developed in a book that stands as a landmark in his thought and influence. *The Genius of American Politics,* published in Chicago in 1953, owes some of its formulations to ideas that can be traced in his earlier work; nevertheless, it seems to be the product of some profound reflection that began with the work on the intellectual world of the Jeffersonians. This work has the concreteness and simplicity of exposition of a publication intended at least in part to be didactic; he wrote it during the period when the international crisis of the Cold War was compounded by the domestic crisis of McCarthyism, and part of the purpose was to give his countrymen some historical bearings by which they could help to steady themselves.

The thesis is that the special character of American democracy and institutions is due to the special, and unrepeatable, circumstances of American development; that the concrete experience of that development, in all its ramifications, and not fixed ideology or preconceived political theory, has given America both its values and its characteristic methods of political action; and that as these

26. *Ibid.*

experiences were unique both in place and time, they cannot be exported or made a basis for imitation by other countries. Boorstin is at pains to repudiate the idea that American development—particularly the successful side of it—has been due to the successful application of theory; his argument supposes the existence of an almost schematic opposition between theory and practical experience. It is not perfectly clear whether his principal assertion is that Americans have repudiated political theory, or rather that they have shared a common theory presented to them as part of the deed of gift that went with the continent, a gift that rendered all further speculation needless. 'For the belief that an explicit political theory is superfluous precisely because we already possess a satisfactory equivalent, I propose the name of "givenness," ' he says. ' "Givenness" is the belief that values in America are in some way or other automatically defined: *given* by certain facts of geography or history peculiar to us.'[27] At this point, then, what is given is not a theory but an equally satisfactory substitute. He proceeds to explain the sources by which this belief is given. The first is 'the notion that we have received our values as a gift from the *past*'—from the explicit ideals of the Founding Fathers; he calls this the 'preformation ideal.' The second, which seems at first sight to conflict with the first, is that American values are a gift from the *present*, 'that our theory is always implicit in our institutions.' This view depends heavily on geography, and in its full extension, which significantly takes the title, 'Values Given by the Landscape: The Land of the Free,'[28] it is more reminiscent of Turner than any other side of Boorstin's work. The city does not seem to play much part in this picture. 'We have been told again and again, with the metaphorical precision of poetry, that the United States is the *land* of the free.'[29] The meaning of the land itself plays a dominant part here, and is emphasized in later works, where the vagueness of the land, its vast promise and lack of defi-

27. *Genius of American Politics*, pp. 8–9.
28. *Ibid.*, p. 22.
29. *Ibid.*, p. 25.

nition, are held to have determined the American imagination.[30] It is in this connection that Boorstin invokes Turner, pointing out that much of his work and that of his followers constitute 'a theory to justify that absence of an American political theory.'[31] 'If American ideals are not in books or in the blood but in the air, then they are readily acquired; actually, it is impossible for the immigrant to avoid acquiring them. He is not required to learn a philosophy so much as to rid his lungs of the air of Europe,'[32] Boorstin comments, leaving us, however, in some doubt as to whether the 'if' at the beginning of the sentence has closed the argument, or opened it.

The third element in the idea of 'givenness' links the other two, which are described as axioms. It is the homogeneity, the continuity of American history in a steady stream, free from violent oscillations of regime and void of violent ideological challenges. 'Because our road has been relatively smooth,' he concludes this chapter, 'we have easily believed that we have trod no historical road at all. We seem the direct beneficiaries of our climate, our soil, and our mineral wealth.'[33]

From these premises, or maxims, the historian goes further, to maintain that the United States has been built up without theoretical foundations, owing its very success to its peoples' readiness to embrace experience and to reject or ignore the teachings of theory. This view—this theory, for it is that—becomes one of the organizing principles of his later work, *The Americans*, where it plays not an exclusive part but certainly a part without which the more positive elements would tend to fall away from each other.

The historical evidence in *The Genius of American Politics* is chosen in support of each phase of the argument with a precise sense of relevance; the book stands as a cogent warning to Americans, badly needed at that phase of the Cold War, to avoid trying

30. *The Americans: The National Experience* (Chicago, 1966).
31. *Genius of American Politics*, p. 26.
32. *Ibid.*, p. 28.
33. *Ibid.*, p. 35

to superimpose their political habits of mind on other peoples with other histories and other ideals. Moreover, the central observations of the book are so significant and so far-reaching that they are likely to have lasting influence even after they have been separated from the didactic theories which they were intended to sustain.

Near the end of the book, Boorstin, having built a case that seems irresistible by virtue of having covered all relevant ground and encircled such opponents as might have been inclined to resist, proposes the course by which Americans should try to reconcile themselves to their history and formulate attitudes to it. He rejects any attempt to build a democratic philosophy. 'When people already agree,' he comments, 'the effort to define what they agree on is more likely to produce conflict than accord.'[34] This remark, even if not too seriously intended, does not strengthen the presumption of real agreement; but that presumption in fact controls much of the argument by defining outlines of relevance beyond which disagreements are merely factious or trivial. It was a remarkably buoyant and optimistic assumption to make about the political health of the United States in an age which witnessed the rages of an anti-Communist hysteria potent enough to close the gates of reason in many of the highest offices of the land and most of the smaller ones, which was cowed and dominated by the contemptuous triumphs of the late Senator Joseph R. McCarthy, and was only to be slightly muted by the presence in the State Department of John Foster Dulles.

What Professor Boorstin asked Americans to do, instead of building an artificial democratic philosophy, was 'to bring to the surface those attitudes which have been latent in the notion of "givenness" itself, to discover the general truths about institutions by which we have actually lived.'[35] But this programme, whatever might be its merits as a counterblast against either McCarthy or Soviet Communism, is weakened by a defect in its logical foundations. The Boorstinian description of the maxims of 'givenness'

34. *Ibid.*, p. 169.
35. *Ibid.*

creates a reasonable expectation that he will explain the origins
and reception of a mystique, perhaps an illusion, certainly a partly
fantastical view of American life. The doctrine of 'preformation'
contains an obvious bedrock of truth: we knew that the principles
of the Founders, including the principle of compromise, had been
handed down and resorted to by generation after generation of
Americans, though often pursuing opposed ends with devious
arguments; yet it was precisely in the interstices between the
agreements of the Founders that the infection grew that would
later burst into sectional conflict. Thus although 'preformation'
provides a valuable concept and a useful clue, it does not close the
argument about what kind of country was being built. When we
come to the qualities given by the land itself, the argument is even
more elusive.

Does Boorstin really believe that the encounter with the land
gave Americans concrete values to live by, and does he himself
proclaim these values, or is he only telling us that Americans were
hallucinated into a rapture, not unlike the mystique about the
desert entertained by the British contemporaries of T. E.
Lawrence, and that this rapture acted as a substitute for systematic
or connected thought? Such an explanation could in itself be valid;
the sources of our beliefs, or ideals, are not necessarily rational;
the trouble is that Boorstin fails, in his own analysis, to make the
relevant distinctions. The title of his opening chapter is: 'How
Belief in the Existence of a Theory Has Made a Theory Superfluous'; and the shortened version of this, as page headings, reads,
'Why a Theory Seems Needless.' These formulations are not ac-
cidental. What he is describing is not the existence of a theory but
only the *belief* in the existence of a theory; but either the belief is
correct, and a theory did exist, or the belief is incorrect, and no
such theory existed. What he is giving an account of here is not
represented as a fact, but as a belief about a fact. 'For the *belief*
that an explicit political theory is superfluous precisely because we
already possess a satisfactory equivalent, I propose the name of

"givenness," '[36] as he explains. When we go on to consider the issues in American history which he maintains can be reconciled with an emphasis on persistent shared experience of 'givenness,' we expect that a moment of revelation is coming; Professor Boorstin has so shrewdly discerned some of the ideas, some even of the sense perceptions, which have contributed to shaping American minds that he seems to have prepared himself for the task of separating illusion from reality; is he not about to warn Americans against the dangers—for surely there are dangers!—of absorbing uncritically the images and ideals that have seeped into them from such vague and contradictory sources and confusing them with the substance of history? Boorstin's own earlier comment has raised this expectation; 'Because our road has been relatively smooth,' he has said, 'we have easily believed that we have trod no historical road at all. We seem [not 'we are'] the direct beneficiaries of our climate, our soil, and our mineral wealth.' But the moment of exposure never comes. In the end it turns out that Boorstin is himself encircled, that the illusion was the fact.

Boorstin's concept of 'givenness' makes it possible to extract a more historical theme from his own work. Passages in *The Genius of American Politics* show that he thinks the sense of 'givenness' began to appear with the decline of the first generation of Puritans (at least in New England), prevailed throughout the settlement of the continent, and began to fade at the end of that period, when the land and its values began to be displaced from the American imagination by the city and the automobile. But he continues to speak of a 'belief' in 'givenness' rather than in the fact, and he never comes to the point of saying how much was valid, how much was illusory, what might have been valuable, what might have been pernicious, in either the illusion or the fact.

This ambiguity can be understood in the light of another logical difficulty, which, like the first, follows from one of his deepest

36. My italics.

shafts of insight. A clue is dropped very early, when in his book on Blackstone he notes that Blackstone's use of the 'maxim' repeated a confusion already present in the idea of the law of nature—on which Blackstone heavily relied. 'The law of nature confused the world as it was with the world as it ought to be'—and the maxims stating those rules showed a similar confusion.[37] The same point is picked up again, briefly, when Boorstin explains the 'apotheosis of nature' in Jeffersonian thought. 'All facts,' he observes, 'were endowed with an ambiguous quality: they became normative as well as descriptive. . . . By describing a work of art as successful, we mean that it is hard to separate description from judgment, the "is" from the "ought," the facts about the work from the standards against which those facts are to be judged.'[38] In an absorbing chapter on the rise of sociology in America, and the incorporation of sociological data into the sectional argument, Boorstin adds a significant development to this theme, for statistical details became clues to a way of life. ' "Givenness" was here expressed in the assumption that life as it was in America—whether in the North or in the South—gave the outlines of life as it ought to be, that values were implicit in experience.'[39] Boorstin has repeated the point recently—again discussing statistics, but in more general terms—observing that 'more and more Americans, in more and more departments of their lives, look to statistics not merely for facts but for norms. By making the fact the norm, we all make it somehow the law, the measure, and the external deposit of our moral life. We make the "is" the substance and not merely the shadow of the "ought." '[40]

In these remarks, Professor Boorstin has touched on a critical problem in the interpretation of American history. Men and women in America have achieved so much of what they have

37. *Mysterious Science*, p. 116.
38. *Lost World*, p. 54.
39. *Genius of American Politics*, p. 106.
40. 'The Rise of the Average Man,' *The U.S. Book of Facts Statistics and Information* (New York, 1966).

aspired to, so many simple dreams have come true (if at the cost of acquiring a rather greater degree of complexity), that the historian, relying largely on material that is in fact evidence of these successes, has difficulty in writing as though the history of facts were not also and necessarily the history of norms. This is, in a sense, the prevailing American extension of the old 'Whig' interpretation of history; and the strength of this standpoint can be seen from the difficulty of constructing an alternative; for whatever one's sympathies, the history of failure, or defeat, can hardly become that of a *continuing* norm, even though it may recognize the existence of a conflict of values at some time in the past.

Boorstin's respect for the integrity of the past might have led us to expect a fuller recognition than he is willing to accord, not only to the passionate intensity of the major conflicts in American history, but also to the intellectual depth and seriousness of the opposed positions. 'Success' he shrewdly observes, 'has made us unphilosophical';[41] but it might be added that a preoccupation with the conditions of success has induced him to minimize the element of conflict; major issues of principle are treated rather as though, within the total context of 'givenness,' they ought to have been seen to be irrelevant. His chilly dismissal of the abolitionists is accompanied by the accurate observation that much of the politically effective Northern opposition to slavery was based 'less on love for the Negro than on concern for the white working man'; but it was the abolitionists who succeeded in infusing into the Northern conscience a concern with the totality of the problem of slavery, which merged into a conviction that the conflict was not, as Boorstin insists, merely sectional, but was a conflict about what the United States, as a country, was to become in the future. That is the burden of Lincoln's 'house divided' speech at Springfield, Illinois, but it is a burden which Boorstin declines to assume, leaving it on Lincoln's shoulders while quoting him on the virtues of compromise and the importance of preserving the West for free white labour.[42]

41. *Genius of American Politics*, p. 39.
42. *Ibid.*, pp. 111, 113–14, 130–31.

Professor Boorstin evinces a revulsion against Reconstruction even more intense than his contempt for the abolitionists. The 'crimes' and 'senseless bitterness' that were visited on the South were 'vindictive' and 'narrowly provincial.'[43] It is doubtful whether this explanation does full justice to Thaddeus Stevens, who did appreciate that the distribution of power in the South was an economic problem requiring an economic solution; and it leaves a considerable vacancy in the place that might reasonably have been assigned for discussion of the Thirteenth, Fourteenth, and Fifteenth Amendments.

The burden of *The Genius of American Politics* is a deeply committed argument that the experiences which Americans share as members of one community are vastly more important than those which have divided them. But it might have been possible to propound this argument without going so far as to deny that Americans have ever been seriously divided on fundamental principles. Thus, after the Civil War 'both sides were still thinking on similar constitutional assumptions.' True; but on the other hand Alexander H. Stephens has just been quoted as saying that the war was over 'different and opposing ideas as to the nature of what was known as the General Government.'[44] If this is true, these ideas (not the facts of experience, but ideas) could neither both prevail nor live side by side, and whether the differences are theoretical and speculative or not is beside the point. At the most pragmatic reckoning, the absence of any tendency to philosophical speculation failed to avert the bloodiest civil war of the nineteenth century.

It is on the same basis that Professor Boorstin makes his celebrated statement that the American Revolution was 'a prudential decision taken by men of principle rather than the affirmation of a theory.'[45] Insofar as the decision was vindicated by events, and the Americans were subsequently happier under their own rule than they would have been under British rule, the decision was cer-

43. *Ibid.*, p. 131.
44. *Ibid.*, p. 129.
45. *Ibid.*, p. 95.

tainly prudent, though the word 'prudential,' with its tone of the board meeting or the insurance policy, effectively conceals the frantic activity, passionate agitation, and background of military operations that brought the leadership up to, and past, the point of independence. And assuredly they were men of principle. But what principle? The answer, which Boorstin does not give, is that these men were Whigs; their unifying principle was Whiggery; and despite their many and serious differences, it was enough to enable them to speak a common political language and to declare a common purpose. Why then, is it important, or even significant, that they did not affirm a theory? What theory, other than that of their Whig principles, could anyone have expected them to affirm?

Here Boorstin's didactic purpose seems to have led him astray from his history. The kind of total theories of society, the desire to use revolutionary means to impose a schematic new order, that have caused such indescribable pain and suffering in our own twentieth century were almost unknown in the eighteenth. Even the French *philosophes,* though holding physiocratic theories about political economy, wanted to achieve their aims not by revolution but by strengthening the monarchy. It was a consequence of the French Revolution, not a motive for it, that social and political theory began to remodel the state (a process, incidentally, that brought a great deal of permanent improvement to France). Boorstin's carefully poised antithesis therefore becomes historically irrelevant and gives rise to the suspicion that he is using the weapons that belong to the eighteenth century to fight the battle of his own generation.

This brings us to a point of some importance. If, as Boorstin says, the American leaders were men of principle (in a political sense; it would be trivial to say merely that they were 'upright' or 'men of honour'), then in fundamental matters they did possess a theory, and thus in a very significant sense Professor Boorstin has been right. His 'performance' theory describes a fact, after all, not simply a belief held by generations of half-bemused Americans; and it provides later generations with a common political language and does much to explain the modern strength of the theory of consensus. But it is one thing to look on the theory of the state as a plan of action, as socialists, fascists, and communists, among others, have done; it is quite another to attempt to reduce to a system, to codify (as Blackstone did) the accumulated principles, institutions, and customs given by history. In his major work, *The Americans*, Boorstin continues to write of Europe as though, in contrast to America, its institutions represented the deliberate enactment of preconceived theories of the state. His identification of America involves an antithesis with Europe in which the contrast between systematic theory on the European side and pragmatic experiment on the American side plays a part as basic as—and interdependent with—the contrast between 'aristocracy' and 'democracy' in social life, education, and politics.

This contrast involves a good deal of oversimplification—and rather too often disparaging oversimplification—of European culture and institutions. Even when discussing modern European political parties, which, as he knows, often define themselves by adherence to theoretical principles, he fails to observe how much European government is in fact coalition government.[46] European education and social thought become, under this treatment, aristocratic education and thought limited by dogma and authority. The Enlightenment is said to have 'acquired much of the rigidity and authoritarianism which it set out to combat.' It was, he adds, 'in fact little more than a confinement of the mind in a prison of 17th- and 18th-century design. . . . The best European minds of that age labored to build the new-model walls in which they were to be confined.'[47] By the eighteenth century, we further learn, 'many European thinkers had arrived at the idea of progress by devious and painful intellectual paths. . . . But in America . . . progress seemed confirmed by daily experience.'[48] English culture also

46. *Ibid.*, pp. 138–39. Elsewhere he describes European culture as 'dying of poverty, monopoly, aristocracy, and ideology' (p. 182).

47. *The Americans: The Colonial Experience* (New York, 1958; London, 1965), p. 173.

48. *Ibid.*, pp. 179–80.

takes some painful blows. 'It was an age which chose David Hume for its arbiter of Truth, Dr. Samuel Johnson for its arbiter of Beauty, and *Pamela* and *Tom Jones* for its epics.'[49] While pausing only momentarily to reflect that if these dicta be true, the age could have done worse, it seems desirable in the interests of distributive justice to notice that most of the leading influences in the intellectual and scientific life of Europe were not products of aristocracy and many owed little or nothing to the aristocratic patronage of education. Such careers as those of Pope, of Johnson, of Voltaire, Rousseau, Diderot, of Hume or Priestley, not to enumerate most of the luminaries of German literature and music, suggest an extraordinary flexibility and receptiveness to talent in these prisons of the mind. Even in such eminently nonmetaphysical matters as scientific agriculture and technology, the basic advances, both theoretical and experimental, began in Europe and were often picked up slowly in America.

However, Professor Boorstin is not writing European history. Europe stands in contrast, a backcloth against which America is staged, and it is because of this backcloth function that Europe appears more static, more tradition-bound than it really was or is. Even without these somewhat artificial contrasts American society comes vividly to life. And this remains the most important thing to say about *The Americans*, because there is probably no living historian of America who is quite Boorstin's equal in the essential historian's power of bringing the past to life. The expert economy of his literary style is an instrument of this power, and his ability to turn a phrase is used not for decorative purposes but to sum up and give point to an explanation. But with Boorstin the historian as with an artist it is really the eye that controls: the hand is merely an agent; and the eye sees the past in its own terms of reference. He is always willing to explain his meaning by illustration—a method that he employs more freely in *The National Experience*—and his keen eye for the revealing incident gives his mature writing an anecdotal vitality without detracting from its seriousness of purpose.

49. *Ibid.*, p. 90.

The Americans is planned as a trilogy, of which *The Colonial Experience* reaches the Revolution, and *The National Experience* describes the growth and character of American society during the settlement of the interior and the formation of a separate Southern consciousness; the third volume is yet to appear.*

The Americans is general history, but not in the comprehensive style of a William Lecky or Channing, or Osgood or Rhodes. It is neither social history without politics nor political history without society nor economic history without either; it is the history of a society in the widest sense. Boorstin is therefore a historian concerned not to establish sequences of events but rather to establish their context. American events arose from a social texture that might have given rise to different sequences, but could never have given rise to the events that belong to European history; and this applies to such differing contingencies as a common law judgement by Justice Lemuel Shaw, the presidential election of Jackson, or the explosion of a steamboat on the Mississippi. Above all, Boorstin is the historian of the character and consciousness of the American community. His themes are rich, varied, and textually subtle; and they are interwoven with a certain deliberate looseness. He is too sophisticated to be interested in being 'definitive,' and the somewhat loose and open framework hints at the open character of American life. Style and method are part of the interpretation. The artistry is, perhaps, unobtrusive, but it is conscious and even elaborate.

In this view, the history of society is conceived as that of certain broad types of experience, some of which are shared by the vast majority but some of which are the result of special circumstances. It is essential to appreciate this implicit theme in Boorstin's work, that of the experience of the community, which continues whatever defeats some sections may suffer, whatever changes the rest may undergo. What is retained through change, what has been absorbed into the bones of American life, is constantly implied as he moves over the varied ground both of the society and of the geog-

* Since this essay was written Boorstin has completed his trilogy with the publication of *The Democratic Experience* (New York, 1975).

raphy on which it stands. It is, in the view he takes, the task of the historian of America to meet the people's need to understand the history they are made of—the myth as well as the reality.

Political history is displaced from the central position conventionally accorded to it. Politics becomes a function of the community; political activities emerge as manifestations of the energies, interests, and rival ambitions of sectors of the society whose character and style of life is under review. It is a view of politics peculiarly appropriate to the American past; and it enables Boorstin to show with complete authority that government was one of the most potent agencies of economic growth and also in many cases the principal source of capital.[50] These points, which dispose of a great deal of weighty and still-active political mythology, are not made in a polemical spirit; the historian is not arguing a thesis with a view to present politics but is collecting the evidence from the past and arranging it, for the benefit of present readers, in a maner which compels one to feel that it would have ben acceptable to contemporaries.

The method, or rather the concept which employs this method, is open to the criticism that the historian's principle of selection is liable to result in the dismissal, as incidental or even irrelevant to the 'mainstream' of American history, of whatever past conflicts either obstruct the passage of his implied argument or more simply do not interest him. According to the American norm many events ought not to have happened; admittedly such events often did happen, but they need not have done, and so can be treated as of secondary importance. The concept of 'givenness' controls the historian's selections and weakens his critical apparatus. It is in this that Boorstin's earlier criticism of the Jeffersonians seems to anticipate the flaw in his own method. While it would be impossible to write any general history that was not at some point susceptible to this kind of criticism, Professor Boorstin shows, both by implication in the structure of *The Americans,* and expressly elsewhere, that he does believe in a mainstream of American history—more so, in all

50. *The National Experience,* pp. 134–47; 249–56.

probability, than in the history of many other countries. His emphasis on the 'homogeneity' of American history is a statement of this approach; 'We view our national history,' he elsewhere remarks, '—and the facts support us—as a single broad stream, the unbroken living current of the American Way of Life, not as a miscellaneous series of great epochs.'[51]

But which facts support us? Epochs are generally the creation of historians trying to reduce to intelligible order the mass and continuity of their materials; but it would be a little strained, in the interests of homogeneity, to deny any epoch-making significance to the American Revolution, to the Civil War, or to the closing of the frontier. A more serious difficulty, however, arises because the same method insists, *ex hypothesi*, that the major conflicts of interest and opinion were due to prejudice, ignorance, or intellectual error rather than to genuine convictions about the fundamental principles. Thus Professor Boorstin gives very slight attention to the divisions of American opinion on Independence, or the Constitution; the bitter disputes of the Confederation period do not concern him, and although in *The National Experience* he treats the rivalries of Whig and Democratic parties as facts of politics, he gives very little indication of why political parties should ever have come into existence in the United States. Alexander Hamilton appears in the index only three times, and never with reference to his major economic policies; the Second Bank of the United States appears only incidentally in one passing reference to Nicholas Biddle.

Yet it is arguable that if Hamilton had not been Secretary of the Treasury, if Jackson had not vetoed the Bank recharter, or if it had been carried over his veto, the lives of the masses, the development of the society which primarily interests Boorstin, would have been different. Conflicts of opinion on these issues, it may be argued, were on matters of vital importance, and the way they were resolved determined the course of events. At the centre of

51. 'An American Style in Historical Monuments,' in *America and the Image of Europe*, p. 83.

Boorstin's reconstruction of American history lies the belief in the consensus of aims. The divisions which he regards as legitimate have been divisions over method; and the relative absence of ideological division between the leading political parties becomes a source of comfort and strength.[52] To this whole theme it might be possible to oppose an alternative. The differences between the Robert Morris–Alexander Hamilton school and the John Taylor–Thomas Jefferson school; between the pro- and anti-slavery camps; and between the Populists and the new industrial order—to name only three major issues—arose because of conflicts of ideals about the future of America as a whole. In reply, the consensus school argues that the United States possesses in its Constitution, supplemented by its party system, a mechanism for resolving major conflicts of principle; even the Civil War appears not to have been a conflict over Constitutional principles, though obviously the Constitution, as a mechanism for resolving conflict, broke down. Behind this view of the Constitution there does lie a theory, either implicit as in Boorstin's argument, or explicit as with Louis Hartz, and this theory affirms the constancy of a unifying agreement on aims. Thus for Hartz, much as for Boorstin, the conflicts were in principle avoidable. Hartz argues for the omnipresence of the Whig-liberal stream of political theory; Boorstin amasses the evidence, not from the rarefied sources of speculative debate, but from the records of life as it was lived and known, for a community of shared experience.

Hartz introduced into the modern discussion a negative concept which has helped us to understand American development. American history knew no feudalism: the commercial, liberal strand was extracted from England and planted in American soil, where it grew into the commercial, liberal, and modern state. To this concept Boorstin has added another negative. He insists that America flourished in the absence of dogma, in the absence of preconceived

52. 'A pretty good rule of thumb for us in the United States is that our own national well-being is in inverse proportion to the sharpness and extent of the theoretical differences between our political parties' (*Genius of American Politics*, p. 3).

theory, and even in the absence of too much formal knowledge. This theme is made to bear a greater burden of explanation than is usually required of absences, of spaces reserved but not filled.[53]

Boorstin has little difficulty in showing that highly schematic plans, which omitted to take account of local conditions, met failure. The Puritan settlements survived becaue of the willingness of the second and subsequent generations to modify their dogma and adapt themselves to conditions; the Virginians flourished because they transplanted working institutions that were easily adapted. The Quaker experiment in government failed, in the last resort, because it could not satisfy the needs of the people of Pennsylvania for defence in a non-pacifist world. The philanthropic experiment in Georgia failed because its planners ignored local economic conditions. Boorstin himself notes that Puritan dogma began to decline in England in the second half of the seventeenth century, so that its decline in America is not a peculiarly local phenomenon, though it may well have been a necessary one. The Quaker attempt to set up a pacifist government would, of course, have failed anywhere in the world when violent enemies appeared; and it seems equally remarkable that in Pennsylvania it should have lasted a lifetime. As for Georgia, one would not have to be an enemy of economic theory to agree that a theory that takes no account of local economic conditions, or of the motives of those participating in the settlement, would be likely to fail. America proved these points, but it would hardly have been necessary to call the New World into existence to do so. The argument insists that success was achieved almost exclusively in the absence of preconceived theory. It makes room for a great deal of instruction, particularly where Boorstin discusses the professions, which in England were clogged by tradition and a jealous and cautious monopolism. But it could be rejoined that the principal point to emerge

53. Support for the same general theme could be supplied from a most unexpected source: 'The Revolutionist's Handbook' brandished by Tanner in G. B. Shaw's *Man and Superman.* Shaw kindly appends the handbook to the text of the play, and its key turns out to be: 'The golden rule is that there is no golden rule.'

is that the problems Americans were confronted with in the process of settlement tended, for the most part, to be of the limited type that could be handled with drive and ingenuity. When fundamental advance was in question, it had to take place where the speculative faculties were more highly respected and had full play. The whole course of this overextended argument shows that Boorstin has lost sight of one of the points he emphasized in his Blackstone; for then he insisted on the transference of law and ideas across the Atlantic and showed the prolonged influence of Blackstone on American legal training. That most acute of critics, Miss Cecelia Kenyon, asked Professor Boorstin to take to heart his own remark at the end of his chapter on Pennsylvania: 'Finally, the Quakers made a dogma of the absence of dogma.'[54]

Positive themes, however, are everywhere implicit—though they are often less openly stated—in Boorstin's argument. The ambition of Americans surges forward to open up a continent of boundless possibilities; and the very lack of definition is here an implied theme: the vagueness of America's physical limits and the myths about its fantastic West—which Boorstin rediscovers with such brilliance that we see why they were believed and almost wish to share those impossible dreams—imply that an open, classless society was in the making and begin to take over the role of historical explanation.

With these, Boorstin links the more specific sectors of legal, educational, and technical history, to which he brings a depth that would be worthy of an expert in each separate field. The common-law tradition in America is seen to be one of adaptability rather than strict precedent and so is enabled to serve the needs of a society in which change tends to be both rapid and normal; it is interesting to contrast the fact that in Massachusetts, trade unions were freed from the threat of charges of conspiracy by a common-law decision in 1842, while in Britain they were legalized by statute (twelve years earlier, incidentally). Education, because of its social

54. Cecelia Kenyon, Review of *The Americans: The Colonial Experience, William and Mary Quarterly*, 3d ser., 16 (1959), 585–89.

range and distinctive practical bent, tends to serve immediate needs, and in doing so helps to sustain the democratic character of society and politics. Boorstin is particularly fascinating when he turns to language and its adaptation in a mobile, expanding, and, it should be added, irreverent society. Not all Americans liked what was happening to language on their continent, and Noah Webster himself was a pillar of linguistic conservation. But once again, the collecting and distilling of vast funds of information serve the irresistible purpose of describing the quality of life in America as though we had been there ourselves.

Although his approach seems to attach more importance to 'scene' than to development, the idea of development is in fact implicit throughout Boorstin's work. Thus the conservative press that served the colonies and was restricted by colonial governments becomes the free intensely partisan press of the early nation; the culture of the colonies, which was defined by its lack of a capital, becomes 'culture with many capitals' in *The National Experience.* The growth of the city begins to change the face of the land; like the growth of transport, it is a product, as has been noted, of much public enterprise, and this brings us back to the central theme of community. Boorstin insists on it. In the process of settlement, the community precedes formal government, and calls government into being just as settlement itself so often in fact preceded the formalities of survey.

As the innumerable facts and flashes of connecting insight gather strength, the whole work mounts a tremendous power: even to disagree with some of its thematic implications is to be instructed not only in the history of American society, but in how to think about it. Yet much of this instruction will be in dissent rather than agreement. Although movement and change are implicit as the subject of Boorstin's themes, his interests seldom call for intense analysis of specific processes; a vague determinism, mainly geographic in bias, underlies both events and social forms. The missing dimension would conventionally be called that of historical explanation. Why, we may ask, did political parties come into being?

Why did community precede forms of government, and still more significant, why did Americans adopt these rather than other forms? The encounter with the land obviously presented hard necessities, but the land did not itself put into American heads the ideas of government and social organization on which they chose to act. Why did they choose as they did rather than otherwise? By ignoring the realm of preconceived ideas, the substratum of institutional thought, he has weakened his power of explanation.

Yet behind the institutions, the inventions, the ways of life, lies a deeper implication still. Boorstin brings to light the texture of life in which the American imagination came into being. Henry Nash Smith's reconstruction of the vision of the nineteenth century,[55] in which 'the myth of the desert' is transformed into 'the myth of the garden,' here flows into Boorstin's stream, and he describes the subject matter of those numerous naturalistic paintings which delighted Americans with the sheer spectacle of the interior of their vast and various continent. This leads to one of his most fascinating themes; for much of what Boorstin says implies that wherever Americans overcame their obstacles, the experience gave them— in part their success arose from—a new vision. A new way of looking is implied. The pragmatic mind, the open land, the open society—all are fused in a new and distinctively American imagination and mode of thought. Yet it is worth recalling that it was Locke whose psychological theories introduced an experimental epistemology and that empirical method is fundamental to English science from Bacon; and as a note on the theoretical possibilities that remain to be discussed it may also be remarked that, while nineteenth-century American painters were using thoroughly conventional techniques of representation to portray new scenes, in France painters were experimenting with new ways of seeing.

Boorstin is not alone among recent historians in his preoccupation with the collecting of facts which then speak for themselves and in his deliberate extrusion of ideology from the substance of

55. Henry Nash Smith, *Virgin Land* (Cambridge, Mass., 1950).

history, or rather from what he holds to be the best and most worthy to endure. In spite of differences, there is a comparison with Sir Lewis Namier; and he resembles Namier in his keen, humane eye for incident. Not, however, for character; little in Boorstin's writing suggests Namier's interest in character or his penetrating psychological insight into the minds of the dead. Neither should the comparison be stretched: Namier believed the past should have undergone crystallization before the historian touched it; Boorstin believes the past does speak to the present and that the historian has a social duty to transmit what it says.

All is not as it has been. The sense of 'givenness' that Boorstin has discovered in the creation of American values has declined since the completion of settlement; and the decline has been accompanied by the rise of a mass media, the artificial stimulation of responses and cooking of events. It is wholly in keeping with Boorstin's sense of social duty that he has concerned himself with these changes. His witty but serious book *The Image* [56] is a work of social criticism, to which we already owe the concept of the 'pseudo-event,' that event which is called into existence solely for its value as news or propaganda, and which provides a large amount of the materials used by newspapers and television. He is commenting here not only on the invention of 'news'—as in press conferences and the numerous sessions of the sort that Professor J. K. Galbraith has called 'no-business meetings' [57]—but on an underlying phenomenon in the nature of experience; for what disturbs him is the decline of the immediacy of experience. Increasingly we see, hear, and know things at second hand, and increasingly, he suggests, our experience comes pre-selected, arranged by various sorts of advertiser, editor, or impresario, pre-packaged and pre-digested. The fact that a wider range of information is thus available would not satisfy Professor Boorstin that the quality of our experience is unimpaired. It used to be the Americans' peculiar advantage that they were in direct touch with facts; but now images

56. *The Image: A Guide to Pseudo-Events in America* (New York, 1962), p. 9.
57. *The Great Crash: 1929* (London, 1955), pp. 128–30.

have displaced facts: 'we have used our wealth, our literacy, our technology, and our progess, to create a thicket of unreality which stands between us and the facts of life.'[58] Americans have lost their power to delight in natural things.

The Image is thus an attack on the degeneration, under the conditions of modern technology, of all that was best because it was most natural in the American heritage. It thus represents a grave departure from the confidence that marked Boorstin's earlier thought. As another critic has observed,[59] the corruption and the threat are now within the community itself and cannot be ascribed to the temptations of alien ideology.

Yet much of the story he has so far recounted is of success. In fact his method has placed a premium on success, for what fails by definition misses or drops from the 'mainstream' of American history. It might be objected that there is a defective sense of cost and loss in all this. Yet Boorstin is not unaware of these dimensions, as he has shown in a sensitive essay on the possibilities of a dialogue between the American and the Jewish traditions.[60] 'To see history *sub specie Americani* is to be encouraged in an excessive (if well-substantiated) optimism,'[61] he remarks; but Jews, whatever their Zionist utopianism, are not historically inclined to exuberant optimism and, until the founding of Israel as a state, were not given to the conquest of nature so much as to speculation and introspection. There are marked signs that the 'well-substantiated optimism' for which he finds grounds in earlier American history is giving way, that he discerns the disintegration of the values he has ascribed to 'givenness,' that the fabric that joined the 'Is' and the 'Ought' is splitting at the seam. Boorstin has never been committed to a single theme or a single mood. As his vision of American triumphs has not been wanting in a tinge of irony, so it seems

58. *The Image*, p. 34.
59. David W. Noble, *Historians Against History* (Minneapolis, 1965), pp. 173–74.
60. 'A Dialogue of Two Histories: Jewish and American,' in *America and the Image of Europe.*
61. *Ibid.*, p. 175.

likely that his account of recent America, with its immense material gains and its pathetic atrophy of vital experience, will not be untinged by a sense of comedy.

Selected publications

Books
The Mysterious Science of the Law. Cambridge, Mass., 1941.
The Lost World of Thomas Jefferson. New York, 1948.
The Genius of American Politics. Chicago, 1953.
The Americans: The Colonial Experience. New York, 1958; Harmondsworth, Eng., 1965.
America and the Image of Europe. New York, 1960.
The Image: A Guide to Pseudo-Events in America. New York, 1962; Harmondsworth, Eng., 1963.
The Americans: The National Experience. New York, 1965; Harmondsworth, Eng., 1969.
The Landmark History of the American People. New York, 1968.
(Ed.) *Delaware Cases, 1792–1830.* 3 vols. St. Paul, Minn., 1943.
(Ed.) *Chicago History of American Civilization.* About 30 vols. Chicago, 1956 to present.
(Ed.) *A Lady's Life in the Rocky Mountains.* Norman, Okla., 1960.
(Ed.) *An American Primer.* 2 vols. Chicago, 1966.

Articles
'Tradition and Method in Legal History.' *Harvard Law Review,* 54 (1941).
'The Elusiveness of Mr. Justice Holmes.' *The New England Quarterly,* 14 (1941).
'The Autonomy of Scholarship.' *The Journal of Higher Education,* 19 (1948).
'The Humane Study of Law.' *The Yale Law Journal,* 57 (1948).
'Self-Discovery in Puerto Rico,' *The Yale Review,* 45 (1956).
'The Place of Thought in American Life,' *The American Scholar,* 25 (1956).
'America at the Moment.' *Forum,* 2 (1959).
'The Rise of the Average Man.' *U.S. Book of Facts, Statistics and Information for 1967.* New York.

13

Richard Hofstadter, 1916–1970
(1971)

Richard Hofstadter wrote history out of a tense, but reflective, engagement with the world of ideas, politics, and people in which he lived. There was no disjunction between his working and social lives; he carried on with his friends and colleagues an almost ceaseless dialogue that was always serious but often delightfully gay. His intellectual energy was relentless; and, towards the end, his work literally helped to keep him alive. Sometimes he described himself as less a historian than a historical critic, a remark that might, from one of the most influential historians of the age, have seemed ironically self-deprecatory, but was meant as a serious comment on his own historical style.

This style concerned itself primarily with the social history of ideas and their relation to political movements. What he sought to interpret was not the ideas as entities, but the collective mood from which they emerged. He was characteristically engaged, moreover, not only with the past but with its repercussions. He loved the play of mind on mind, but was deeply concerned with

This essay was first published in *American Studies*, Vol. 4, No. 2 (1971).

the action of past on present, and always wrote history with a sense of his own responsibility for the consequences. He responded to crises of his generation with the intensity that often seems to impel his work; the mania of the McCarthy era is present by refraction in *The Age of Reform;* and that incomplete *mélange* of brilliant, partly autobiographical reflections, *Anti-Intellectualism in American Life,* is charged with the tension between populistic democracy and the American intellectual. His preoccupation with historical states of mind sometimes rendered him vulnerable to the findings of archive research, though corrections in points of information or emphasis detracted little from the value of his own original insight. He was early in grasping the significance of problems of social status in American politics, which he saw as marking the leading distinction between the politics of prosperity and those of depression. The theory, which was worked out through his interest in the ideas (rather than the techniques) of certain sociologists, did not provide an exhaustive explanation of the Progressive Movement, but it permanently broadened the dimensions of the sociology of the past. He was better aware of the total complexities of the situation than perhaps were some of his more vigorous critics; and his famous reappraisal of the Populists opens with an appreciative reflection on their predicament and on their contribution, as well as the 'stress and suffering' from which their thinking emerged.

Hofstadter's literary style was an artistically perfected instrument for the analysis of such complexities. For a writer of such eloquence and power, his prose is surprisingly economical. The subtle rhythm of the sentences and the weighting of short against long are means to convey the content of his thought; and his trenchant ironies are intrinsic to his argument, never attracting attention away from it. Some of his works are full-length interpretative essays, in which his prose carries his argument forward, and the reader with it, as that of a great narrative historian might carry the story of events.

His thought was formed under the influence of the progressive historians, and it was in keeping with his interests, and with the culturally autobiographical streak in his work, that he should eventually have devoted a book to them. These scholars had emphasized America's historical divisions. In *The American Political Tradition,* as a mild reaction to this emphasis, Hofstadter suggested the value of studying the continuity and consensus in American politics. But he never developed this view into the dogma that it became in other hands; for him it remained a comment, not an interpretation.

The city was Hofstadter's base of observation, psychologically and socially. His mind was informed by the social and cultural riches of New York. He was one of the greatest in a modern urban aristocracy of intellect which has altered the entire perspective for the critique of American culture. With all this, his personal appreciativeness of others was not an additional quality, but an essential element in a singularly complete and harmonious character; it was an attribute of mind that was able to give so much to his times, and to his students, colleagues, and friends. The beneficiaries of all these good things now find themselves hugely alone.

Index

339

Harvard College, 103, 173
Harvard Law Review, 310
Harvard University, 301-2
Herodotus, 212
Heussi, 292
Higginson, Thomas Wentworth, 205
Hillsborough, Viscount, 232
Histoire socialiste (Jaurès), 277
History of Historical Writing (Barnes), 273
Hobbes, Thomas, xx
Hobson, J.A., 277
Hofstadter, Richard, xiv, 265-66, 268, 276, 300-301, 335-36
Holmes, Oliver Wendell, Justice, 101
Holt, Lord Chief Justice, 58
Hooker, Richard, the judicious, 83
Hoover, Herbert, 76
Horwitz, Morton, 83-84, 89-104
House of Burgesses, Virginia, 4, 6, 8 n.20, 9, 10, 235-36, 237; then House of Delegates, 12, 20, 21, 22
House of Commons, 50, 132, 134, 140, 231, 235, 239, 241
House of Lords, 50
House of Representatives, United States, 50, 51, 129
Howell, T.B., editor of *State Trials*, 59
Huguenots, 267
Hume, David, 323
Hurst, Willard, 76, 89-90, 99, 102-4
Hutcheson, Francis, 56
Hutchinson, Thomas, 233

Idea of Progress, The (Bury), 291
Illinois, 114, 149, 150, 154, 156, 160
Image, The (Boorstin), 332-33
Indentured servants, 6
Inner Temple, 301
Innocent III, Pope, 281, 287-88
International Working Men's Association, 121, 141
Ireland, 84, 158; Irish, 111, 133
Israel, State of, 333
Italy, 113

Jackson, Andrew, xiii, 37, 97, 155, 156, 263, 324, 326; Jacksonians, 99, 265; democracy, 249; period, 105, 259
Jamaica, 58 n.2, 59
James I, 271

James, William, 289
James, River, 17
Jane, a slave, 174, 177, 198
Jaucourt, Chevalier de, 74
Jaurès, Jean, 277-79
Jay, John, 65
Jefferson, Thomas, xiii, 3, 9, 13-14, 17, 18, 21, 22, 25, 64, 65, 72-73, 80, 86, 155, 158, 194, 195, 217, 219, 228, 236, 248, 250, 306-8; Jeffersonians, 269, 308-9, 318, 325; *Notes on Virginia*, 22, 34, 246
Jenks, Edward, 278
Jews, 216, 333; Jewish religion, 207
John, King of England, 279
Johnson, Andrew, 166, 167, 260
Johnson, Chapman, 25, 30-31
Johnson, Dr. Samuel (*Dictionary*), 212, 323
Jones, Charles Colcock, the Reverend, 171-76
Jones, Charles Colcock, Jr., 171-76; 188
Jones, Mary, 171-76, 198-99
Jones family of Georgia, 170, 176-78, 198-99
Jordan, Winthrop, 64, 69, 71 n.13

Kansas, 114, 150, 158, 159, 160-61
Kennan, George F., 258
Kenyon, Cecelia M., 226, 329
Knight v. Wedderburn (1778), 60
Knott, Josiah, 196
Know-Nothings, 149, 158

Lairds, shipbuilders, 140
Lamb, Sir Matthew, 7
Lambeth (Eng.,) 130
Lamprecht, Karl, 293
Lancashire, 113, 134, 135, 136, 138
Land, as property, 13, 27, 75
Lawrence, T.E., 316
Lecky, W.E.H., 324
Lectures on the Industrial Revolution (Toynbee), 276
Lee, John, Deacon, 75
Lee, Richard Henry, 17, 236-37
Lee, Thomas, Colonel, 7
Lee family of Virginia, 236
Leeds (Eng.), 131, 246
Legislatures, American, *see* Assembly